OUT
UNDER
THE SKY OF
THE GREAT SMOKIES

"I acknowledge the transcendent circumstance
of the Great Smoky Mountains themselves."

Out Under the Sky of the Great Smokies

A PERSONAL JOURNAL

HARVEY BROOME

ILLUSTRATED BY LARRY HIRST

UNIVERSITY OF TENNESSEE PRESS

Knoxville

The publisher gratefully acknowledges the assistance of The
Wilderness Society in making this edition possible. Much of the
material originally appeared in *The Living Wilderness,* a journal
published by The Wilderness Society.

The paper used in this book meets the minimum requirements
of ANSI/NISO Z39.48-1992 (R 1997) (Permanence of Paper).
The binding materials have been chosen for strength and durability.

Library of Congress Cataloging-in-Publication Data

Broome, Harvey, 1902–1968.
Out under the sky of the Great Smokies: a personal journal /
Harvey Broome; foreword by Michael Frome; illustrated by Larry Hirst.
        p. cm.
"Originally published in 1975"—T.p. verso.
ISBN 1-57233-113-5 (pbk.: alk. paper)
1. Broome, Harvey, 1902–1968. 2. Natural history—Great Smoky
Mountains (N.C. and Tenn.) I. Title

QH31.B857 A3 2001
796.52'2'092—dc21
[B]   00-059997

TO *B*ENTON MACKAYE

For extraordinary contributions
to land use and
to wilderness preservation

I WONDER AS I WANDER OUT UNDER THE SKY . . .

From a southern white spiritual
collected by John Jacob Niles in
Cherokee County, N. C.

CONTENTS

 # OREWORD

Harvey Broome, a gifted man of the law, was also in the forefront when it came to ecology. In hiking, backpacking, and camping he was a joyous companion. When it came to the preservation of the unique wildness which this continent once knew, he was advocate extraordinary. And when it came to writing about the outdoors and the wilderness, I always rated him along with Henry Thoreau and John Muir.

—William O. Douglas, 1972

To those words of Justice Douglas I say, Amen!

And again, Amen to the words of Senator Howard Baker, of Tennessee, who declared in tribute, soon after Harvey's death in 1968: "Mr. Broome's love of nature was the hallmark of his life. America has lost a great citizen."

Harvey would be embarrassed by such words of praise, for he was modest to a fault. But few Americans, in any era, ever achieved his special relationship with the out-of-doors. His close friend Benton MacKaye called him "Earth Man," and that he was. He honored the earth and knew it intimately in all seasons. But he generously shared his love for the earth. As president of the Wilderness Society, an organization that he helped found, for example, Harvey was an able, inspiring spokesman for a movement that has penetrated deep into the conscience of America. That was one way he shared.

He traveled widely across the continent and recorded his explorations for us to read and appreciate, and that was another way. Starting in 1928 Harvey kept journals covering all his hikes in the Smokies and beyond. He edited the annual handbook of the Smoky Mountains Hiking Club, which itself constitutes exceptional nature writing. Later, his friend Howard Zahniser, executive director of the Wilderness Society, invited Harvey to contribute a series of "Mountain Notebooks" to *The Living Wilderness*, the quarterly journal of the society, which Zahniser edited.

Following his death, Anne Broome, Harvey's wife, felt inspired to assemble and publish his work in book form. They were the closest of companions, and she felt it her happy fortune to have shared his life and work. Anne consulted Paul Oehser, who served with Harvey on the governing council (board of directors) of the Wilderness Society and had long been in charge of publications at the Smithsonian Institution in Washington. With Oehser's encouragement and guidance, *Harvey Broome: Earth Man*, a collection of miscellaneous essays, was published in 1970. This was followed two years later by *Faces of the Wilderness*, a collection of largely personal accounts of field trips taken by the council of the Wilderness Society in conjunction with its annual meetings, from its first in 1946 up through 1965. Through those pages the reader became privy to the discoveries, discomforts, and exhilarations of wilderness travel in various sections of the country—on seashores, in deserts, and high in the mountains, from Alaska to the Everglades.

And then in 1975 came *Out Under the Sky of the Great Smokies: A Personal Journal*, a substantial volume illustrated with line drawings by Larry Hirst. Harvey actually had worked on this book before his death. He wrote the acknowledgments and introduction as they appear in print, and the work preserves the sequence just as he envisioned it. While preparing these lines, I have just picked up my clothbound copy of the original edition. I note the inside flap presents three endorsements. One from A. J. Sharp, a distinguished botany professor at the University of Tennessee, called the book "A superb account of the recurrent joys and spiritual rejuvenation found in wilderness." Stanley A. Cain, who also taught at Tennessee before going to the University of California, Santa Cruz, wrote: "This private journal, the most intimate of writings, is part of Harvey Broome's bequest to those who love people other than themselves." And I see the third endorsement is from myself: "The focus may be on the Smokies, but Mr. Broome expresses a sense of universality that should appeal to lovers of nature the world over."

That was more than a quarter century ago, to be sure, but Harvey's work now influences a new generation as well. Kenneth Wise, for example, has been hiking in the Smokies since he was twelve and has used the Broome journals as an academic research source and hiking guide. In a memorandum to the publisher, he cites the historic value of the journals as the only written accounts of old trails and paths that no longer exist. He believes that "No other writer conveys to the reader a better visual image of the Smoky Mountains wilderness. It is remarkably free of errors." As author of the contemporary popular guide *Hiking Trails in the Great Smoky Mountains,* Kenneth Wise should know.

Out Under the Sky is a timeless work. Here we find Harvey, the wilderness apostle, on his home turf. He reveals himself exactly as I knew and loved him: a gentle spirit, sensitive to the needs of nature and humankind, always with tolerance and good humor. On my first hike with him in the Great Smoky Mountains, we ventured to the Chimney Tops, a steep climb, almost vertical for several hundred feet, hand over hand from one rocky perch to the next. It was raining and I dared to complain. Harvey brushed me off with a laugh. "You don't complain about weather in the Smokies. You learn to accept it!"

Harvey saw the Smokies in every season and every mood. He was out under the skies when the temperature dropped to fifteen below zero, and the trees cracked and popped throughout the night, and the ice froze on his eyebrows and eyelashes, and the water froze in his canteen. He met and marveled at bears, snakes, and spiders, along with the more acceptable plants and trees. "Trees are very satisfying. They stay put; they don't go out at night; they don't have dates. Living less complex lives, they are not as stimulating as people, although, on the other hand, they are less disappointing than many people."

He began his lifelong love affair with the Smokies in another age in history. It was already the twentieth century but little changed from the nineteenth. Clusters of rural settlement like Sugarlands and

Cades Cove were largely isolated from outside civilization. Mountain people lived as their parents had lived before them. They grazed cattle on the grassy balds, following old pathways. The most significant intrusions by logging outfits and their railroads into the wild Smokies were then underway, but few trails led to the inaccessible peaks.

Harvey B. (for Benjamin) Broome was born in Knoxville in 1902, when it was not yet a city, but a provincial valley town, like most of the South still in arrested development following the Civil War. People walked to work, school, and church, rode the few electric trolleys, or rode bicycles, which outnumbered automobiles. As he recorded in *Out Under the Sky,* Harvey was born at home, since there was one hospital in town and it was rarely used for birthing. Harvey's father, George William Broome, had come to America as a child with his parents from Shropshire, England, in 1872. His mother's family was of early revolutionary stock. His grandfather, James Harvey Smith (on his mother's side), died at the age of ninety-two in the brick house where he was born, near the intersection of North Broadway and Tazewell Pike.

The defining moment in Harvey's life came early, when he was fifteen. Because he was slightly built and sickly, an uncle offered to take him on a camping trip in the Smokies. He came to the mountains to build his health hiking and camping, and then came again and again, in much the same way as another sickly boy, William O. Douglas (who the doctors feared would never reach maturity), camped and hiked in the Washington Cascades, and in the same way as sickly Theodore Roosevelt in the 1880s when he fled the East to the Badlands of North Dakota.

Harvey traveled from Knoxville on the Little River Railroad, an adventure in itself, into logging camps and through deep-water gaps. His first hike, in 1917, was to Silers Bald; his first climb to the Chimney Tops in 1920. In Knoxville, he was a good student planning a professional career, but his heart and mind were bound from the start with the Great Smoky Mountains wilderness.

Harvey was graduated from the University of Tennessee in 1923 and three years later from Harvard Law School. For all the benefits of formal education, his best learning came from two other connections that continued through the rest of his life. One was with Benton MacKaye, regional planner, philosopher, and wilderness apostle, to whom Harvey dedicated *Out Under the Sky.* The other powerful lasting connection was with the Smoky Mountains Hiking Club. I'm not sure that Harvey was a member when the club was organized in 1924—he may have been away at law school in Cambridge— but he certainly became involved with the group in the1920s, and remained close to it until he died.

Benton MacKaye was a New Englander, graduated from Harvard with a forestry degree in 1904, and then was employed by the U.S. Forest Service for twelve years before pioneering in regional planning and social and land reform. In 1921 he wrote an article titled "An Appalachian Trail: A Project in Regional Planning" in the *Journal of the American Institute of Architects,* which he circulated widely. The Appalachian Trail, or AT, as it has become known since MacKaye's time, has become a considerable recreational resource, but he saw it then and thereafter as something more: the means of making each metropolis a place of cultural individuality and unity, based on its own natural setting, "a sanctuary from the scramble of everyday worldly commercial life." He was thinking of protecting wilderness, much like his contemporaries Arthur Carhart and Aldo Leopold. In his 1921 article, MacKaye wrote: "Wilderness is two things—fact and feeling. It is a fund of knowledge and a spring of influence. It is the ultimate source of health."

Scattered groups and individuals responded to MacKaye's proposal and within two years completed sections of the trail. Early in 1925, leaders of various clubs convened in Washington, D.C., for the founding meeting of the Appalachian Trail Conference. MacKaye attended and outlined the philosophy he hoped would guide it. He wanted local initiative to count most. He felt it proper that government agencies administer the land but essential that volunteers, through the clubs, maintain and protect the Appalachian Trail.

Following the 1925 conference, individuals and groups along the trail did wonderful things to advance the conference's goals. The Smoky Mountains Hiking Club assumed responsibility for the length of the trail across the Smokies, then still wild and little known, at a time when the movement to establish a national park was just getting underway. The club aimed to increase interest in hiking and love of the mountains by disseminating information and taking beginners on hikes, initially scheduled once a month to key landmarks like Mount LeConte, the grassy balds of Thunderhead and Gregory, the Chimney Tops and the big trees in Porter's Flats. In 1927 the schedule was increased to two hikes a month throughout the year and the hiking program enlarged from a leaflet to a substantial handbook. Harvey Broome by now was corresponding secretary and editor of the handbook, and thus left us a record of his own and the club's activities.

Trip leaders in those early days (in addition to Harvey) included Jim Thompson, the photographer, whose pictures illustrated the handbook; Laura Thornburgh, author of an early guidebook to the Smokies; Ed Meeman, editor of the *Knoxville News-Sentinel* (who led a moonlight hike from Cades Cove to Gregory's Bald) and Jack Huff, whose family built and ran the Mountain View Hotel in Gatlinburg. The handbook is filled with cheery, positive writing, mostly Harvey's. In the 1929 edition he published a poem of his own titled "Winter" (signed H.B.B), which includes this stanza:

> It's the powdery snow in the moonlight,
>   A canvas for brilliance and gloom;
> It's the close, peaked ranks of the balsams,
>   Creaking and popping as at doom;
> It's the air, crisp and bitter as poison,
>   Which chills me and cuts to the bone;
> The resistless spell of dead winter,
>   That seizes and makes me her own.

Harvey returned from Harvard to pursue a successful law career in Knoxville, first as law clerk to a judge, then in private practice. That was the professional side of life. On the personal side, he became the fifth president of the Smoky Mountains Hiking Club in 1932, the year all the trails in the park were completed and when Harvey and seven others hiked the full length. It took them nine days.

He also established continuing contact with MacKaye. To show the closeness of their connection, Harvey in 1926 had met Anna (subsequently Anne) Waller Pursel, a native of Bloomsburg, Pennsylvania, at Cambridge while she worked as a secretary at the Harvard Law School. They corresponded, kept in touch, and fell in love. Harvey introduced her to his friend MacKaye, who invited them to be married in the living room of his home at Shirley Center, Massachusetts; and so it took place in 1937.

MacKaye himself was married for a few years early in life and then became a lifelong bachelor, with little ambition or need for material wealth. He worked here and there as a planner and consultant, but he most enjoyed projecting his philosophy on the role of nature in regionalism. I recall visiting him in retirement at Shirley Center. He was over ninety, still cheery with new ideas. He insisted on taking me to lunch and drove his car to get there. (He died in 1976 at age ninety-seven.)

MacKaye broadened Harvey's ideas and probably influenced his writing style as well. For example, in the article "The Appalachian Trail: A Guide to the Study of Nature" in *Scientific Monthly,* April 1932, MacKaye wrote: "Primeval influence is the opposite of machine influence. It is the antidote for over-rapid mechanization. It is getting feet on the ground with eyes toward the sky—not eyes on the ground with feet on a lever. It is feeling what you touch and seeing what you look at." On November 15, 1933, he wrote Harvey's sister, Margaret Broome (later Howes), as chairperson of the Smoky Mountain Hiking Club's handbook committee, in response to her request for a message of greeting for the handbook:

> Friendship is a hard thing to define. To me it is a portion of creation held in common. Our special portion (yours and mine) we call the wilderness—the portion untarnished by act of man. Such is our common bond. To cherish it (even as human fellowship itself)—such is our common goal.
>
> For we need this thing wilderness far more than it needs us. Civilizations (like glaciers) come and go, but the mountain and its forest continue the course of creation's destiny. And in these we mere humans can take part—by fitting our civilization to the mountain.
>
> This, friend Margaret, is the thing that you are doing (you and your Clubmates)—you who have wrought your portion of the Appalachian Trail—you who cherish the Great Smoky Mountains for yourselves and all America.

In 1934 MacKaye came to Knoxville for a two-year assignment on the planning staff of the Tennessee Valley Authority. Likely he and Harvey welcomed the opportunity to work together closely, but they could hardly have foreseen the momentous consequences of their collaboration.

That year, 1934, they met twice in Knoxville with Robert Marshall, a young man in his thirties who was pioneering federal programs in wilderness protection. Marshall as a boy in New York had tramped all across the Adirondacks (in the same way that Broome had tramped the Smokies) and gone on to adventurous hikes all across the continent and to a successful career in government. On this occasion he was on assignment from Secretary of the Interior Harold L. Ickes to view the effects of New Deal road-building projects on the Great Smoky Mountains. After Marshall and Broome climbed Clingmans Dome, Marshall reported to Ickes in a memo (August 18,1934): "I hiked to Clingmans Dome last Sunday, looking forward to the great joy of undisturbed nature for which this mountain has been famous. Walking along the skyline trail, I heard instead the roar of machines on the newly constructed road just below me and saw the huge scars which this new highway is making on the mountain. Clingmans Dome and the primitive were simply ruined."

Then on another visit to Knoxville one month later, Marshall met again with MacKaye and Broome and also Bernard Frank, then a TVA forester, to conceive a new organization to be called the Wilderness Society, and a few months later the society was duly constituted. From the very beginning until the end of his life, Harvey Broome was a central figure to development of the society's ideology and implementation through law and regulation.

Aldo Leopold, who had seen national forest wilderness disturbed and destroyed, joined the group. So did Olaus J. Murie, a well-respected field biologist who had conducted important studies in Alaska and Wyoming. Robert Sterling Yard, who had been journalist, editor, and early publicity chief of the National Park Service, in 1935 became the part-time executive secretary (and later president) of the society. Yard had become disillusioned with commercialization of the national parks and had dreamed of starting "an organization to preserve the primitive."

Bob Marshall, the young crusader, died in 1939 at the age of thirty-eight, and then Robert Sterling Yard, the old crusader, died in 1945 at eighty-four, but they left the wilderness movement well defined and the Wilderness Society in the hands of committed and caring colleagues. Following Yard's death, Olaus Murie became director, based in Wyoming, and Howard Zahniser, formerly a government editor, became executive secretary, based in Washington. Zahniser, or "Zahnie," I well remember from personal contact as studious, soft-spoken, patient, always willing to listen, always resisting the seduction of compromise. He drafted the Wilderness Bill in 1956, found sponsors, and worked tirelessly for its passage.

Zahniser and Broome were colleagues and comrades. Edward Zahniser, the son of Howard, remembers from childhood "Harvey's wry, affectionate smile, his attentiveness and gentleness, a strength in his love for Anne." Because their own grandfathers were dead, the four Zahniser children felt free to call Harvey "Grampa." The whole Zahniser family would visit Harvey and Anne in Knoxville and at their cabin at Cobbles Hollow, in Emerts Cove, at the edge of the national park. The cabin was built with logs, an open fireplace, kerosene lamps, its own spring, and a view down a ravine to Mount LeConte. It was a great starting place for hikes into cove hardwood forests and into the high country.

Zahniser appreciated Harvey's writing and invited him to contribute regularly to the quarterly *The Living Wilderness*, which Zahniser edited. Considering the Wilderness Society was still a small struggling organization with a few thousand members, that magazine had little circulation and was often late in publication, but it carried articles of lasting value by gifted visionaries like Aldo Leopold, Benton MacKaye, Olaus Murie, and Sigurd Olson. Harvey Broome, after visiting the Big Horn Crags in Idaho in 1961, wrote in *The Living Wilderness* as follows:

> I think how precious in such an environment and
> under such circumstances is one human life. It is one
> of our problems today that our huge cities have
> become frightening colossi. The individual exists,
> for himself and a few who know him. Otherwise,
> he is one of a mass to be thought of in the mass
> and shunted about in streams of traffic, in streams
> of thought, and in easy academic classifications. It
> took this wilderness experience to etch again the
> importance of a single person.

In this same period William O. Douglas, associate justice of the Supreme Court, became another intimate friend and trail companion of Harvey's, in the Smokies and elsewhere. A native of Washington State, frail and sickly as a child, Douglas found strength and purpose in the outdoors. He called the Cascades home but knew the mountains of the world and considered them all sacred.

As a strong-willed civil libertarian, Douglas bucked the political or public tide when he felt need to. "We must have freedom of speech for all," he insisted, "or we will in the long run have it for none but the cringing and the craven." And at times Douglas thought little of stepping down from the bench to become involved in earthy affairs.

For example, in 1954, the *Washington Post* published an editorial favoring construction of a parkway on the towpath of the Chesapeake & Ohio Canal, intruding into a section of the Appalachian Trail in Maryland. In what became one of the most famous letters to the editor, Douglas challenged the author of the *Post* editorial, Robert Estabrook, to join him in hiking the 185 miles of canal towpath between Washington and Cumberland in western Maryland. Subsequently, Douglas and thirty-six others, the editor included, rode the train to Cumberland and started down the towpath parallel to the Potomac River, through rolling pastureland, mountain gaps, and historic towns. The "Immortal Nine," including Bill Douglas, Harvey Broome, and Olaus Murie, averaging between twenty and twenty-seven miles a day, completed the full journey in eight days, returning to Washington in cheers. It was a bit of a Gandhian protest, as Douglas called it, and it worked. The parkway plan was discarded.

During the late fifties and early sixties, the battle for the Wilderness Bill wore on. It was a hard uphill campaign. Key members of the governing council wavered and had second thoughts about pushing the bill any further. Stewart M. Brandborg, Zahnhiser's close associate and later successor, well remembers: "When Zahnie was always open to endless discussion of the topic of 'What should we do next in working for the bill?' some complained that he overdid it. I recognized its value and resented deeply the tough interrogations." It became so bad that Zahniser despaired and was ready to quit. Edward Zahniser remembers his father's anguish, but also that "Harvey Broome emerged as the council champion of keeping at it."

Zahniser saw the campaign through, but died in May 1964, five months before the Wilderness Act became law. He was the Moses denied entry to the promised land. Harvey was already president of the society. He had been elected in 1957 and the following year had quit his law practice to work as clerk for a federal judge in Knoxville, with the understanding that he could take reasonable time as needed to labor on behalf of the society. Brandborg recalls as follows:

> I consulted with Harvey as a source of mentoring. He always shared in his generous, loyal way in my tribulations. Harvey usually would arrive in Washington on Friday nights for the three quarterly meetings of the executive committee on Saturdays. As a rule, he stayed with us on Saturday nights and we hiked on Sugar Loaf Mountain or the C&O Canal on Sundays until his afternoon plane for Knoxville. The kids went along and were pleased with his humor and observations on the woods and its critters.
>
> At no time in that period from 1964 until his death do I remember a single unpleasant occasion while working closely with Harvey. It was always a matter of reasonable discussion, gentle persuasion and presentation of alternative lines of action, but never an argument. It was terribly important to me as a young guy feeling my way that he was unfailingly willing to share his wisdom and guidance.

In 1966 Harvey lived his finest hours, the summation of a life devoted to the cause of the Great Smoky Mountains and to wilderness everywhere. In that year the National Park Service announced its first wilderness proposal under terms of the Wilderness Act of 1964. The agency chose for its precedent the Great Smokies, of all places, but its proposal could not have been worse. It was, in fact, an anti-wilderness proposal. As the *New York Times* editorialized on June 14, 1966, on the eve of public hearings: "The Park Service has come up with a meager, unsatisfactory and essentially bureaucratic proposal that six different areas covering less than half the park be held inviolate as wilderness. It is the Park Service, supposedly the prime protector, that has plans to destroy major parts of the Smokies wilderness by constructing several highways."

The anti-wilderness design was the personal concoction of George B. Hartzog Jr., the crafty director of the National Park Service, who had made a commitment to local North Carolina politicians for commercial-boosting highways across the Smokies and who resisted wilderness designation everywhere. "The Hartzog proposal for Great Smoky Mountains National Park was fortuitous in a way," Stewart Brandborg recalls. "It stirred Harvey's deepest emotions. We began a day-by-day strategizing process, with Harvey 'feeling the pain' of each Hartzog ploy for destroying the Great Smokies wilderness and wilderness of the entire national park system. I was green in facing this challenge and the ultimate confrontation with George and all his political chicanery, but with Harvey's thoughtful, gentle counsel we chose and steered the right course."

Harvey may have been gentle, but he was resolute as well. I saw that at close hand during this period. For three years I had been working on *Strangers in High Places,* my book about the Great Smokies, and had benefited from Harvey's experience and friendship. He took me out on the trails and into his home. Now I saw him as tough and tenacious, never once countenancing the possibility of defeat on the issues of principle.

He and his closest comrade-in-arms, Ernie Dickerman, were disciplined and determined. They gave the spark that fueled the fight. Harvey was like the commander-in-chief and Dickerman the chief of staff in charge of mobilizing grassroots support in defense of the Smokies wilderness. They were old Knoxville buddies, long active in the Smoky Mountains Hiking Club. *Out Under the Sky* includes reference to many trips they made together. These range from early 1941, when they hiked to Wooly Tops, plunging into "the dead of winter, with great snow blankets, gray-green ice falls, and time-covered trees" to the historic "Save-Our-Smokies" hike on Sunday, October 23, 1966. On that day a total of 576 people walked some portion of the route from Clingmans Dome parking area out along the Appalachian Trail to Buckeye Gap, where the proposed road was intended to cross the crest of the Smokies, and then down to the Elkmont Campground. A total of 234 persons walked the entire 17 miles, the last completing the trip by moonlight.

"It is amazing how many persons from all over the country supported wilderness designation in the Great Smoky Mountains," Dickerman wrote to me in a retrospective years later, "and opposed any new roads in the course of the campaign which lasted six years until George Hartzog finally threw in the towel." Or, as Stewart Brandborg recalls: "Victory in the Smokies gave us a precedent and the confidence and experience to face down the bureaucracies which continued in their opposition to wilderness designation. Harvey gave the leadership on focusing on mobilization of grassroots people who would carry the day in wilderness designation for lands in their states."

Following Harvey's death in 1968, Dickerman carried on. He organized a trip to Washington by almost one hundred conservationists from North Carolina and Tennessee on June 23, 1969. Hartzog's political sponsor and superior at the Interior Department, Stewart L. Udall, was now gone as secretary, and the delegation called on the new secretary, Walter J. Hickel, who met with them and shook each person by the hand. "I am impressed by your numbers and sincerity of your purpose," Hickel declared. Then he humbled Hartzog by directing him and his agency to come up with a new and better plan. The transmountain road idea died there.

Dickerman was part of Harvey's circle of loyal, gifted, and giving people. A lifelong bachelor, Dickerman lived simply and carried little baggage. During the campaign in the Smokies he joined the professional staff of the Wilderness Society, training and mobilizing grassroots activists, continuing on his own even after retirement in 1976. In 1986 the hiking club presented him the Harvey Broome Distinguished Service Award. He died in 1998 at age eighty-eight.

I felt privileged to be included in Harvey's circle. Staying in the house with him and Anne on Mountain Crest Drive was always uplifting and enlightening. Brick and timbers in the house had been moved to the site when the old family homestead was razed. A little of the front yard was mowed along the walkway, but the rest was strictly *au naturel* wooded and shrubby. Harvey and Anne were focused on wilderness, but had a breadth of interests. She was a weaver, with a loom in the house, doing something creative with her hands. He was a local historian, president of the East Tennessee Historical Society from 1945 to 1947, and author of four chapters in *The French Broad-Holston Country, A History of Knox County*. Anne's parents had died when she was a child, so Harvey's family became her family and one of his nieces, sister Margaret's daughter, is named Anne Broome Howes.

I saw Harvey for the last time early in 1968, a matter of weeks before he died. A few months earlier he had climbed Mt. Katahdin in

Maine. Then, near Thanksgiving, he learned that he had a heart ailment. Still, he came to Washington on Wilderness Society business and had dinner with a small group of friends. While walking with him back to his hotel I saw that he looked pale and weak. The once tireless hiker felt he must stop to rest every few steps.

On Friday, March 8, 1968, Harvey collapsed and died in his yard while sawing a segment of a little hollow log to make into a wren's house. Several days later eight or ten of Harvey's intimates gathered for a service in the study of his home on Mountain Crest Drive. I remember Anne Broome, Alice Zahniser (Howard's widow), Stewart Brandborg, Ernie Dickerman, Ernest Griffith, Michael Nadel, and Paul Oehser. Anne read selections from Harvey's journals, including this entry from April 23, 1950, about a climb in the Ramsay-Buck Fork country, at the Chapman Prong confluence with the Ramsay:

> In the deepness of twilight, we noted an elusive fragrance, and I was reminded of the fragrance which Thoreau noted several times over the course of years and which was to him so sweet and captivating that he was almost afraid to trace it to its source. He never did. We, however, followed ours to an oasis of phacelia which flanked the trail like snow—acres of it. And the heavy, tense, strenuous day came slowly, evenly, peacefully to an end, like the subsiding notes of a great symphony.

Each took a turn to express some special reminiscence. When my turn came I stared at Harvey's boots perched on a filing cabinet. I wanted to make some reference to them but felt inadequate and words stuck in my throat.

Then we drove to the park to hike to Harvey's favorite area in the section called Greenbrier. It was raining in the Smokies, a steady, drippy downpour that turned the forest misty, mellow, and a little mournful. I hadn't realized what was coming and wasn't prepared for it. Anne removed from her backpack a container about the size of a Mason jar. It held Harvey's cremated remains, looking like ground chalk—all there is to any of us in the end, and no mausoleum, no matter how majestic, can make more of it. While we stood silent and thoughtful in the rain, Anne scattered the ashes. It was time to leave, but no one seemed ready or able to lead. Ernest Griffith, treasurer of the Wilderness Society, an old scholar who had already lived a full life, broke the silence. "This is a time of thanksgiving, not of mourning," he began a brief impromptu eulogy that brightened the mood. He called it a day of triumph, gratitude, and dedication, and so it became.

A few days later in Washington, Representative John P. Saylor of Pennsylvania paid tribute to Harvey on the floor of the House, as Howard Baker had done in the Senate. Saylor had introduced the Wilderness Bill in 1956 and fought an uphill battle until it became law. He said that he was proud to consider himself a fellow to Bob Marshall, Olaus Murie, Howard Zahniser, and Harvey Broome: "They were all great leaders for the saving of wilderness for our time, for all time. They have passed on, but their legacy falls to new leaders, as their spirit lives on."

They have gone to their reward, John Saylor included. Anne Broome died in 1983. Of those at the service, only Alice Zahniser, Stewart Brandborg, and I remain in the twenty-first century, but the spirit of them all lives on. Paul Oehser was a considerable poet, and from one of his pieces, called "Song," I will conclude with these appropriate two verses.

> Let songs be crystal clear
> From countless throats, till stars shall hear
> The unyielding notes;
>
> Till songless men shall share
> The echoes coming, each unaware
> Of his own humming.

— Michael Frome

I acknowledge with appreciation help given to me by others than those cited in the text above, specifically William S. Broome, Jr., nephew of Harvey Broome; Leroy Fox, stalwart of the Smoky Mountains Hiking Club, who reminds me the club is still on guard in protecting the national park, and Scot Danforth, editor at the University of Tennessee Press, who enabled me to write these words.

CKNOWLEDGMENTS

Anne Broome has for thirty years shared fully my enthusiasms.[1] She assumed the enormous burden of transcribing my Journals and that of the retyping; and her counsel has borne fruit in tightening the text.

As editors of *The Living Wilderness*, the late Howard Zahniser and Michael Nadel published several articles based upon my Journals under the general heading "Mountain Notebook." I am indebted to them for their warm encouragement and to the Wilderness Society for permission to use materials found in chapters 1941 through 1950 which appeared in somewhat different form in *The Living Wilderness*.

I enjoy a particular rapport with Michael Nadel, who sanctioned both the coining and use of a new word in "Mountain Notebook . . . 1950."

Paul Oehser has led me through editorial trails so very familiar to him and so unfamiliar to me. His competence has been spiced with quip and pun.

Miss Eleanor Goehring, reference librarian at the University of Tennessee, has been unfailingly helpful.

---

[1] Shortly after this paragraph was typed we were on a holiday in a remote part of the Smokies. The trail had vanished. We were negotiating slippery rocks in midcreek. I wanted to go higher. Anne chose that moment to say whimsically, "I wonder if the word 'fully' shouldn't be omitted from that first sentence."

Acknowledgment is made of many persons whose lives were at various times mingled with mine in the physical and mental adventures recorded here. There have been literally hundreds of trail companions, whose names drift in and out of the pages like mists through ridgecrest pines. Recognition of all of them is beyond possibility.

But the volume would not be complete without specific acknowledgment of Uncle Charlie Mooers, who introduced me to the mountains on a camping trip half a century ago; of Russell Gilmore, at whose home I stayed one summer near the foot of Mt. Le Conte and who gave me a first course in the identification of trees; of Lucien Greene, tireless and cherished companion in the rugged pre-Park days; of "Dutch" Roth, a pint-sized juggernaut in human form who was oblivious of fatigue, weather, thicket, or steep, and who went climbing with me when no one else would go; of Guy Frizzell, robust, sometimes earthy, gay, sensitive, articulate—a superb camper and matchless companion on countless trips.

Robert Marshall touched me not only with his enthusiasm for wilderness, but with his conviction that primitive America was vanishing "with appalling rapidity."

Many have helped me to understand what I was seeing in the back country. In this considerable undertaking, Benton MacKaye and Aldo Leopold have been outstanding—Benton, through his writings and a friendship lasting over a third of a century; and Aldo, through association on the Council of the Wilderness Society and through his lucid and dazzling books. Bernard Frank, a member of the Wilderness Society Council, was a genius at reading the landscape for me. There was "Prof" Jennison, an easy companion in the 1930's with a vast knowledge of the flora. A quartet of ecologists around the University of Tennessee—Stanley Cain, the late Royal Shanks, Edward Clebsch, and Randolph Shields—were most helpful.

I acknowledge an immeasurable debt to the councillors of the Wilderness Society with whom I have served since 1935. There is not the space to name them all. Some have passed on. Several are now my closest associates and friends. I have mentioned a few of them elsewhere. Others, all of them my elders, who affected my life deeply include: Robert Sterling Yard, an indefatigable and dedicated purist among wilderness advocates, who was active at fourscore years; Harold Anderson, a nonprofessional interested in the Appalachian Trail, who pursued that interest inevitably into advocacy of wilderness preservation; Irving Clark, another nonprofessional, a reserved man with a twinkle who was a foremost defender of the Olympic Mountains and of the North Cascades; Ernest Oberholtzer, who transmuted a frail body and an uncertain future in the Boundary Waters Canoe Area into rugged health and a lifelong and spectacularly effective career on behalf of the Quetico-Superior; and Olaus Murie, a distinguished mammalogist of immense learning, gentle nature, and undeviating probity. My debt to Olaus and to Howard Zahniser (my contemporary in age) for an understanding of modern trends is incalculable. With them I had deep and lasting friendships.

I acknowledge my debt to three conservationists (writers and hard-bitten observers of the modern scene) with whom I have walked in the Great Smokies—the late Edward J. Meeman, William O. Douglas, and Michael Frome.

Finally, I acknowledge the transcendent circumstance of the Great Smoky Mountains themselves—a priceless legacy from an inspired company who worked so selflessly for their preservation.

Knoxville, Tennessee   H.B.
July 1967

$\mathscr{I}$NTRODUCTION

From January 1941 I have kept Journals. They were maintained at first for my eyes only. But there were frequent entries dealing with experiences in the Great Smoky Mountains. And as time passed there began to appear reflections upon basic outlooks, and upon social and technological changes which were not only blasting our wild country but disastrously affecting the quality of living everywhere.

With the exception of the first chapter, in which I bridge in skeleton fashion the gap from my birth and formative years to the year 1941, the chapters which follow were taken with sharp editing from the Journals.

Most of the entries deal with the wilderness of the Great Smokies and nearby mountains. The commentaries upon the corrosion of environment have a deep relevance; wilderness is at one end of the environmental spectrum, and the blight-ridden land, air, and water at the other.

It was in the wilderness that man first became conscious of himself and mastered the art of speech. Such a world was for long ages the naked arena in which he lived and learned. Where wilderness can still be found, the ancientness of the land and the nobility of man's struggle emerge. Wilderness is vastly different from the clutter and clatter of much of our civilized world. In wilderness one experiences exhilaration and joy. In its freedom and simplicity, in its vitality and immense variety, happiness may not only be pursued; it is ofttimes found.

As I have written elsewhere, wilderness has many faces. This is not the place to enlarge upon that subject, other than to observe that whatever its face—desert, swamp, lake, stream, forest, mountain, plain, ocean, shore, tundra—the intrinsic differences are overshadowed by a basic identity. The sovereign quality of wilderness is the same wherever encountered. Its overtones are universal whether found in the coyote's wail in the alpine dawn, in the measured dead-of-night call of the owl from riverbank cottonwoods, or in the unexpected discovery of rhododendron blooming in deep forest. Each manifestation has an unshackled quality—each stirs untapped longings—each gives a fillip to living—each has an unsuppressed lilt which bursts from the deepest wellsprings of life.

These are the realities found in the wilderness of the Great Smoky Mountains.

OUT
UNDER
THE SKY OF
THE GREAT SMOKIES

$\mathscr{F}$ORMATIVE YEARS

From my birthplace on a hill in east Knoxville the Great Smoky Mountains were a pale blue band on the southern horizon. It is significant that my birthplace was also my home. The town had one hospital, seldom used for such natural events as births.

The majority of the streets were rutted surfaces of bare earth over which a layer of stone had been scattered. There were then few automobiles. People walked to their work, to school, to church, or rode the few electric trolleys. There were some private stables among the well-to-do. Bicycles were common, threading the treacheries of gravel and ruts. Sidewalks and a few downtown streets were of brick. But interurban roadways were unknown.

Most people read by the light of coal oil (kerosene) lamps or gas. Some streets were lit by gas—a few by the novel electric arcs. The daily newspapers and a few magazines—*Literary Digest, Review of Reviews, Youth's Companion,* and *World's Work*—kept the people aware of an outside world. They read the Bible and the newspapers; went to church; went to bed early and arose early for long ten- and twelve-hour work days.

People took an interest in the churches and the new minister, in their children, in politics and elections, in shootings and murder trials, in fires which were frequent and destructive, in deaths and weddings. There were modest excursions on the river, and boating was popular on the tiny lakes of the town park.

Walking was popular on Sunday afternoon after a soporific noontime dinner. With cousins I often went to a bluff which hung above the river. Sometimes we went to the plant down on the river where throbbing steam-powered pumps hoisted water 300 vertical feet to settling basins and the great standpipe which served most of the town from the crest of the hill above our home. Sometimes we went to the "water works" and looked at the raw water, rust-colored and turbid as it came up from the river, and then at the same water, cleansed and sparkling, as it poured into the final tank to be raised thence to the standpipe.

On rarer times we crossed the river and climbed through wooded foothills to the Cherokee Bluffs, where we could see gun emplacements from the Civil War. There we could pick up Minie balls of lead, relics of the war.

About once a month my parents, brother, sister, and I took the steam "dummy" line—a miniature train—five miles toward Fountain City to Grandpa Smith's farm, where there were a two-storied brick house, two barns, several horses, cattle, pigs, chickens, fields, rabbits, an orchard, a springhouse, a smokehouse, woodhouse, and outhouse, each carrying its own odor, delectable or pungent. There were free-flowing springs from which clear pure water was dipped.

Grandpa was someone special. He had been a cavalryman in the Civil War. But he was always a farmer. He could shoe a horse, cradle a field of wheat, make a pair of shoes, slaughter a pig, milk a cow, chop wood, grind a blade, grease a wagon, and handle a horse with certitude. Grandma could weave, knit and quilt, make lard and butter, blackberry jam and apple butter, and soap. Her brown-sugar cookies were incomparable.

On Sundays Grandpa hitched up the surrey and spring wagon and we drove three gritty miles to church. After Sunday School, the catechism, the sermon, hymns, and the socializing, we returned to the Old House where we feasted from Grandma's bountiful table. Then we propped ourselves in chairs on the front porch and watched the people drive by.

In the later afternoon, before the pigs had to be fed and the milking done, if we were lucky we could persuade Father and Grandpa to climb the wooded ridge to the east, whence five long miles away we could just make out the red standpipe on the hill above our house in town. I was astounded that one could see five whole miles.

In this pleasant, peaceful, isolated, and self-contained world I don't recall when I first became aware that there were mountains to the south. But I could not have been very old.

As I have implied, the church was the center of much of the social life. The more sophisticated town churches sometimes chartered a train for their summer picnics. Cinders and black smoke poured in the open doors and windows of the swaying coaches, and the screech of the steam whistle raised the hair on our heads and allowed the cinders to settle closer to our scalps.

I loved the train rides. I loved the expectancy and the first lurch of the coach. One time we went beyond Maryville and rolled and jolted to the way-station of Walland. There our locomotive was detached, rolled onto a turntable, and was rotated by two straining trainmen. A curious engine with a battery of vertical pistons on the side was coupled on and we were jerked and towed for miles along a small clear river to Townsend.

This was a sawmill town with great piles of logs, a log pool at the foot of an inclined elevator, the high whine of the handmill, and smoking cages of sawdust burners. Everywhere were bark and lumber piles, and the sour tang of fresh-sawed boards. I didn't question where the logs came from.

Beyond Townsend we entered a wooded gorge and were snaked up the stream. The wheels screamed on the curves. Such thrills! We looked down on raw boulders in water, foaming and clear. The cars crossed the stream on a bridge and everybody moved, as one, to the windows on the opposite side to continue a love affair with the river. It was alive and moving and beautiful.

Something was said about Elkmont. I know now that it was a logging camp, where there were some rough houses, a small railroad shop, and a commissary whose steps and floors were chewed and pitted by the needle calks in the Cutter boots of the lumberjacks. But we rolled on through Elkmont and were pulled a short distance beyond. We hardly had time for lunch and a furtive retreat to a screen of bushes to change our clothes for a quick, sharp dip into the clear biting water. I didn't ask where the water came from.

I do not recall any particular impression made upon me by the rugged surroundings. I do recall that I was reluctant to leave when the long blast of the locomotive whistle signaled the end of the day.

As the train swept out through a deep water gap into the valley, the glorious façade of the mountains was broadside to the train. I leaned on the windowsill of the coach and watched that soft blue wall until it vanished in the twilight.

I had become aware that there were mountains. And after two or

5

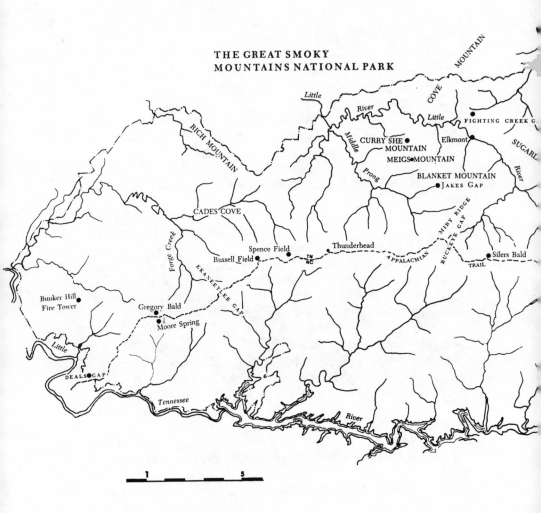

THE GREAT SMOKY
MOUNTAINS NATIONAL PARK

COVE MOUNTAIN

Little

River

Little

RICH MOUNTAIN

FIGHTING CREEK G

CURRY SHE
MOUNTAIN

Elkmont

Middle

MEIGS MOUNTAIN

SUGARL

BLANKET MOUNTAIN

River

JAKES GAP

Prong

CADES COVE

MIRY RIDGE

BUCKEYE GAP

Forge Creek

Spence Field

Thunderhead

Silers Bald

Russell Field

TN
NC

APPALACHIAN

TRAIL

EKANEETLEE GAP

Bunker Hill
Fire Tower

Gregory Bald

Moore Spring

Little

DEALS GAP

Tennessee

River

1   5

WHITE ROCK●(MT. CAMMERER)

LOW●GAP   Creek

Maddron Bald

Old Black   Big
(MT.) GUYOT   MT. STERLING (N.C.)

Tricorner Knob

MT. CHAPMAN

Cat Stairs

Greenbrier Pinnacle

Little Pigeon River   Middle Prong   Ramsay Prong

Emerts Cove

Creek

Dudley Cr.

Winnesoka

PORTERS MOUNTAIN

Porters Flat   Woolly Tops

TRILLIUM●GAP
Grotto Falls   Laurel Top
Rainbow Falls
(MT.) LÉ CONTE
Alum Cave Prong   DRY SLUICE
Bear Pen Hollow   Horseshoe Mt.

Charlies Bunion

HUGHES RIDGE

ANAKEESTA RIDGE   Jumpoff GAP
Chimney
Tops
(MT.) MINGUS

NEWFOUND GAP
INDIAN GAP

Bradley Fork

MOUNTAIN

●MT. COLLINS

lingmans Dome

Andrews Bald

Smokemont●

Indian Camp Creek

7

three such picnics at Elkmont, I became aware also that the pale blue band which could be seen from the upstairs front window of my birthplace was mountains. Two new measures had become a part of my world, a longer horizontal (much farther than the five-mile view from grandpa's ridge) and a vertical dimension—mountains.

Such was the first phase in the linkage of my life with mountains and the wilds. The second phase also had an early origin. Illness had touched the first decade and a half of my life. My body was frail, or so everyone thought; and I was shielded from contact sports. Though I performed my share of the chores—splitting kindling, carrying coal, cutting grass—and though at the age of eleven I got my first bicycle, I was undersized and weakly and a concern to members of my family.

In 1917, when I was fifteen, an uncle thought a camping trip in the mountains might boost my health. He approached my parents. Father agreed with alacrity; mother, who was always a cautious person, finally yielded to my enthusiasm for the trip. Father and I went to a harness maker with specifications for a knapsack in which to carry my personal belongings. It was made of canvas and leather; and though it cost but $2.00, I was to carry it for a decade.

The great day of departure started with a train ride to the Elkmont of earlier years. We were met by three grizzled mountaineers, whose clothes carried the odor of sweat and of the earth. The scent was not unpleasant but I was aware of it whenever I came near them, and the very experience was a part of this great new adventure.

Our mountain friends had three horses tied in the shade nearby. After an interminable period of weighing and balancing and roping the nondescript bundles of duffle to the pack frames, we got under way. Our destination—twelve miles away and 3500 feet higher—was Silers Bald, near the heart of the Smokies.

Only the camping equipment was to be carried by the horses. The three mountain men, my three uncles, and a cousin and I were to walk. I was uneasy about the hike. I had no inkling of what was involved in walking twelve miles, and of climbing 3500 feet.

It was a hot August afternoon. Ridges towered to unbelievable heights. After climbing a few miles we digressed from the Jakes Gap trail to take the more direct, slippery and inhumanly steep Dripping Springs route to the summit of Miry Ridge. Each of us was carrying an item or two which could not be packed handily on the horses. I had the rifle. Burdened with it and my own inexperience, my struggles in brief slippery spurts up the Dripping Springs mountain added nothing to my self-assurance. My legs were weak; my lungs were shallow. Every lunge upward seemed to bring me close to exhaustion. But the ascent finally dwindled away. The slope leveled off and we moved out on top of Miry Ridge.

That night we slept in a rude enclosure constructed around the "claim cabin" of a lumber company. We lay on the ground with only the folded canvas of a tent underneath us. A round moon arched across the sky. Stimulated by the openness above and by the hard earth beneath, as well as by the day's excitement, I slept little on this my first night, ever, out under the sky.

The next morning we started early. A mist hung close and in its dimness we and the horses wallowed the length of Miry Ridge. Pans clanged as packs collided with trees, and my cherished knapsack was torn on a snag. We avoided the quagmire of the trail and sought out a narrow and incredibly greasy bench of humus alongside. The morning was cool. The mist mingled with the forest in a muted world of rhododendrons and hemlocks, of birch and maples. By midmorning it had vanished, and we emerged into sunshine at a rocky look-off near the junction of Miry Ridge and the Great Smoky divide.

The magnitude of the view was lost upon me. Every sight, every sound and sensation since leaving Elkmont, except the punishing climb up Dripping Springs mountain, had been strange and exciting. The whole trip had been akin to a first breathless glimpse of the Grand Canyon. I had been plunged into wildness. When Uncle Charlie pointed out the one thing in that vastness of which I had previously heard—Silers Bald—I centered my attention upon it.

About noon we pitched our wall tent on a little flat. Slender beech trees, cut from the forest, furnished poles for the tent and frames for our canvas cots. Sam Cook, our guide, found a small overhanging cliff and laid his bedding under it. Sam split bark from a buckeye and flattening it out made a table. A pole squared on one side and braced between two trees provided a seat. We assembled rocks for a fireplace. Our water was obtained from a scooped-out place down the side of the mountain. It was a long walk down, and it was a longer carry back with 40 to 50 pounds of water sloshing in lard cans between us.

A single layer of canvas discouraged the elements. We cut, chopped, and split trees for firewood. Candles supplied light. The day's activities began with the dawn and ended with the dark. There was no

9

outhouse. One quickly found the pattern for more primitive ways. We experienced 48 consecutive hours of rain and fog, and lived with mud and dampness. The rain falling on our tin plates splashed food into our faces. Smoke saturated our clothes as we rotated before the fire on a corduroy of logs laid to raise us above the mud.

On the east horizon four miles away was the rounded bulk of Clingmans Dome—what seemed to me a very high mountain. It was covered with an evergreen forest—denser, darker, and more mysterious than our grove of beeches.

One fine day we followed the divide from Silers to Clingmans. At one spot we looked far down into Tennessee and saw logging trains which resembled toys. At another spot we could both see and hear lumberjacks working in North Carolina.

At the summit of Clingmans we entered a dim, thickset stand of evergreens smaller than telephone poles. I did not inquire why the growth was different from the majestic forest, brilliant with wild flowers, through which we had ascended. But the memory of that dark and closely growing timber has remained with me all my life. Later I was to learn that it constituted a few acres of second growth and that there are differences between a primeval and a regenerating forest.

After two weeks we returned home. I had survived in the outdoors despite rain and bad weather. From Sam Cook I had discovered that one did not need a tent for a snug shelter but could use a cliff. I was sturdier and had gained a few pounds in weight. Under the sharp surveillance of three grown men I had been permitted to use an ax. But I could not have built a fire in the rain or have found my way without a guide. I had not learned what it meant to climb with a pack on my back.

On Silers we had been surrounded by a vast expanse of mountains, blue and inviting when the sky was clear. On the east rim was Clingmans Dome. Far to the west was Thunderhead. And on the north rim were the bold outlines of another great peak, Mt. Le Conte. The huge triangle defined by those summits was a complete unknown to me. My eyes were on Mt. Le Conte, which had come to hold for me an irresistible appeal.

Three years were to pass before I was to climb it. The first World War intervened, curtailing much civilian activity but bringing one boon. Teenagers became a useful commodity upon the labor market and twice I worked for a short period at an apple orchard a few miles from the base of Mt. Le Conte. This spot lay in rough foothill country, and a whole day by truck, wagon, and foot was consumed in covering the 40 miles between Knoxville and the orchard.

The mountains were close and twice we took quick trips around the end and back of Le Conte to a stream of surpassing beauty. We hiked far past the last rough homestead where visitors were so rare that it was the prudent custom to pause outside the fence and call before approaching for fear of being shot.

Here we purchased eggs and obtained permission to use a cabin belonging to a lumber company. Beyond the cabin we entered upon an old trail which had served as access to saltpeter deposits in the Civil War. Since that date it had had limited use for passage between North Carolina and Tennessee. Overgrown and narrow, the trail crossed and recrossed a stream of absolute clarity.

The crossings I approached with real fear. We were backpacking and I reached the stream with rubbery legs and scorched lungs. There were no footlogs, and we waded or leaped from boulder to boulder. If a person slipped, or his knapsack pulled him off balance, he would bang a shin or fall into the water. On the Silers trip my introduction to mountains had been along their ridge tops, but now I received my baptism in their streams.

Our destination was a tiny log cabin which had been erected in a rough clearing above the stream. The gaps between its logs were closed by clean, hand-split shingles which had been nailed horizontally on the inside. The work was crude and the air circulation remained excellent. The cabin had a puncheon floor and a roof of split shingles.

A small iron stove with a flat cooking surface was propped on billets in one corner of the cabin. Pole bedsteads with corn husk mattresses occupied two corners, and a pile of firewood, mostly waste from the cabin construction, was stacked handy to the stove. This was our shelter.

We fished the stream for brook trout. One of my companions was an expert who caught all that we could eat. Our fire of hemlock and spruce chunks popped and crackled as it flickered through the cracks in the stove. The smoke of these woods also has an extreme pungency, and the night breezes swirled it like incense both outside and inside the cabin with separate but equal abandon. At nightfall the vastness and darkness of the uncut forest settled about us, and our whole world centered around the liveliness in that rickety stove. The high beech woods and meadows of Silers Bald had never been like the overwhelming, inky-black forested wilderness at the bottom of that narrow, chill, north-facing valley.

After the camping trip I worked again at the orchard. In good weather the summit of Le Conte was visible eight tantalizing miles distant and 5000 intriguing feet higher. On the weekend before I was to return to Knoxville to the university, I planned to make the climb with some mountain friends. Quite unexpectedly my father appeared on the day before, and quite characteristically joined the party. He knew that his way of life had not conditioned him for such a trip. But he lived his life with a certain quiet élan, often counting the cost of an adventure afterward rather than before. I have always been grateful that he turned up to share this climb with me.

There was a trail less than half the way. When it played out we took the first hollow to the right. And when it became impassable from vertical cliffs made slippery by moss and water, we bore to the left to the ridge on that side of the gulch.

We were now on the side of Le Conte itself and again encountered cliffs and maddening thickets of laurel and rhododendron. We scrambled and we slipped; we clawed and we pulled. This lofty mountain seemed to have no summit, and I was becoming weak from hunger and fatigue. When it seemed I could go no farther I dragged myself over a low ledge and found we had reached the top.

The view from the immediate summit was disappointing because of a screen of balsams. But after lunch we fought our way to a look-off point, and a truly magnificent and tremendous view burst upon us. We were on one of the points of the great triangle of which Silers was the center. But the superior elevation and location of Le Conte produced stupendous views not only of mountains but of the fields and hamlets in the Great Valley. Though the day was brilliant, to the north over Knoxville was a long sooty band touching the horizon. I had not then heard of smoke pollution.

The middle peak, or Cliff Top, to which we proceeded after lunch, was covered with dense stands of windswept balsams, a low-growing rhododendron, and masses of a gorgeous, hedge-like shrub with tiny glistening leaves suggesting a boxwood—Huger's sand myrtle. The leaves of this resplendent plant had a waxy content and were highly inflammable. This fact was discovered by the youngest member of the party, who set fire to an isolated clump. He was scolded by his father who quickly stamped out the blaze.

But when we left the cliffs for the descent this youngster lingered. Later when we looked up from the open summit of the Rocky Spur far below, we saw a column of white smoke hovering over Cliff Top. The sand myrtle was afire and I felt a youthful outrage. For the first time in my life I had wanted to protect a bit of nature from destruction.

We followed no trail down the mountain, as we had followed one but little on the ascent. This trip had been an introduction to bushwhacking by my mountain friends who were masters of the art. My fears of the unknown and of getting off a trail had been blunted. The experience led to an awareness that every foot of the mountains was open to me, and that trails, though a convenience, were not a necessity. And on the same trip a lifelong concern for the vegetative cover of the land was kindled by that senseless blaze in the sand myrtle on Cliff Top.

The next years had their frustrations. I was busy at the university and plagued by lack of time and money. Once or twice I managed a prodigious excursion, prompted equally by my love of the mountains and by my desire to measure myself against them.

At Easter we skipped classes and took a trip to Thunderhead—the massive grassy bald which had formed the western tip of the great triangle revealed from Silers. This was a 40-mile jaunt crowded into three days. We were elated by seeing acres of bird's-foot violets in the foothills and by the sight of a yellow lady's-slipper—my first orchis. Soft from unwonted exercise, we had crammed six months of yearning into one relentless excursion.

Another summer I worked at the very base of Mt. Le Conte. My employer was versed in botany. From him I learned the identity of many trees in this land of many trees. On the weekends his home became an overnight stop for visitors from the "outside" who coveted a look at these great, verdant, little-known mountains. On one weekend two research professors, a botanist and an entomologist, were there. From them I learned the name of the fresh and beautiful pink turtlehead, a flower which grew near the summit of Le Conte.

On another weekend a taxonomist of some note came from a midwestern college. His excitement, as he discovered plant after plant which he had not even seen before, was contagious. In the party that day were several mountaineers. During a rest our visitor reached down and picked a leaf of the dog hobble which covered a whole slope. Musingly, half to himself, he spoke its scientific name, *Leucothoë*.

One of the mountain men replied, " 'Leucothy,' that's what we calls it." Who was the ancestor who had known and handed down the scientific name of this shrub, and why had he come to these mountains?

In a moist cleft on top we found an exquisite ivory-toned flower, its petals strongly veined with green—Grass-of-Parnassus. I have since seen its long-stemmed cousins in the area of the great limestone springs in Florida and a dwarfed version at timberline in the North Cascades of Washington. The memory in later years of that enchanting plant on Le Conte contributed to my first dim perception of plant ecology on the North American continent.

One autumn I departed East Tennessee for three years at an eastern law school. I came home each summer and worked in a law office, but managed a trip or two to the mountains.

On one of these we hiked from Thunderhead to Clingmans Dome, camping along the way. Sam Cook was again our guide. At Spence Field we found many domestic animals grazing on its expansive summit meadows, the practice of valley farmers being to summer their stock in the mountains.

At our campsites I learned from Sam how to start a fire, how to set up a crane from which to hang a bucket over the fire. At Buckeye Gap we heard a call in the night. The eyes of young John Tittsworth widened with fear.

"What's that?"

Sam chuckled, "That's an owl; he's your friend."

The "whoo whoo" of this bird is one of the startling sounds of the great woods. Its call is yet heard in many areas of our country. Where there are woods enough for it, there is hope for wilderness.

From Buckeye Gap we walked to Silers Bald; John and I went on to Clingmans.

The next day we all hiked to Elkmont via Miry Ridge. As we descended through the rain there was smoke in the air and we began to see blackened stumps and snags. The area had been logged, had burned, and was still smoldering. I could not perceive in this open rocky charcoal-black area, the lush and magnificent forest I had traversed in mist eight years earlier. Down in the hollow we ran into the logging operation itself in a land I had known under different conditions on my first trip into the high mountains. I had found the origin of the logs which fed the sawmill at Townsend. The following summer, at Charlies Bunion, I was again to see first-hand the consequences of careless logging.

Whereas Mt. Le Conte had once been my great goal, I now wanted to try Mt. Guyot, a peak second in height only to Clingmans Dome and located in a remote complex of mountains far to the east of Le Conte. I had interested Wiley Oakley in going with me. He was a mountaineer who looked upon the mountains as a source of beauty and inspiration, rather than a resource to be exploited.

We were to hike from Gatlinburg to Le Conte and out the meanders of the ridge, now known as the "Boulevard," to the state line, and thence along the untrailed state line to Guyot.

The Boulevard ridge was trailless. We were slowed by frightful undergrowth and by the battering of a summer storm. By late afternoon we had barely reached the edge of the burn near Charlies Bunion, on which were now stands of blackberry briers eight feet high. We plunged into them hoping to reach Dry Sluice Gap by dark, but were held back by the briers and by partially burned trees which had fallen across our course. The briers had completely engulfed the windfalls so that we were unaware of them until we walked into protruding limbs. Progress was slowed to a quarter of a mile an hour.

Near the gap the briers thinned a bit. The fire had burned the humus down to the mineral soil, and water from the storm was running over the area. We attacked blackened logs with an ax and chopped out dry wood for our camp fire.

A second storm struck and we thatched the fire with bark. Under this cover it outlasted the storm. But there was no dry spot for sleeping. Finally we collected large stones and heated them in the fire. Some of these we placed at our feet and others on the slope as seats. I shall never forget Wiley's tentative test, and how he quickly sprang upright when he found it too hot. Whimsically he said, "My seat is hard as a rock." Over this spot we stretched a poncho and sat out the night.

Dawn came eventually. Our eyes were red from smoke and sleeplessness; our hands and faces were scratched and besmudged. We decided to return to Gatlinburg by the shortest route. This was down the trail from Dry Sluice Gap, and through the Porters Flat of the Greenbrier.

On the descent we followed a deep ravine just east of the Charlies Bunion peaks and ridges. Looking up at them, we were appalled. They had been incinerated down to the bare rock leaving only the blackened trunks of a once virgin forest. Since there had been no logging on the Tennessee side, the fire must have started in the loggings in North Carolina. It had swept across the divide into several hundred acres of virgin woods in Tennessee.

Two miles farther, the valley leveled out into the Porters Flat where grows one of the surpassing deciduous forests on earth. It was as unspeakably beautiful as the area of holocaust had been unutterably blighted.

In the decades following the first Silers trip I grew in assurance and strength. My love for mountains and wild country became a major motivation. My trips there numbered into the hundreds in every season—from the cold dormance of winter, through the perfections of spring and the heavy humidity of summer, to the sharp scintillating delights of the fall. They involved short one-day excursions and week-long back packs. Camp fires were built from wood so damp that moisture pockets, exploding in the wood, blew out the flames. Camps were established in storms so violent that they dumped four inches of rain in a night. I waded streams so cold that my feet became numb, pushed through snow up to my middle, and camped in the deep forest at $-15°$.

My knowledge grew not only of the terrain of the mountains but of their plant and animal life. Recognition of first- and second-growth forest developed, and likewise perception of the succession of plants involved in the long journey back from disturbance to climax forest. The differences between north-slope and south-slope vegetation became clear.

The movement for a National Park in the Great Smokies got under way during an absence of mine. But upon my return to Knoxville I supported Colonel David C. Chapman and other leaders of this complex and successful undertaking.

In 1930 I learned of the Appalachian Trail and participated in the location of remote stretches of the trail through the mazes of little-known ridges in the Smokies.

I became acquainted with Benton MacKaye, father of the Appalachian Trail; with Stanley Cain, a great and articulate ecologist; with Robert Marshall, a professional forester and a towering figure in the field of wilderness preservation; and with Bernard Frank, a specialist in forest influences, from whose searching eyes little escaped.

On trips into the mountains with these and many others, there came a disturbing awareness of the rift between the untrammeled wilds and the rifled countryside where man had established his civilization. It was not enough to enjoy wild country; one felt compelled to try to conserve and defend the land against further spoliation. With MacKaye, Marshall, Frank, and four other dedicated conservationists [Harold C. Anderson, Aldo Leopold, Ernest Oberholtzer, Robert Sterling Yard], I was associated in the founding of the Wilderness Society.

Some persons hunt for the origins of the wilderness movement in the consciences of big city dwellers, who, seeing about them the shambles of the natural world, seek to protect and restore it elsewhere. But my own beginnings in a provincial valley town, and my youth among a gentle and unassuming people, rebut such a sweeping assumption. The very first time I journeyed the few miles from my home village to the foothills of the Smokies, I found something beautiful, different, and intensely desirable. I had not been conditioned by the fevers of a metropolis. The great bent of my life had been fixed before I set foot beyond the boundaries of Tennessee.

NINETEEN FORTY-ONE

January 16　　　　　　　　　Tonight the line from Whitman's "When Lilacs Last in the Dooryard Bloomed," referring to the "gorgeous, indolent, sinking sun," raised such a nostalgia in my soul that I delved into my memory for my choicest experiences of things of the earth. I glanced over some of my writings; I found vignettes—tiny sharp etchings. But I wish I could do something more sustained and masterful, like Whitman's "By Blue Ontario's Shore."

I wish I could catch the erratic, humid, madcap, and slightly awesome gustiness of an early spring wind in the Greenbrier or the sharpness of dawn in the evergreen zone—a sharpness that penetrates sight and feeling and sense of smell. I wish I could recapture the drowsy "caught-up-ness" of Cades Cove in the early twilight of an April evening. No peace that I have known seemed more permanent.

I wish I could spin into a thread of words the thin, exuberant piping of the peepers on a warm February night. I wish I could convey the feeling of the night wind in the high Smokies as it envelops one and suggests the need of more clothing.

I wish I could catch the slowly unfolding inexorableness of a moonrise, the pinpoint brilliance of the heavens on a cloudless night. I wish I could catch the heavy, brutal, almost frightening fecundity of summer—the slightly sweet shuffling tang of dry leaves in the fall. I should like to catch the dying breath of the growing season, as a restless wind brings down the dead brown leaves of the beeches onto limpid pools. I wish I could unite this detailed beauty, sadness, and roaring delight into a great, deft, exultant "Song of the Seasons," a song which would speak with all the richness and infinite nuances of our natural world.

April 1 Bernard Frank, Ernest Dickerman, and I went to Woolly Tops. But for the blue sky and a comparatively warm atmosphere, we plunged into the dead of winter, with great snow blankets, gray-green ice falls, and rime-covered trees. The powdery snow was dreadfully slick as we plodded up slopes as steep as Popo.* I came to dread an open snow slope, for there the briers and viburnum or wild hydrangea stalks gave little support against the slipping. And as long as I live I shan't forget that interminable stand of rhododendron on the descent, blanketed down by snow into an almost impenetrable mass of obstruction and pitfall.

After squeezing through barrier after barrier of this, and falling knee- and crotch-deep through interstices, only to see the rhododendron continuing to wall us in on all sides, we were driven to the creek and its ice- and snow-covered rocks. For three hours every step was an acrobatic maneuver. Squeezing, twisting, swinging, jumping, cooning, testing each foothold, we finally came unexpectedly upon the old Eagle Rocks trail. And that old overgrown trail, which infuriated us in July 1939 because it was so overgrown, seemed like a boulevard.

April 30 I wish I could re-experience the awe I once had for that great ever-changing façade of Mt. Le Conte. In 1920 I walked back and forth from George Ogle's to the Watson home with my eyes glued on its vast bulk which I had never climbed. Then came my first climb, when I nervously wondered whether I would have the strength to make the top. Later came a second climb, by way of Bear Pen Hollow, when I first experienced the sight of clouds drifting through the trees just above my head. Fearfully I wondered whether we would lose our way should they envelop us.

In the intervening years the great outlines and moods and framework of the mountains have become familiar. Those early unknowns have yielded to subtler ones which move and pass us by and vanish. I think of the sough of the wind in the tops of the high spruces, one of the most haunting sounds I know. I try to seize upon the soft yellow-green wash of spring. It fades even while I observe it. Acres of spring

*Popocatépetl

beauties push up silently, catch at our throats with beauty, and are gone before we can return.

The mountain streams roar and swirl on through eternities, gathering incessantly in the chill clefts of the high ridges, renewing themselves unceasingly from the heavy-falling rains. They go on and on, while we watch and while we don't watch.

We see dogwood blossoms clustered in great flat platters of white. We see patches of dwarf iris growing impudently in an old roadway. A gaunt snag, gaping with holes, is a silent monument to the life of woodpeckers.

I have thought that the word *America* must mean different things to the people who live under its aegis. I would that for each of them it might be symbolized by one—at least one—memory of some aspect of unspoiled nature. America—wide, far-reaching, insouciant—has been the amphitheatre for our civilization. I wish each of us could appreciate its vast beauty, and could see how far the elements of our civilization fall short of the sheer majesty of our America.

It is curious to think that if by some calamity our civilization should pass away, or be eclipsed or uprooted and cast out, America the land will continue on its slow, imponderable geologic heavings; that the plants eventually will reach out and seize and cover and heal the raw slopes we have so improvidently ripped open; that the bird life which somehow lives with us, and yet above and beyond us, will return in abundance and merriment; and that our great dams will crack, seep dry, and disintegrate before timeless forces of frost and rain and sun.

Wilderness first met civilization in the person of a single woodsman with an ax in his hand. He did it little harm. But another man came in. Rules were set up to define spheres of activity. Another came, and another, and the freedoms of the individual became restricted and later fettered and swamped in law and rules of conduct. Combining the force of its various units, our culture pushed itself like the web of the tent caterpillar across the face of nature. The might and beauty and freedom which inhered in singlehanded concourse with nature were overridden. Men became obsessed with the rules of civilization instead of absorbed in the golden intimacies of nature. Men who had never lived on that front line where civilization and nature met, men who were versed in the amenities and laws and mores of society, injected a ruthlessness into the front line. Nature came to be used, disemboweled, ignored, instead of being husbanded, respected, and loved.

Competing cultures began to vie for the right to use the natural world; turmoil and confusion swept the face of the earth. That's where we are now, nervously, ruthlessly protecting our society, our customs, our luxuries, instead of lovingly with the sublime understanding of people of the earth protecting our bit of its domain.

May 7 The spell of Sunday's hike up Buck Fork and over to Ramsay is beginning to wear off under the bludgeoning of city life. Incessant noise, auto horns, the whine of electric trolleys, pneumatic drills, and sirens have supplanted the peace of the wilds.

Everywhere I have gone in the mountains this spring I have found numerous blowdowns. We followed them Sunday on the Guyot lead. Sometimes the logs supplied a pathway straight up the mountain; sometimes we crossed from one to another on a sort of "Jacob's Ladder," as Henry Gray said. But the old logs were a fascination. Lying on the ground through several winters they had become mere shells, retaining the shape but none of the firmness of trees. We crushed through the disintegrating bark into a spongy mass of pulpy fiber. Yet a few years, and they would be merged with the cushioned humus.

At the crest of the ridge we emerged into a flat mossy spruce woods, which reminded me of Deer Creek Gap and of High Top on Le Conte in the old days. One wonders if this was the first time man had ever edged through this copse, for we had missed a turn and were a mile east of where we should have been. We were recompensed for our mistake by coming upon that silent stand of boreal forest.

I yearn now to move along the length of that ridge, through the great aisles in the rhododendron at Drinkwater Gap, to the fir thickets on Guyot itself. It must be one of the least frequented places in the Smokies—the land of the bear and of the winter wren and of the sad winds.

May 27 Sunday we encountered specimens of the rarely appearing yellow lady's-slipper. This orchis is fragilely beautiful. One tends to think of it almost as a phenomenon, without any roots or place in the natural world. And yet it, too, has had its tough old ancestors which have eluded fires and drought and freezes to pass on in this lovely form the boon of existence. If a plant so delicately lovely can at the same time be so toughly persistent and resistant to all natural enemies, can we doubt that hopes for a better and more rational world may not also withstand all assaults, be bequeathed from generation to generation, and come ultimately to flower?

President Roosevelt says he has not lost faith in democracy; nor have I lost faith in the transcendent potentialities of LIFE itself. One has but to look about him to become almost wildly imbued with something of the massive, surging vitality of the earth.

June 11 We were working upward in the damp giant forest of the north-facing gorge of Big Laurel Branch. The earth beneath our feet was soft with the disintegration of ages of forests. The stream was alive with light as it swirled between boulders or slipped down the cliffs in a film to be gathered into dim, cool, moss-rimmed pools below. The atmosphere was subtle with the perfume of blooming things and the damp freshness of the well-watered forest.

Suddenly the air was filled with a slim torrent of exuberant music. What a rush of notes, tripping over themselves, spreading through the green caverns of the forest in a thin riot! It was the winter wren, hardly bigger than my thumb—bursting with zest and rending its tiny body at intervals with its riotous notes. No song, no sight in the forest, fills me with half the thrill. A bear is a clumsy animal, littering the trails with heavy piles of excreta, or biting and clawing the bark off young trees. The great inflorescences in the spring have a static quality. The occasional vistas are immense, the forest overwhelming. But this bird, frequenting the higher, wilder forests, too frail to harm any but the tiniest insects, shrilling forth its overlapping melody, vitalizes the world for me. In one jetting effusion it seems to compass the whole story of life, of tiny seeds springing into gigantic might, as out of the silence of its breast there bursts this gleeful, lilting spasm.

I would not spoil this meaning for myself by hearing the song too often. I want to hear it sparingly, that I may always yearn for the repetition of what my memory preserves so scarcely.

July 7 Yesterday at the conclusion of a three-day holiday in the Cherokee National Forest, Herrick Brown and others of us looked out over the vast forest from a fire tower. After widespread rains we could see clear across the great valley, even to Walden's Ridge and the Cumberlands in the background. But that nearer view of unbroken forest, stretching like a wrinkled green carpet to the southern horizon, brought home to me, more than anything I have ever seen, just what met the eye of the first pioneers as they crossed the range. Limitless, absolutely limitless, forest! No wonder those men were prodigal in the treatment of that forest, and no wonder that the race which trickled through and finally swept over it was a lusty, swashbuckling breed, master of the tall tale, huge of strength, and mighty of exploit . . .

At Stratton Meadow we camped on the edge of a once lovely, still grassy open space. Thorn trees resembling hollies had been nibbled into fantastic shapes by grazing cattle. Great wild cherries grew nearby. Falling into the excessive spirit of this remarkable region, we fought a prolonged and drenching rain, which thudded into the forest like pellets of lead, with a huge campfire made of log butts six feet long and twenty inches in diameter. The battering might of the rain and the roaring warmth of the fire swept into our souls like wine, and we were intoxicated with the joy of living. The struggle of man against man seemed but a dim illusion.

August 26 The road mounted high on the shoulder of Grandfather Mountain in North Carolina. On happy impulse Anne and I decided to climb it that day.

The Grandfather, with its straggly growth and enormous up-juttings of rock, appeared gaunt and forbidding. However, the climb was stirring. We had just enough rock climbing for thrills and just enough sand myrtle and spruces and balsams to remind us of Le Conte. The views were superb. We topped the day with a canteen full of huckleberries, which we collected in a swag near the first peak.

The next morning we drove down to Wiseman's View, a breathtaking overlook from which the yawning, perpendicular-walled immensity of Linville Gorge could best be appraised. A Forest Service patrolman sauntered over and struck up a conversation.

"Ain't that the lonesomest looking place you ever saw? The sound of that river down there would make anybody homesick."

The gorge was too steep for profitable timbering, and too rough for a road. It was penetrated only at intervals by trails. In between, a person would be effectively boxed in by the castellated walls. Known only to fishermen, gutted at the base by floods, it possessed one tiny shelter and no camping places. This was the Linville Gorge, watched over by Hawksbill and Table Rock, guarded at the lower end by Short Off. Except for the warming of the stream due to logging far upstream, it was precisely as the forces of creation had made it.

The patrolman was Cal Hall, born of a Hatfield mother in Harlan County, Kentucky. He had vague memories of chicken raids by the McCoys. As a boy he "bagged it out" over the mountain to Watauga County, North Carolina. He " 'lowed" this was the roughest place east of Yellowstone Park. The lower two-thirds is a Forest Service reservation. He suggested that we reverse our proposed route in order the more certainly to find the up-trail, where a wire across the river marked the Forest Service boundary.

Into the gorge we went. The banks were shorn clean of undergrowth by the August 1940 flood; and the river being low, we made excellent time picking our way carefully from slab to boulder to rock. The densest undergrowth matted the banks. Through openings in the trees, and towering mightily above, we saw the gray walls of immense cliffs—sometimes with flat surfaces, sometimes with lines of perpendicular and horizontal cleavage, which had loosed great chunks of rock into the river. We were aware of this; we were aware that our getting out easily depended upon our finding the Bynum's Bluff trail, and that sometimes a wall of water raced through the gorge without even the warning of a shower. We knew it was a bad summer for snakes, an awareness which didn't leave us as we felt along the ledges above our heads for handholds as we flattened ourselves to the rock in skirting a pool. Only once were we forced across the creek where a sharp bend piled the water against an untraversable wall. We doffed our boots and inched ourselves across the slippery bed athwart the current.

Actually the going was easy, except for the uneasy awareness of being cut off. Once we crossed an acre of jagged fresh-fallen rock, and looked up to see yellow cavities 500 feet above us whence they had fallen. I sensed the hollow by which we should leave the gorge, but so many were the horizontal fracture lines in the rock that I missed the wire across the gorge. Anne spied it, directly over my head. We felt some relief; and then the full beauty of the river, of the 25-foot cascade below us, and of the great pool at its foot, smote us. We walked out on a huge battlement 50 feet above the river and were silent. Then the luxury of a skinny dip bath . . . and the steep, sweaty climb up Bynum's Bluff.

$\mathscr{N}$INETEEN FORTY-TWO

February 22   I want to recapture if I can the atmosphere of that trip to Brushy Mountain two weeks ago. There was deep snow, lying softly in a fluffy blanket over every surface. Fog had frozen onto trees and limbs and branches in slender needles of white. The air was sharply cold, biting at face and neck and hands. There was whiteness everywhere, relieved only by the darkened stream channels at the bottom of each hollow and by tree trunks which had not intercepted the blowing snow.

Across this world of white we saw black shapes moving—wild turkeys at home in their wild. Their three-pronged tracks stirred the overall whiteness. There was whiteness around the track—lesser whiteness in the faint shadow of the print. Four trails, without beginning or end, crossed our own in a grandeur of timelessness. We were intruders here, unless the great, unspoiled, overwhelming vastness of this turkey home asserted itself in our souls and minds. One is impressed through his senses; one appreciates through his mind.

Up through this gray whiteness we churned our way. Fluff furnishes no footing; and it was only as we sank through to the frozen ground that we could move at all. On the cliffs we essayed frigid handholds and icy footholds, grabbing eagerly at long, pipe-like laurel roots and shunning brittle and rotting branches. Among the broad-leafed rhododendrons, we struggled through canopies of whiteness, while above them the twigs of the myriad-forking birches were swollen into heavy white fingers which fretted the background of the fog.

The fog faded and we saw the arbored labyrinth of the mountain against a cast of blue. Then the wilderness gilded its own lily as a broad beam from the sun seared those upper limbs with white fire. I straightened up from a pocket of snow in which I had been floundering, kicked again and again to ease the cramp in knotting thigh muscles, and was glad, painfully glad, for the rush of beauty that poured through half-blinded eyes into my soul. I was climbing like an old man, but I could appreciate with the garnered wisdom of my twoscore years.

Up the last wall of rock we climbed, shoulder-high rhododendron tearing at my clothes and sifting snow down my neck. Then the burst of distance and we were in the clear, although fog drifted about us in a formless curtain. Through the fog, shifted and thinned further by the wind, the Stateline developed slowly, until we could see its customary blue-green contours outlined in a faintly emerald white. Snow, sun, fog, frost, and mountains played havoc with emotions and the capacity to take it all in.

February 26 Last night I looked out a window of our house. Not a car was in sight; all that I saw was the embracive peace of a snowy landscape. Again I wondered if the machine age had brought any real contribution to human happiness. Without the automobile, the everyday world about us would perforce take on some of the peace of the deeper woods, which we drive so far to experience. The prospect is rather bleak. Once the war is over, the world will fairly crawl with the machines which are being denied us today. And overhead where today there is one plane, there will be ten.

April 24 Perhaps because the tender green and the flowering loveliness of spring are still everywhere evident, I had not noted that the severe drought of last year is still with us. Already the rainfall deficiency for this year is five inches. In the lower Greenbrier last weekend, the leaves rustled underfoot as in the fall; and over toward Cosby, in the otherwise clear air, a great blue fog of a cloud hung over a forest fire. Many national forests have been closed to visitors.

Tonight's newspaper reported that in eastern Tennessee this spring 200,000 acres burned (a third the size of the Great Smokies Park). All day there has been a whitish haze in the air through which the sun has shone dim and pale. Against the ridges and hills this pall has had a bluish cast; and long before sundown the sun shone as a dull, orange-red orb through this deathly shroud. It is sickening to me that the fresh, moist richness of the woods is being eaten away. Streams will not only languish, but will grow dingy. And unbelievably, some of these fires are wantonly set! One wonders that the civilization for which we fight can harbor persons so ignorant of its resources, or so indifferent.

Over against these hellish events and ominous forebodings recorded just above are the serene memories of the last weekend. It strains belief that two such opposite worlds can exist concurrently on the same planet.

Under a tranquil sky, we pushed to the end of the last thread of civilization, crossed the footbridge of the Middle Prong, and were in forest. Under the trees the ground was an undulant carpet of leaf and shy bloom. The hushed roar of the Middle Prong rose through the trees from the valley below us. An occasional bird burst into liquid melody. Through it all there was not one discordant note of sound or sight. The peace of climax forest reigned.

In two hours we had gained the Rock Den on Chapman Prong. There we shed the world, and for 30 hours became one with this magnificent forest. The new moon shone behind the minutely branching birches. Thirty feet from us, hidden by underbrush, we heard the soft splashing of the stream. A fallen magnolia had knocked limbs from a black cherry and once again the prodigal ways of the woods seized us; and with hardly a thought of its value in the world we had left behind, we made our campfire exclusively of this lovely, hard-grained cherry wood. We ate heartily, rested grandly, and in the gloom of disintegrating embers and of a starry sky sang of "Barbary Allen."

In another place I once wrote of the simplicity of life in the woods. Its enjoyment does not depend upon complicated arrangements, of getting hosts of people together. One tingles with the crispness in the air at dawn, his teeth ache from cold water drunk directly from a stream. We "rassle" with a tough piece of wood in splitting it for a fire. There is the musky tang of humus. There is the feel of the forest around us. Sometimes the enjoyment comes from avoiding discomfort, covering up from the stealthy chill of the night, removing a rock from under one's bed, or, as at the Rock Den, bursting from under it to escape the stinging smoke that swirled in from the campfire.

The next day we walked up Eagle Rocks Prong along the old trail which is so far gone that we were off it as often as we were on it. In the laurel, new growth whipped at our faces, but beneath our feet pressed the firm earth of the trail. At the Laurel Top fork we took to the creek, and skirted great pools as we moved readily along the dry rocks at the edges. We climbed gradually through comparative flats and open woods until the Stateline loomed ahead of us, appallingly steep.

At the first great cliff, lying close to its base, we found snow—a drift 40 feet long and two feet thick. There was momentarily a wintry sting to the air. We climbed the spikes of a leaning spruce and surmounted the first falls. Once we pushed over a loose rock which dropped with sickening momentum, hit with a splintering crunch and bounded on, gaining speed as it fell. It was frightening even to think of falling in such places.

Then we saw the Black Cliff—a dry, warm, gnarled, lichen-covered surface with the water trickling in a fissure at the side. The cliff opened out over a gulf so steep we could look into the tops of trees, and on across a wide-flung blue world of mountains. There was not the slightest evidence of man. It was quiet; a mild breeze coursed up from below, and once we heard distantly the jeweled, tinkling notes of the winter wren rippling on and on and on.

We felt the power of creation; but how could anything so vast be so in repose? Only because of infinite time, only because there was no time—no schedules, no quotas, no deadlines. This was not created for us. It had been this way for endless centuries and would change only in the course of endless centuries. We were just passing by. We cling to a cliff for a part of a day and our cup runneth over, overwhelmed by incomparable stillness and the soul-wrenching fullness of wilderness.

June 14   I read an article in *Audubon* which shocked me. As I have gone through the Smokies in the past 25 years and have seen evidences or heard reports of increase in, or at least a stabilized position of, certain species of wildlife, I have not been aware of the large number of species of animals already "gone from the earth." It is another example of the fallacy involved in viewing one's surroundings from the perspective of a single lifetime, rather than from the vantage of scores, or hundreds, or even thousands of years. For every species which seems on the increase or stabilized—such as the bear, deer, turkey, ruffed grouse, raven, and duck hawk[2]—there is another species which is gone or in danger of going—the bison, elk, otter, beaver, ivory-billed woodpecker, and passenger pigeon. The rareness which has endowed with a particular thrill the sight of a duck hawk, or an eagle, is a rareness which springs also from the depredations of man and not simply from ecological scarcity.

It shocks me to think that my life has spanned the period of the passing, or near passing, of the American chestnut, the cougar, the ivory-billed woodpecker, and others. The readiness of my mountain guide of 25 years ago to shoot down a deer and a wild turkey in violation of game laws, a readiness which struck me as being deliciously lawless at the time, has undoubtedly speeded the process of extinction.

Biologically the passing of a species may or may not be serious. In most cases there will be readjustments. Perhaps the death of one species may occasionally carry with it into oblivion another species which has been dependent upon it. The adjustment in many cases may be simply replacement, or the occupation of a larger sphere, by another species which has been contemporary. So great is the competition for a place in this temperate world, the movement into it by another species would seem almost automatic.

But the thought that leaves me desolated is that a branch of evolution, which over the eternities has been at work bringing to a climax a striking species, is cut off, never to be reinaugurated. The same thing happens frequently among individuals, such as childless couples, but the species goes on. There is a grandeur in the continuation and perpetuation of some great animal species like the moose or elk or caribou. Its extinguishment through preventable causes is like an unfinished symphony.

I rejoice that I have known even slightly the duck hawk, raven, ruffed grouse, and wild turkey.

September 4 And now for a trip to another world. It was not a dream world, for it was as real as gnats and flies and hard beds and blisters and sweat could make it. Except for a few battle planes flying high and impersonally over us, we were for the entire last week of August cut off from this world of woe. No visitors, no radio, no

[2] This was written 25 years ago. The duck hawk seems to have vanished from the Great Smoky Mountains.—H.B.

papers, no phone—a mountain cabin was capital of a kingdom in which we were the sole subjects and kings.

Outstanding in this other world was the total eclipse of the moon which seemed a lonely, somber phenomenon for our eyes alone, but which looked down on warring countries too. We saw the earth's shadow cut the white brilliance of the moon into an acorn shape; then into a tam-o'-shanter; then as the last fleck of light radiated from the shadow, it resembled a diamond ring. Once as I watched, very late, a cloud drifted across, erasing all evidence of the moon; and for that moment I felt, like the ancients, that some devil was indeed abroad.

All this I watched from the terrace in front of the cabin, keyed alike to the scene above me and also to dark, bumbling shadows which might reveal the presence of our giant bear. We had seen enough of him to know that he was not a creature of habit, and that he might as easily appear from behind us or from behind the cabin, as from the cookshed or springhouse areas in front of us. We had not then seen enough of him to know that, despite his colossal size, he was easily frightened and was in normal circumstances probably entirely harmless.

And so, as I stood in the open at the height of the eclipse, focusing my binoculars upon that smudged disc with its baleful ring of redness, the hairs upon my head would tingle as I strained for sounds from behind me.

Happy indeed was I to see the gleam of returning light at 11:30 and to note the awakening nuances of the woods as the growing light drew them out. Surely the ancients could not have welcomed the uncovering more heartily. It was curious to note, just as the light reappeared, that there was a freshening of the indolent air. Progressively with the waxing light a sharp breeze sprang up, blowing briskly out of the north. It was as though the air itself welcomed this second showing of the moon.

Each increasing moment limned more of the grounds and woods until, when I retired about 12:30, everything was so brilliantly clear I could have detected the slightest movement of Mr. Bear from 40 yards away.

The bear we saw several times. The first night we were aware that he visited the terrace and pawed the threshold. He had stretched fully eight feet to rake a cache of garbage from the eaves of the cookshed. The bear was heavy-shouldered, with much fawn color around his face. With his teeth he punctured cans like bullet holes; one night he doubled the already tightly flattened disk of a Pet milk can. I had a wholesome appreciation for his enormous strength in both claw and jaw. Another night he aroused us by clanging the iron on the auxiliary fireplace. Twice, obviously unseeing and unaccustomed to human scent, he came within fifteen feet of us as he approached the cookshed. We found him to be easily frightened and sensitive to movement or noise on our part, and twice we accelerated the movement of his huge bulk by touching off flash bulbs. He did not stalk silently through the woods, but secure in his strength moved noisily about, once or twice betraying his presence before we had seen him. His pelt was mangy, and from his square bulky lines I believe he was a male.

Those first few days at the cabin time moved in a measureless void. We worked upon no schedule, under no compulsion. The few things we had to do, like chopping wood and cooking, took infinite, heedless time. Only once was this flawless rhythm really broken. That day Anne and I got up in advance of the dawn and walked across the dew-drenched sward, under the stars, to the cookshed. The setting moon gleamed like a jewel through the branches of the trees, and moments later tiny streaks of clouds were touched with rose. This was the day we hiked fifteen miles, traversing Porters Mountain, obtaining incomparable views of Charlies Bunion, the Jumpoff, and Porters Valley.

September 24 Last weekend, starting out from Knoxville under an overcast sky, we moved toward the mountains under increasingly heavy clouds. The mist hit us short of Emerts Cove, and the rest of the day we were either in rain or heavy mist.

How we cringed at first from the damp bushes and undergrowth—but by the time we reached the end of the trail along Porters Creek it made little difference whether we avoided them or not. We were by then well soaked. Progress up the Charlies Bunion Prong was rapid. A second flood had gouged out some of the accumulations of the '27 deluge and we moved easily over the open rock. I was wearing Bean boots and was concerned for my footing on the rocky slopes and cliffs of the Bunion higher up. I needn't have worried. The rock was clean-sharp, and only occasionally did I find a film of lichen or moss. For the most part I climbed as securely as though my feet at each step were glued to the rock. Although we moved in rain and through dirty white fog and were met by a merciless wind on the ridge crest, I have never made the climb more easily. A few times we dislodged scree, and once or twice a fallen tree moved as we passed over it, but otherwise my climbing was serene.

Some of the boys climbed in shorts, and as they dallied to let others catch up they shook with cold. We couldn't see 75 feet ahead of us. The slopes dropped off hideously steep each way from the narrow crest, to be lost in a foggy void. As we progressed upward, the Bunion took shape out of the fog in a dark precipitous blot.

Seven of us reached the top and plowed down through the underbrush to the trail. There the wind tore greedily at our bodies and even those of us who were warmly clad began to chill. Three of the party were lagging unaccountably down that fog-wrapped ridge and I pushed back through the bushes to investigate. By this time it was raining hard and my clothes had become completely saturated. The water gleamed where my trousers stretched over my knees and thighs. I reached the unsheltered crest and met a wind so blasting that when I shouted it seemed to blow my voice back down my throat. As I strained for a possible answering shout, the wind roared across my ears drowning out all other sound.

I climbed down the rocks a hundred feet or so, braced myself, and called again. No answer. I began to shake convulsively. I couldn't see. The wind shook me and I was chilling rapidly. I could hardly have been more alone, more buffeted, had I been on Everest.

Eventually we met up with the missing hikers at Newfound Gap and all of us returned to Knoxville together.

$\mathcal{N}$INETEEN FORTY-THREE

January 12   It was a raw day, with wind and clouds. There was snow on the ground, just deep enough to show a track. There were almost no birds. We went a mile east on the trail from Newfound Gap before we saw a few chickadees, all fluffed up with cold. A few scattered snowflakes began falling. Fox tracks in the old snow began to fill up slightly with fresh white granular snow, and soon we came to realize we were in the midst of a tough, tugging blizzard.

We ate lunch at Ice Water Springs—out of the snow, if not out of the wind and cold. On down the trail we plodded, in a storm increasing in violence. I slipped and fell heavily on ice concealed beneath the snow. At Charlies Bunion we were not disposed to pause. Veins of ice covered the tree branches, and Dry Sluice Gap was a windy torment.

We crept back on the trail through the sharp-ridged drift. We couldn't face the storm, and in the mist there was nothing to see anyhow. Ice froze on my eyebrows and eyelashes. Water froze in my canteen. The snow, as loose as soot, grew deeper and we kicked a little spray ahead of us with each step. The trail breaker did not pack the snow down; he did little more than rearrange it. The fox's tracks reappeared, fresh since we had been along. Our own out-tracks were long since erased. Two trees had blown across the trail in the interim—winter decadence.

Newfound Gap was a scene of wildest violence. Snow was drifted up to two feet, and was shrieking across horizontally from the Tennessee side. The car was plastered. A tiny crack in one window had let in gallons of snow. But the drifts were loose, and we proceeded slowly down the highway without chains. Seven inches had fallen in a little over six hours! A wild, wonderful day in which all thoughts of war and the other world were buffeted out of us.

June 30 Sunday we went to Gregory Bald with Sam Meyer, Royal Shanks, and the Alvin Nielsens. The bald is deep with grass but is not ragged looking, and does not yet seem to be affected by the termination of grazing. It looks well kept. And the gorgeous azalea clumps of diverse hues, running from pure white through all the pinks, yellows, salmons, and flames, to deep saturated reds, were ranged in such delightfully unstudied stands around the edge it seemed as though it had been done by design. Perhaps the answer is that good landscaping follows some pattern of natural informality. In any event, the effect was breath-taking, mentally inconceivable—50 grassy acres bordered with hundreds of sturdy clumps of this spectacular shrub. A few scattered plants had sprung up out in the sward, but the great masses were found near the dividing line between forest and fell.

On the drive through Cades Cove, we saw John Tipton sitting on his front steps in overalls, with knees spread wide, looking out with good humor. His mustachios were rather more sweeping than usual, and he was wearing a great, wide-brimmed, fawn-colored hat whose undented crown rose like a dome over his head. I regret that there was no time to talk with him to inquire of the need for the tall scarecrow and many satellite and diminutive agitators which were stuck willy-nilly in his corn patch. Later I heard that he was trying to scare off raccoons which were ruining his garden.

The cove seemed even more populated than usual and appeared well tended. There were great fields of corn; and at least four substantial herds of beef cattle, peacefully grazing in pastures which spanned the entire cove. There seemed to be a resurgence of life which belied the impression I had gained last fall as I studied the cove from the little burying ground.

July 22 On the last weekend Herrick and I made the long-planned trip to Guyot; Dickerman, here for ten days on furlough, joined us.

We went up by Buck Fork and crossed over the range to Drinkwater. We reached the crest below the pool and moved through magnificent rhododendron to the Ramsay Prong. We did a round trip of probably eighteen miles. Around Drinkwater and on the side of Old Black I had the impression of being in another world. I have sensed this many times and have attempted to put it into words—but have never really succeeded.

It is not that the area is peaceful. There are the roar of the creek, the battering of the heavy rains, and the suddenly mounting, savage winds which produced the great blowdown near the top of Guyot. There was other movement also. Lower down we saw the hind-quarters of a bear bouncing out of view; on the Buck Fork we watched an amiable, slow-moving rattlesnake; and we saw a bright blue kingfisher taking without the slightest hesitation the Buck Fork at the junction with Chapman Prong. Now and then we saw a squirrel and a junco and a robin in the blowdown. Once we heard the dual-noted veery, and several times the tiny king of wilderness singers, the winter wren.

I think the feeling is one of maturity. Certainly there is an element of sadness and I think that goes with maturity—also a dash of inscrutability. There is not the clashing of impressions one gets in man's world; nothing staccato, nor titillating, nor jarring. What is noisy in this wilderness is mellowed by space and soft yielding surfaces of leaf and needle, fern and moss.

There is an impression of unhurried stability. These moss beds, inches deep in soft woods-green, covering rock and ledge and fallen tree, took years and years to form. The great rhododendron thickets were not grown in a day; and the unceasing splash of the creek into Drinkwater Pool did not spring from groaning, pulsating pumps, but from the union of innumerable trembling drops seeping down through the springy moss beds miles from far above us. Lying under the gloom of the firs and spruces on Old Black, the widespread, unbelievable carpet formed of thin flat clusters of oxalis leaves and unmarred by fallen trunk or fern, came from conditions which reached back beyond any span known to man. Here there was no pressing for effect, no drive for results, no straining for goals. Each bit of forest, each fresh delicious aspect seemed content. Even the blowdowns seemed to know of the springing greenness of hundreds of seedlings appearing under their trunks.

There is an imperturbable quality to the woods which one finds only in a mature man, or a mature civilization. Ah, this woods association is one of the oldest on the face of the globe. Even the raw, senseless scar of the graded trail will be healed in time, but not, alas, in time known to men now living.

Away from the trail, man had not left his imprint on this area. Man is not here. There is an insouciance he never attains. If the woods were sentient, and some seedling should say, "Here comes a man," the whole forest would answer, "What of it?" The rain falls when and where it listeth. When the skies are clear, many say the forest is wonderful. When the skies are leaden and pouring forth their moisture, it is as welcome to the forests as is the sun. The forest takes what comes, what is offered—the rain, the sun, the devastating winds, the blights, fire, death, animals, destruction, growth, maturity. Nothing disturbs it, in its loins are the seeds and conditions of recovery; in its calendar are endless ages.

And so, as I sense the soothing gloom and power and strength and long-suffering of the woods, I realize here is an ancientness, a patience I cannot touch, can never attain.

I live in the woods for a day at a time; they have been here for millennia. I could not live in them for a month without bringing them harm and change. Even around our two-meal campfire, we had trampled down ferns and the pink turtleheads. I can only visit and wonder and be humble in these woods. Unless I can live as the bears off the berries and roots and ants—without gun, or ax, or fire, or man-made shelter—I am alien here. I can never be wholly a part of this, even as my soul strives deeply to absorb and assimilate it.

It would be sheer boorishness to put motor roads through places like this. It borders on ignorance to say that one can "see" or "feel" the mountains from a motor car.

I dimly see why these woods seem unattainable. The winter wren has adjusted to them; I haven't. If I could, without thought, take the rain, the cold, the sun, the vagaries of weather, instinctively sensing within me the seeds of renewal and resistance, then I could encompass the Smokies. Until then, they will seem more than slightly inscrutable to me; there will be loveliness but with an edge; there will be concern for passing aspects of that which is infinite, and a feeling of inadequacy and of strain because I am not in myself within this environment, overwhelming and everlasting.

Two other items deserve mention. I have spoken of the reptile. I failed to note that under proddings from Herrick, the amiable rattle-snake straightened out the S-curve into which the forepart of its body was fashioned; and from the heavy coil of the midpart, as a base, extended its head forward thirteen or fourteen inches, at an acute angle eight or ten inches above the ground. Thus it nosed the stick which Herrick held in front of it. The extended part was probably a third of the snake's total length, and would appear to be the portion under control should it strike out. After one or two further gentle pokes from the stick it uncoiled, almost wearily it seemed, and crawled off with a flowing motion, very slowly. It certainly was not retreating; it seemed bored, as though there was something strange which it did not understand and which annoyed it slightly.

The other phenomenon was that of a spider web, which we noted in the early morning because it was made conspicuous by tiny dewdrops. It was strung from beside the falls across the width of Drinkwater to the ledge at the lower side of the pool. The span was fully twenty feet, almost entirely across water and with a jungle at either end. There were trees overhead, of course, but it is still difficult to figure out how the spider contrived to throw that strand across the pool. It would be possible for him to work from above, but it was a mighty undertaking indeed.

July 30 An article I read in *The Scientific Monthly*, "Man's Long Story"—which points out the recency and the short span of civilization as compared with the whole of human and its antecedent evolution—explains the feeling of sadness and almost uneasiness which we feel in the presence of ancient natural wilderness. Can it be that innately we are still primal and that when we return to the woods we are feeling a kind of homesickness? It is demonstrably true, I think, that our ancestors were as much at home in the woods as the wrens, reptiles, and mammals which are yet able to subsist there today. Perhaps something deep and subconscious in us sets up that mystic stirring, blended of sadness and joy and inexplicable peace. We have simply gone back home—to our primordial home—and within us arise inarticulate feelings experienced by our ancient forebears.

INETEEN FORTY-FOUR

March 19   Last Sunday we took our long-
planned trip to the Greenbrier with the Nielsens. There was that
familiar and ineffable feeling of peace that accompanies a preponderantly natural as against a preponderantly man-made environment. The rain was warm—one that can wet without chilling. Porters
Creek was a foaming, potent riot. Several places we had an illusion
that it was actually higher than the bank. The wind moaned and tore
with a madcap frequency through the trees around the cabin. There
was a sort of fearsome wantonness about it all.

We did not get beyond the cabin. The rains were too persistent
and unpredictable.

On the return, we stopped at a little bluff which overlooks the
creek. The water below us ranged from tawny to creamy white. The
relentless, endless potency of it made me think of a huge herd of
white horses galloping violently downward through a narrow defile.
Is there the same significance in the name of the Whitehorse Rapids
on the Yukon?

I think the water of Porters Creek was higher than I have ever
seen it. The rainfall high in the mountains must have been enormous.
Farther down, in the flats, we stopped at the old mill, and just as we
drew up saw a kingfisher resting on a branch.

June 2 I look forward to working with a wilderness group in
Knoxville after the war. We shall fight to preserve the status quo in
the Greenbrier. We will be fighting for the right of Americans to see,

there, a bit of inviolate forest. May the Greenbrier, in Aldo Leopold's biting phrase, remain axless, pathless, and roadless, as an act of contrition for Little River, Charlies Bunion, Forney Ridge, and Big Creek.

The problem is enormous. How can people be persuaded that there is something of priceless worth to the human spirit in the very existence of tracts of the primeval, which they have never seen or experienced? And how can they see or experience such when they have no incentive to exert themselves to that end? Can the finest and most sensitive writing in the world make upper Ramsay really live for those who have never been there?

June 23 While Knoxville was recoiling from 102° heat, we were pushing up through the Greenbrier to the moist verdant charm of Long Branch. As we passed under the great trees, their calm spirit fell across our own tensed spirits. Such calm, such repose! In the gloom of that lush north slope, our bodies seemed to soak up moisture from the very air. The little cliffs were easy to negotiate; the earth was a cushion to our feet.

These remnant woods are glorious. But how quickly man is slicing into them. Scarcely 100 years ago, our County Court was paying bounties for wolf scalps. One can only picture the boundlessness of the forests which gave the wolves cover. Now there are left only patches of the primeval forest here and there. And people whose thinking is attuned only to what they have known, and not to what can be imagined, see no harm in another trail, another road, another accommodation in these remnants of the virgin forest that are left to us. Then the next generation, familiar with smaller patches yet, will not be shocked by a further carving.

Thus man is slowly closing a door between himself and his natural environment. Will there be richness and balance enough in the environment that is left to him—most of it stamped with his own mark —to bring him happiness, and perspective? I don't know.

I was thinking again of that incomparable forest. There, in harmonious setting, we heard the rounded melody of the wood thrush and the exuberant outpourings of the winter wren.

September 10 There is something wonderful about the cabin in the 'Brier. The second night we were there the bear came, moving with an unbelievable silence for his great bulk. Anne saw him in the jungle just opposite the cookshed. He moved deliberately as befitted his enormous size, paused uncertainly at the little brook, and then made off into the woods, only to return for another look.

It was then that Bud and I, acting on a hunch, went over to the garbage pit and found him, a 600-pounder, with both front paws on a can. He got his mouth into it and we could hear the rasp of teeth against metal. He heard our shouts, which seemed to puzzle his primitive brain. Then he came over toward the barn—we were in the loft and almost over him. He must have sensed our presence, for he stood for a moment looking up at the barn, his great shaggy head not more than eight feet from us. His eyes wore a look of uncertainty, but no fear. Something disturbed him and he turned and ambled off, his great hind feet turning in as he walked.

December 9 Pure water, which was the free blessing of every early inhabitant in this country, is becoming a coveted resource. How tragic that the pendulum must swing to an extreme before a prodigal and heedless people become aware of the truth that every mountain man knows—the joy of a spring of pure water. Of course many city folks will never learn the blessing of "sweet water." Many a mountain man has left the city and gone back to the ranges because he didn't like town water.

When will people become equally sensitive to smoke and hideous surroundings? When will they covet for their communities pure air and a pleasing prospect and a more happy blending of the natural and artificial? When will they think as much of good living as of production? of serenity as of change and "progress"?

NINETEEN FORTY-FIVE

June 20   We went back after three years to
Silers Bald. It was memorable. We saw six ravens and heard both
the winter wren and the veery. No horses had been on the trail for
the several war years. In some places the leaves and duff had accumulated inches deep in the trail, becoming a cushion to our feet.
The winds were restless, and late in the afternoon the fog swept in
as we toiled up a grassy slope on the west shoulder of Clingmans.

I felt that we were surrounded by all the sadness and loneliness in
the universe. It was as though we were three pilgrims on a lonely
moor on a far planet. Oh, there was brightness, and there was gayety,
too. The purple-fringed orchids, bluets, and oxalis touched the landscape with flecks of color—and the first two gave off the most subtle
and pleasing aromas. On the lower point of the bald there was a
bright little garden of azalea. One plant of sheer yellow set back in
the fringing woods looked strikingly springlike with its colors of
yellow and green.

The character of the landscape had changed during the war period.
We could see several segments of Fontana Lake, as well as some
very raw and fresh road cuts. Although the sky was dull, and although
there was moisture in the air, it was also strangely clear. I believe
we saw more ranges stretching back into North Carolina than I had
ever seen before. Forney Ridge was shrouded in mist, although once
we saw the fresh green grass of Andrews Bald glinting on the skyline
in the sunlight.

Silers, or at least the summit, is undergoing encroachment from shrubs and beech sprouts. The tree line is but returning to where it was in 1917 before the top was cleared for survey purposes.

The soughing of the wind through the evergreens went on interminably. When we were watching the ravens sporting and hovering and soaring in the winds, Anne said:

"Think what goes on up here when we are not here."

I have had that thought scores of times, and I always have it when I hear the restless, gusty sigh of the winds in the balsams on a foggy day. I could listen to those winds forever. The befogged world becomes an inscrutable enigma and epitomizes the state of man—the sadness of obscure beginnings and the uncertainties of an unfathomable future.

I noticed with misgivings that the roadsides along the crest of the divide between Newfound Gap and Forney Ridge have not stabilized. Although there is new growth of fire cherry and birch, the spruces and balsams are still dying on both sides of the road. There is no sign yet that the rate of decay is arrested. As Dr. Harry M. Jennison said before his death, the disturbance and interruption of the water flow are deadly. He said that the spruces and balsams need the blanket of moss and humus, and disturbance thereof can not be tolerated by these trees. Even the trees that have been replanted above the parking ground are yellowed in spots and sickly looking. Guy wires hang like broken gallows from dead snags which were living trees when they were attached.

Fred and I decided that a narrow foot trail through the balsams was about all that could be cut without real damage. The whole aspect of the road is changing. Now it seems that we drive through an open woods, where formerly one had the impression of driving through a deep slot in the dense evergreens.

The problem is no longer one of esthetics, but of protecting watersheds and stream flow. Over the country this is of grave import, and its solution will have a bearing on the shape of things to come, affecting even the overall economy of our country.

June 26 Saturday night I lay out on the sward of Gregory Bald. Three of us were 50 yards down on the North Carolina slope to escape a sharp and incessant breeze. A full moon followed an arc across the southern heavens. No dew collected on the grass. We lay on and between hummocks of grass. Near mountains were dark; far ones were lost in a blue-gray murk. Clumps of azalea, with color obscured, stood sentinel about us. All the world we could see lay below the rounding bald. Here was spaciousness, moon-blue beauty, and infinite peace. No sound but the wind; no sight but the aloof and elusive and painfully beautiful natural world. And while George Hines and Guy slept, their inert and shapeless forms bulking monstrously in their sleeping bags, I sat up, deep in the night, and looked.

Here was the break needed between individual man and his civilization. One becomes humble, alone with the wind in a prodigious circle of mountains. Values and incentives clarify; the transiency of man becomes painfully manifest; and selfishness and ignorance seem unworthy before this impersonal and inscrutable vastness. I had no feeling of wanting to retreat from it, but rather of broadening my own spirituality to encompass more of it. Only the richest and boldest of civilizations are worthy of the earth to which they cling so fitfully.

This day the Charter of the United Nations was signed. Time will reveal whether it is another false start or whether it will do for the nations of the world what Magna Charta did for the people of Britain. The work done there at San Francisco has an almost ghastly importance. If it does not succeed, there is no power that can save the world from another holocaust of war.

The Charter, or at least its purpose, seems so obvious in the perspective of a night alone on Gregory. Why shouldn't men who are thrown together for a passing span, existing here for a few swings of the earth, between the dim and unsolved eternities of the past and the far-off and obscure eons of the future, covenant to live together in peace so that they might turn all their energies to the greatest occupation of all—the reconciliation of man and mankind, mentally, physically, and spiritually with the surrounding universe?

Civilization is much like the sleeping bags which kept George and Guy shielded from the winds on Gregory; it interposes its transient and ofttime feeble aims and pleasures between men and the world about them. Maybe men prefer their cups and their tournaments, and the quickly resolvable gamble of the race or the game, to the implacable laws of the natural world and its toughly held secrets. A few men, a few institutions, are tugging the whole world toward light and freedom, when all of civilization ought to be moving gaily and sentiently in that direction.

October 4 I don't think I have recorded here my impressions of that trip up Ramsay. It was a warm night—we had the tent flap thrown back. We had not expected the moon to shine, because two years before, when we camped higher up at Drinkwater, the direction of the creek was such that the moon hardly appeared above the Guyot lead. But as I looked out I realized this night was to be different.

There was a scattering of birches in the immense tangle of forest of which we were the center. And as I looked out of the tent, the trunks on their eastern contours glowed dimly with the light of the rising moon. It was not yet visible to me; and as the birches stood out here and there in the woods, silent and motionless, it seemed as though they were sentinels waiting with oriental patience for some visitation as yet hidden from me. Later the moon itself shone through leaves above the cascade and the whole valley began to show some of its details. There was no clarity, rather an eeriness in which the canopy of leaves seemed unbelievably high above us and the gloom of the forest relieved ever so slightly with a mellow light. It was so beautiful, so fitting, so harmonious, I felt that I would like to stay there forever.

The next morning there was a spot where the trail veered away from the creek, and on a shoulder set with giant birches and evergreens we stopped to listen to the stillness. Far away, we could hear the creek as a faint sigh—a hardly perceptible stir in the air. Back of us, everywhere, were those giant trees. Here was remoteness—and repose!

Later Guy Frizzell and I stopped in one of those grovelike spots between blowdowns. The wind had settled and we were above the sound of the stream. For a moment I thought we were experiencing the rarest thing in nature—absolute stillness. We strained and listened; at first, only to the thumping of our hearts, and then we distinguished three sounds: the call of a nuthatch, the zing of a fly, and the tiny sawing operation of a beetle in a dead snag. Even so the moment was memorable. After the driving activity of the climb and the tortuous maze of the blowdowns, we had come to this place of maturity—almost no undergrowth, a ground cover of needles and a few herbaceous plants, and small, stocky evergreens growing far apart. The groves were God's first temples!

NINETEEN FORTY-SIX

February 26   Last Sunday for the third time the Hiking Club made in February a trip up the north side of Brushy. The day was unexpectedly raw, and though there was not much snow underfoot it came down sharply during the climb, swept in by a bitter north wind. The views were blotted out by fog, and the moisture, freezing on the trees, limned them in grayness.

There were no unusual incidents, except the sight of a barred owl along the road above the forks. But there was the unaccustomed experience of aloof and implacable woods in winter. We were not very cocky, nor very comfortable, as we waited our turn to descend at the upper gap. There was snow in the air, and the wind swept mercilessly against us. Our hands lost feeling. Our very foreheads ached with cold. We had measured ourselves and our spirits against nature, and the margin in our favor was not great. Without implements for fire and without the food we had brought with us, we could not have survived for long in that exposed spot.

There was a severe and frigid beauty to it, a world of searing cold which man in his cities strives to shut out. Yet there was cleanness and simplicity to it—no cunning, no trickery, just a nonhuman harshness, which forced those on the hike to help each other and drew them close in a mutuality of endeavor. I told Anne that I felt I had been purified.

June 19 Last weekend we went to Roan Mountain in North Carolina. We went with comparatively new friends by a new and

45

back country route, and the whole trip took on the zest of an exploration. Iron Mountain Gap, Bulladeen, and Glen Ayre had fascinating names and glamorous possibilities. We were not disappointed. The remote gap opened the expanse of Roan Mountain looming gigantically across the valley.

On top we heard a veery and both heard and saw some ravens and my first winter wren this season. Royal Shanks, Ernest Ford, and I were on a gaunt overhanging bluff, west of Roan High Knob, when I heard the persistent notes of the wren. Royal located it on the tip of a fir about 50 yards away. Through the glasses I saw a tiny silhouette. When it opened its beak and tilted its head in line with its throat and gave forth a gay and lilting song, I could see even the curve of its upper bill and the perky tilt of its tail. What a place to see and hear the year's first winter wren!

July 22 Summer is here. The crape myrtles are coming into full bloom. I love to look at them in the heat of a hot dry sun which they love so well. But there is a bit of sadness to it, paradoxically. With the turning of the apex of the season, there is the unspoken realization that the extravagant promise of spring is again not to be realized. We could not stand it if life and the earth continued expanding with the dynamics of spring. But how we love that extravaganza of promise. And I guess none of us really cares, because we know that in the offing is the exquisite sadness of fall.

August 9 Sunday we went to Le Conte by way of Bear Pen Hollow. I had forgotten the massive fecundity of that lower forest. The tree boles were enormous, and the leaf layer was high overhead throwing a welcome gloom over the tangle of nettles and shrubs through which we climbed. Higher up, the spruces, thickset and tall, resembled an irregularly spaced palisade. We got spruce and balsam gum on our hands, and we smelled the tang of balsam and skunk cabbage. There was a Turk's-cap lily in the little clearing just below the summit.

The blue of the opposing mountain wall from that open spot had thickness and life and an infinite richness. Once we heard a winter wren, and the calls of the juncos were continuous. Two juncos came quite close to us on Cliff Top. The old clearing to the north of Cliff Top, where the first bark lean-to was thrown up, has now grown up in such a tangle that without search I could not be sure where it had stood. It was good to go back to Le Conte after several years' absence.

September 4   In the mountains, on the weekend, we heard charms of goldfinches along the balds, some kinglets and chickadees. Both nights I heard the barred owl; and a scream and muttered guttural note may have been from a great horned owl. This was at Deep Gap, near Maggot Springs.

Logging was going on outside the Park line. Guy Frizzell and Cliff Backstrom and I went down and talked to some of the loggers at the cabin near the spring. They were the usual friendly, noneffusive, joke-loving lot. In speaking of the area across the fence, one of the men referred to it as "that Park." They told of a man who went to Florida and spent a year hunting snakes for an antivenin farm. The story was summed up: "Yeah, he *snaked* just about a year." I had never heard that word used in the intransitive, but it was a use characteristic of the mountain people emphasized by Kephart in *Our Southern Highlanders*.

The rangers had killed about 25 rattlesnakes this year. The highest elevation at which they had found one was 5800 feet. I told Hanna the story of the snake in the Buck Fork country which had straightened the forepart of its body out of its S-curve to nose a stick which Herrick Brown was holding out in front of it. Hanna remarked that it probably sensed that the object was hard and unyielding, but that if it had noted the warmth of flesh, it would have struck.

Coming down the trail along Fork Ridge into the Big Cataloochee on Labor Day, I detected a stir in the weeds along the trail a few inches from my boot, simultaneously heard a high pitched horny rattle, and realized that a heavy-bodied timber rattler was there. I changed direction very quickly! Against my inclination it was killed. Others were following us. About fifteen hikers had preceded us without arousing it.

From the bridge up the several miles of the Big Cataloochee to our first camp site, we were in a dream world—a lovely narrow valley with well-wooded hills on each side. Above, the skies had the burnished look of fall. Long shadows were beginning to line the edges of the fields. The road went through meadow after meadow, fenced with rails, neatly cut, with the hay stacked and a little forelock twisting out around the pole to keep out the rain. Stock grazed in a few of the meadows. Here was land in which the beauty of the wilds merged gently with appropriate, lovely, and beautiful husbandry of man. It was a place of perfection and a place to return to.

November 5   At Smokemont with the DuBoises, the Bowmasters, and the Hosses, we had a genial time. Except for us, the campground was deserted. The camping spaces had been little used and we pitched our tent upon a flat plat without a bump in it. I slept almost like a babe for nearly eleven hours and awoke wonderfully refreshed. Our hike was up Richland ridge. It was a bland hike except for some bright hickories, some yawning views up-gorge, and a palpitating vista down the gorge toward Smokemont which made me think of the view from Negus Mountain in Massachusetts.

But those hickories! The leaves were at their brightest yellow—and as I lay on my back at noon, I could view them against the pale blue autumn sky. Leaves became detached and drifted down one by one. What a myriad movement from branch to ground. From aliveness to shuffling tangy deadness. I loved to watch those leaves drift and sweep downward. There was sadness to it; but there was a ripened fullness to it, a sort of caught-up-ness to living. And there was the exquisite pain of happiness full-packed and running over—the pain of no more kingdoms to conquer. Relaxed and comfortable, I floated in the aura of autumn, surfeited with perfection.

We crossed through a gap, and soon felt the lush, damp spirit of a river and came in time to the wide, clear, boulder-studded Bradley Fork. It had a certain levelness of bed, and was overhung by giant, white-boled sycamores. The scene was beautiful, but the rushing stream robbed it of the restfulness on the boundary ridge.

November 10   Fall hangs on. Spent a glorious day in the mountains in the Yellow Creek section. Dry leaves, warm sun, soft skies, and long-range views. We drove through the beautiful Little Tennessee valley, with its wide, shallow river bed and shifting sheen of thinly rippling, clear water. It must be one of the beautiful streams of the world!

December 16   At home we had a wood fire throughout the weekend. The backlog was a gnarled and knotted oak chunk—the unsplittable focus of many limbs. It is only half gone after a day and a half of fires and another day of simmering. The knots have resisted oxidation, and one has a dark center and a spreading bloom of white ash, resembling the face of a barn owl.

Few people these days have wood fires. Heat and energy are piped or wired into our homes, and we get further and further from the prime sources of energy. It is good to have to stagger in under a backlog and to learn the ways of a fire—how to kindle, how to control the third piece, how to pull the fire apart, how to put it back together. We need some realities like these.

INETEEN FORTY-SEVEN

January 20   This has been a wild, turbulent, blowy day. Outside it is alive with the rush of the wind. It is much too exciting for sustained work on my part. I have been all tense and excited inside.

By 9 a.m., after several violent showers, the skies began to break. Soon deep blue sky was showing—and the day has been bright, dazzlingly bright, sunshiny and windy. The sky has been brightened by great masses of white, swift-moving clouds. On one gust of air, I saw cedar waxwings (fifteen of them) mount high and then turn with the wind and sweep out of sight.

About 10 p.m. I stepped outside. I tingled with the crisp surge of air into my face, and listened to its great, fulsome rush through space. It is magnificently exciting, drowning out all other sounds—an ocean of air passing between me and the pines on the ridge.

March 18 Last Sunday we spent at the cabin. Although it was now mid-March, snow furrowed the deep hollows on Le Conte, Charlies Bunion, and Woolly Tops. There was a chill in the bright, sunny air; and the full waters of the creek, clear though they were, had the delicate greenish hue of winter. Someone has said that the color is not an illusion, but is probably due to suspended fragments of moss and lichens which have been torn loose and ground fine in the roiling water.

The carpet of humus was deep and yielding. These woods had been logged, but my guess is they had never been cleared. If they had, they had reverted rapidly after the people moved out of the Park; and the prolific growth had accumulated this rich cushion underfoot in a very few years. No wonder the waters of the creek came out clear after seeping through this natural filter. There is poetry in forest duff. It is the key to healthy woods and limpid streams.

April 5   On the weekend I had another try at Charlies Bunion in the snow. This climb came nearly six weeks later in the year than my previous snow hike up there, but this time there was more snow. There were probably six or eight inches on the level and drifts belly-deep and more in the hollows. Sometimes the snow clung to the rock

"... the Stateline loomed ahead, appallingly steep."

and you could punch holes in it with your boots. At other times it gave way maddeningly, and occasionally we would break an outer crust to see cavernous depths along the stream bed.

The snow had largely melted from the south-facing cliffs of slaty black rock, and immediately some of the boys took to those cliffs, preferring them to the snow. The rest of us went up a hollow. Where the snow had drifted deeply, Henry Gray, taking a glissade to retrieve his coat, broke through to his neck. Herrick Brown immediately went for the crest of the buttressing ridge and made out. I took a middle course, lizarding back and forth, making altitude at very difficult places. I learned to gauge the stability of patches of snow. I realized how difficult is rock with a downward pitch. Toe holds were precarious. At lunch I reclined against the wall with my feet on a tiny wedge-shaped ledge, about a yard long. Looking down the slopes I had climbed, there were spots where it pitched too steeply to observe.

I was finally blocked about six feet above my lunch site. There was a bulge and although by stretching I got a decent foothold I could find no handhold by which to pull myself up to what appeared to be comparatively easy going. Several times I lunged out but with a sickening sense of what would happen if I gave up my safe handhold. I had to beat a not too easy retreat to the hollow where I followed steps punched in the snow by Henry Gray. Later, on a dry slope, I clambered up the knots of a huge old rotting spruce.

April 21 Every time I start to write something here, something more immediate, more exciting, seems to intrude. Yesterday, it was the exquisite spring hike we had up the Little River above Elkmont. The dogwood, redbud, and freshening leaves changed every landscape with a delicate glamor. In the bright sun the air had the singular appearance of being both sharp and diffused. Maybe the air was sharp. Maybe the manifold shadings in the new leaves produced the diffused quality. Maybe it was our own minds which were taken in by the sweetness of spring.

But there were gaps in the appearance of spring. Some places the trees were hardly advanced at all. In others there were distinct points of color in the blooms of the columbine and wild bleeding heart. And as we drove along we saw, in the grass along the edge of the highway, blurs of color of royal purple violets, of mountain iris and phlox.

The full weight of the season did not rest upon us until we left the car and proceeded up the main river above Elkmont. The air was bright and warm. Exquisite beds of white and yellow violets appeared along the grass-grown roadside. And there were great white blotches spotting the slopes—thousands of enormous white trilliums, some suffused with pink and others with black centers. Such luxuriance—such gigantic size! Then came a clump of phlox into which we buried our noses for a whiff of its delicate fragrance. Blooms on an old apple tree, sprung up by a cabin long since gone, yielded another fragrance. There were several small patches of phacelia with their delicate fringed cups of white and shadowy blue.

Then our attention was diverted by a great russet form winging silently through the trees. Once it came to rest, and then took off again—its body moving with absolute noiselessness. We lost it, but the corner of our eyes caught a spot of scarlet—a tanager. We heard and saw grouse.

Coming to the grassy glade at the forks of the main river and the Fish Camp Prong, we took to the Fish Camp as the more inviting and stood a moment on the bridge to look at its mouth. Anne, who came from an inland community, said that the mouth of a stream seemed a romantic place, and she had never quite got over the feeling.

Later we came to another opening in the forest, which rolled upward through terrace after terrace until it was lost in the trees— white with phacelia, acres of it resting like snow on the uprolling earth. The quiet lavishness of it was breath-taking. For this lift to our spirits we had journeyed far. There is no real describing it—the whitened expanse on which we stood, a vista here, a further vista yonder, leading our eyes upward until the last whitening was lost among the trees.

We came to another grassy spot at the end of the road, where in times past I had camped. The remains of the old logging road trestle were nearly gone, but across from us we could see the flatness of the old railroad grade seemingly unchanged except that it was now shaded by young birches. Those lacerating briers of a few years ago were disappearing under the shade. The pounding cascades were still there, but in a softened setting. This rather raw area was slowly healing; and the water in the pools and little surface ripples again had lights in it. The barren ridge across the creek from us had some cover now, although there were several large bare scars where slides had occurred. There was one point near the ridge which, like a portion of the Bunion, had seemingly burned down to rock.

For the most part the woods around us were in their winter bleakness, although here, as all along the route we had followed, the "sarvises"[3] were blooming—their airy, white blooms blending gently with the green-bronze of their unfolding leaves. No tree I know has more appeal. There is nothing heavy, or obvious, about its blooming—nothing mathematical or flaunting. Here is beauty in restraint, with a baffling, shy, elusive quality.

My impression was one of sadness. I have had it before. The beauty is so timeless as to be overwhelming. These ever-flowing streams—whence do they come, whither do they go, and why? This endless renewal of spring with its persistent healing of man's outrages on the mountainsides brings an end to thought.

On the return, as we came to the junction with the up-river fork, we felt rather than heard a distant call. I thought it was the end of a faint, long-drawn-out hail. Anne thought it was an owl. As we strained we heard it again—softly, like the pulsing of the blood in our ears, like the soft stirring of a breeze, *whoo, whoo-whoo whoo—who whooah.* Once repeated, hardly heard, it was as though that whole mountainous amphitheatre had distilled its spirit into one exquisite thinly gathered sound—the call of the barred owl. It was like an elixir—so potent that it has stirred my heart for days.

After such experiences, I have no real will to *do* things. The restlessness of mankind has a certain pointlessness. Ultimately the glaciers or the floods or man's own excesses will catch up with him and he will yield the surface of the earth to stronger forces. My feeling is that civilization has gotten out of balance. There is struggle in nature to be sure, but the essence of living is not struggle. Much of it is a yielding through our spirits to the embraciveness of nature. I would be the last to complain of the existence of "divine unrest"—but if only it were not so blatant, so never satisfied.

June 9 The next great era in world history may involve the adjustments which all peoples are going to have to make to their dwindling resources. The era may be complicated by wars, labor troubles, and all the plethora of incidents which make up the complex pattern of modern life. People, with their preconceptions and a generous capacity for self-delusion, will blame this *ism* and that group,

---

[3] *Amelanchier laevis,* serviceberry.

whereas the real reason will be that they have come to the bottom of the bin.

It is inconceivable to our people that we may be reduced to the bitter peasantry of the Chinese coolie and the Indian outcast. In those countries population has seemingly long since outstripped the capacity of either country to supply decent sustenance. We herald our increasing, populations as the providers of new markets which will multiply ad infinitum, and ignore the probability that each one of this increasing number will be a competitor ultimately for such basic things as food, as each is already a competitor for such basic things as trees and unspoiled scenery.

August 26 Two weeks ago I hiked with friends for a day through the incomparable forests of Santeetlah Creek and trod warily the huge boulders of the stream course. There was a black-green vitality to the forest. Gray ledges, hung over with birches and hemlocks and covered with moisture-drenched mosses, were almost black in the shadows. Great slopes, deep with rhododendron under the hemlocks and reflecting the light from lustrous leaves, rose from the creek almost like a wall.

There were boulders with angular lines, roughened with lichens and moss, resting like monoliths in the creek bed. Some were as big as rooms. We would inch up one of these boulders and peer over the top to catch a glimpse of a narrow cascade of sheer white foam sliding through a cleft in the rock. The air and undergrowth were moist from the previous night's rain, and there was a slight—ever so slight—dinginess in the water, which, however, did not prevent our seeing to the bottom of five-foot pools. Our trousers, absorbing this moisture, clung to our legs; and our socks, shaken by a thousand jarring leaps, subsided into our shoes. Sometimes we were on our stomachs writhing under a blowdown, or were performing acrobatically through windfalls eight feet above the ground.

In one place a yellow birch had fallen, and its green leaves in varying states of wilt were sloughing off. These leaves were deep green on the face and a lighter green on the reverse. Coming to rest on the brown humus, they reminded me of the pattern and color of jungle suits.

Limbs raked our hair, cobwebs clung to our faces, and dead leaves, broken twigs, and the infinite litter of the forest fell into our shirts.

We scrubbed up the earth with our stomachs, scraped off litter with our backs, soaked up moisture, and splashed through shallow pools until the rawhide laces of our boots became so limber they would slip out of their knots like a snake. Once a vine gave way and we fell into a pool. Once we had to cross from one side to another and there was no way across the swirling current, so we splashed through a deep pool. Damp, disheveled, crawling, wading, we absorbed the odors and colors of the woods themselves.

There was something almost terrifying about these calm pools, restless eddies, and gleaming waterfalls, moving through this exquisite forested gorge in a fluid pattern of beauty—self-renewing, eternal. We were scratched and marked and soaked until we began to take on some of the disarray of the woods, where the infinity of plants and leaves and drops blended into a powerful image of inexhaustible vitality.

September 13 Arriving late last week at Linville Gorge, we dashed out to Wiseman's View in the deepening twilight for some spectacular photographs across the blue-green gulf. A soft roar rose from the barely discernible river, remotely, as from another world. A storm was gathering across in the Piedmont, and the wind whipped across the sheer point on which we stood. Once I stepped backward for better perspective and glanced down to find myself standing at the brink of a 200-foot drop. I was looking down upon the point of a great, dead hemlock 100 feet below me. It was no place for a misstep, and I curbed my eagerness.

On the next day we trudged through wet bushes and a heavy mist to the Hawksbill. On top were small pines and sand myrtle, interspersed with slabs of rock overlapping like shingles but with their exposed edges pointing upward instead of downward. These terminated irregularly, projecting over space in a frightening manner. As we lunched, a thinness came in the mist and we saw the darkness of the opposite wall of the gorge as through a moving curtain. There arose the feeling of being drawn into terrifying depths. But the fog dissipated ultimately and we saw the sheer columniation of Table Rock, the vertical walls to the west of it, and the white thread of the river at the bottom of the gulf.

To the south, the Piedmont spread to the horizon in a brilliant blue-green patchwork of fields and low hills with strips of silver marking the lakes. The forest slopes followed a gentler gradient to the river from the Hawksbill than from the yellowed rocks of Wiseman's View on the opposite face of the gorge. But there were the same huge scale and sense of precipitateness. From our height the giant boulders of the river bed resembled pebbles, and the turbulence of the river and of its cascades came up to us in a soft sound like the sough of the wind.

October 27 Tonight I was reading from Dimnet's *The Art of Thinking*. He wrote that feelings and unexpressed thoughts flit about the edges of our consciousness, the full experience of which is lost in an attempt to reduce them to words. How true that is.

I have wanted to write of the sweetness of a new-mown meadow in the milieu of the hills. Was it autumn and the sad charm of satiation which lay like a wash over that field? And what of the ineffable remoteness of the Abrams Creek gorge? of those placid stretches and lazy shoals? of the mysterious bends shutting off the view and stirring the spirit to turn that corner too? In my mind I wanted to follow that trail to Abrams Falls, to make the connection from the known of Happy Valley to the previously known of the falls. But in my heart, I did not want to do it, and I am glad I did not. Something is left for expectation. Does that gorge really, after all, lead to Abrams Falls? Or may it not lead to some unexplored fastness yet beyond the tread of man?

As an Eskimo put it, I want to camp where no man has camped before. I no longer want to connect up all the knowns. I want to stir my thoughts, cultivate my expectancies. I would like to see Abrams Creek with eyes of the first man who forced the mazes of its windings and looked upon that beautiful flat and called it good; with the eyes of the man who built that ancient rail fence a tiny section of which we saw, and which had not yet rotted away. I want the thrill of discovering for the first time a giant white pine, the existence of which I had not known.

And I want to save places like Santeetlah Creek so that others may have the superb experience of *discovery* which was mine hardly two months ago. Already the fine bloom has been taken from Little Santeetlah by the name Joyce Kilmer and by the marker which somehow clots the subtle streaming of perception which one ought to feel in the presence of superlative forest. Bernie Frank and I were equally guilty when we measured the feathery towers of the hemlocks and the stocky columns of the tulips. I hope I may never again reveal the height of those mighty trees.

December 22   Man has created much loveliness which does not exist apart from his civilization. This is the Christmas season, and I have just been listening to a magnificent program of Christmas music. Man has created some lovely dwellings—some soul-stirring literature. He has done much to alleviate phyical pain. But he has not, in his cities, created a substitute for a sunset, a grove of pines, the music of the winds, the dank smell of the deep forest, or the shy beauty of a wild flower. Why is it that as their numbers grow, individual men see less and less of these things?

Man has notable achievements to his credit in the organization of society. And he has perhaps not yet completely emulated the ant in standardizing living, but he is heading that way. Great hosts of people can exist at one time fairly comfortably and with a measure of happiness. But sheer numbers shut off many from the eternities except through the experience of sex and except through religious observances, which are cut off further from reality since they are observed indoors.

INETEEN FORTY-EIGHT

January 21   If one wants to relax, he should stay out of conservation! The winter issue of *The Living Wilderness* lists a continual series of threats to its philosophy, to the Olympic forests, Jackson Hole, Quetico-Superior, Lake Solitude, ad infinitum. A chap by the name of Baker concedes that the Wilderness Society has a function in slowing down wasteful and needless inroads upon the wilds but, being a forester, he thinks that the chief end of man is economic and such needs must eventually overcome the "snobberies" of wilderness folks.

He is right that the threats will continue for economic use of the wilderness, but he is wrong in thinking we should proceed to the end of our rope before being forced to think whither all this is leading. Under his view, continued economic use amounts simply to the momentary deferment of the inevitable. It points up Olaus Murie's view that the primary problem today is one of burgeoning populations; and there is little disposition anywhere on earth to face this nightmare.

March 6 Last Sunday, in sunshine and comparative warmth and encountering only tiny and infrequent patches of snow, we worked up the Walker Camp Prong to the Appalachian Trail and down through more sunshine to Newfound Gap. Of course we got cold when we stopped in deep shade; but it was hardly a wintry day. The hiking up the creek was marvelous. The water was not too high; the rocks were clean and our boots gripped them like iron. There was just

Walker Prong ". . . the rhododendron continuing
to wall us in . . . , we were driven to the
creek and its ice- and snow-covered rocks."

enough rhododendron along the edges, where the pools were deep,
to supply obstruction. At points where the creek made sharp loops
we cut across the intervening hogbacks, which were soft with moss
and shaded by great spruces.

August 28   The trip to the mountains last weekend, more than any
I have taken in the Smokies in a long time, called up old feelings of
eagerness and excitement for new things. Leaving the Porters Flat
trail, we turned into the west Greenbrier, under the Boulevard. The
bed of Boulevard Prong was 25 feet across. The water was low, very
low, but brilliant in the sun. In the last decade or so it had been
opened up by flood, and the rocks which composed its bed were

scrubbed of their lichens until they gave firm hold even when sharply sloping. There were occasional mighty logs across the stream. One had become jammed in such a way as to dam it completely and against it lodged stones, rocks, and debris of various kinds.

The cohosh was in berry. Henry Gray picked some and offered them as huckleberries to a slightly doubting group. Another place the viburnum, or hobble bush, glowed with brilliant scarlet fruit. Twice we were forced out of the creek by a juxtaposition of pool and rhododendron and for a few paces felt the friendliness of yielding humus under our feet.

One pool lay somberly green at the foot of a slanting ledge. At another spot the water sped down a tilted trough. Curiously, similar rocky troughs occur on many of the Smoky streams. There was a perpendicular wall covered with moss over which much of the stream flow filtered in pendulant drops. I tried climbing the wall, but the handholds gave out at the top and I was forced to scramble up a rotting log.

The stream bed became narrower, the overarching of trees more complete. Looking ahead I saw the rising bulk of the separating ridge, light and blue in the distance. The pitch became steeper. I had been doing balanced rock hopping, picking several footholds at a time and moving forward, easily and rhythmically, even on these oft-treacherous rocks. But as the going steepened, I would often have to lunge for the next foothold, pause, and recover myself. The climbing became harder, and the delusion that I was as good as I was twenty years ago vanished.

Spick-and-span hikers became dirty and disheveled from squirming under brush or rolling over logs. Some of them got soaked feet as they misjudged a jump or stepped on an insecure rock. In two hours they had become one with the wilderness, flopping down anywhere to rest, relaxing gratefully on bare rock. One time half the group lined up in various poses on a single log, like cedar waxwings in the sun.

At last we took to the left up a hellishly steep and encumbered slope. If one craned his neck, he could see the Bunion through the trees. It is beginning to have a slight greenish cast—no longer quite the stark, rocky horror it was a few years ago, although in several of its hollows we could see log jams which had been there since the flood of 1927.

At lunch Dan Hale had held forth on the thesis that a downward slope of a certain pitch is an aid to hiking; but as we twisted down through the rhododendron, holding ourselves back to keep from falling into its tangles, he remarked, "This ain't it!"

Another boy had been through the conditioning mazes of Officers' Candidate School. He said, "This is worse. Those I could do." Just then he slipped on a sheath of damp greasy algae and fell heavily.

The descent of that upper creek bed was a nightmare. The stream was a mere rivulet, overgrown with dense herbage and made treacherous by loose rocks and dripping algae. After the pitch lessened, we could work along the bank beside the stream bed. The boys ahead scared up a bear. We came to a perpendicular ledge, and our rivulet dropped into a much larger stream course, one of those which had been disemboweled twenty years before by the floods from Charlies Bunion. So much loose rock had come from above that it acted as a kind of sieve and the water percolated beneath as we tramped the surface. There was no barrenness. The woods were dense and heavy on both sides and overhead. Here we didn't have to contend either with rhododendron or with slick rocks.

Eventually, and before we had come to the point of praying for it (as Marshall Wilson literally had once done after an exhausting weekend in this same area), we found a trail. It was a mere trace, hung across with rhododendron but firm under foot, and we followed it gratefully.

October 31 Last Sunday I relaxed upon some uneven ground at the Rich Mountain fire tower. The air was fitful and blustery. Clouds raced across the sky holding back the warming rays of the sun. Even wearing many clothes, I was not quite comfortable in the shadows. Lying on the ground, hat over my eyes, my body sharply sensitive, I listened to the incessant stirring of the wind in the dead leaves of the oaks. There was no surcease—a continuous ferment of sound which left me vaguely dissatisfied.

What did it mean? Why did the wind blow? Listening, I was not a part of it. The air would have surged and the leaves rustled, whether I was there or not. It was building up to no climax. A cool front was coming in, but that is just a description, not an explanation. There was something inscrutable, elusive, about this noisy activity in which I joyed, but which I could not interpret. Winds blow where they list, seemingly without end, dropping into a calm or bounding into violence like the moods of a giant and everlasting symphony.

INETEEN FORTY-NINE

March 21   Many times I have written of the boundless prophecies of spring—the warm sun, the soft breezes, manifold aromas, and songs which weave a spell that seems to have no end. It is as though the flowering could go on forever into beautiful and ever more beautiful phases. But the surge of beauty spends its inner force: the petals wither, the sun hottens, drought succeeds the gentle rains, and the promise becomes old and astringent . . .

Is there any analogy in the life of a nation? I shan't press the similarity because of its complexity. After all, one does not know the time schedules involved in the springtime of a civilization or of a race. I have reservations about the ever-expanding dynamism of the present day. It must rest upon definitely circumscribed resources and lands. It springs from an expanding population which must perforce bear an increasingly unfavorable relationship to resources.

Many people with whom I discuss this unfavorable relationship, including some scientists whose experience with facts ought to teach them differently, have a disposition to shrug their shoulders and say that science has always found a way out of other dilemmas and will find a way out of this apparent one. Admittedly we are living in a day of unprecedented scientific adventure, but it does not seem to me to have the broad base of the Renaissance, which, as I understand it, was very widely diffused throughout the population, and which—if there is any lesson in it for us—was very short-lived.

Where is the maturity to restrain this dynamism from almost certain and damaging excesses? Our very advances have brought closer the dreadful clouds of war. Do the people of the earth—or rather the people in these snowballing economies of the United States and Russia—lack the ability to assimilate all the potentialities of their headlong rush? Or is the rush in itself so intoxicating that there is no turning back?

May 14   Anne and I climbed the Chimneys recently. Hiking alone, we moved according to our own inclination and interest. We had no time schedule and stopped frequently to take in the limpid loveliness of the Road Prong and listen to the calls of the numerous birds.

I had forgotten the utter beauty of that creek. It is not remote in distance, but there is little suggestion of man. What there is of man resides in one's memory, not in what he sees or hears. Beech Flats is growing into a thicket of beech sprouts. The appropriateness of the name will soon be lost to those who did not know it a couple of decades ago.

The wilds have done a notable job of reclaiming the old Thomas Road along the stream. In the teens and twenties, when I went up the old road, it was still open in places, and although the width of the original passage is still discernible the passage is now a wide man-way.

At the Standing Rock ford there was no evidence of a road crossing; but Anne remarked that the two approaches were yet plain. I do not know how the mountain people negotiated those fords with their wagons, although conceivably they may have rolled boulders and small stones in among the ledges. But there have been uncounted floods since this old mountain-way was used for wagons. On Sunday we saw debris the height of a man above the bed of the creek. Such floods would tear all but the heaviest boulders out of the stream.

After we left the Road Prong and turned up the little hollow we found faint evidences of a trail. But after passing two piles of bear dung and noting where occasional herbaceous plants had been nipped off, we decided we were following the spoor of a bear rather than that of a human. The hollow is V-shaped and on a steep tilt. It is extraordinarily free of undergrowth and the trees are tall. Most of them were buckeyes. There were some blowdowns, including a doughty old hemlock which had crashed across the hollow, bringing down some smaller trees with it. But by and large we climbed openly, if steeply, through forbs. The pitch was so great that when we rested and glanced down the ravine we would find ourselves even with the tops of trees, well over a hundred feet tall, which we had passed only a couple of hundred feet back.

Birds flitted about and sang in this towering leafage. There were several warblers, a few unmistakable snatches of song by the winter wren, both nuthatches (which Jack Huff used to call that ". . . lonesome-sounding bird"), and a great vocal clatter by the "lord god" bird—the pileated woodpecker.

We finally reached a slender buckeye which seemed to grow out of an earthen pedestal at the very center of the ravine. Here we bore to the right and upward through great rhododendron clumps, to the south ridge of the Chimneys. The transition from a buckeye association to that of great spruces and rhododendron was sharp. Taunted by the gleam of the skyline through the undergrowth, we moved at an exhausting pace to the ridge crest and to the soft, hummocky trail through the rhododendrons and spruces. I love the serene, natural openness of that animal trail along that knife-edge ridge.

So much did I enjoy the seclusion of the woods that the Chimneys themselves seemed an anticlimax. The sight below of the highway and of the moving cars, the swish of traffic and the muted blarings of the horns, took some of the zest from the otherwise magnificent view, and we retreated to a ledge on the south slope from which no human works could be seen or heard.

Shortly we heard a rumble of thunder, and when the storm crossed the Sugarland from the vicinity of Blanket Mountain and whitened the valley with fog toward Cove Mountain, we beat a retreat down along the crest to our packs. It looked as though there might be wind, and we had squirmed down through the rhododendron almost to the hollow when the storm struck. We took refuge under a bulging birch. Actually the rain was not heavy, although two shattering cracks of lightning were so close that we wondered whether we should be under a tree at all. But I reasoned that a birch, even a big one, had a diffused crown and would not be the target that a spruce or hemlock would be. I recalled that I had seen numerous spruces which had been split open by a bolt of lightning, but not a single birch which had been so hit. The storm passed, the shower was reduced to an aimless dripping, and we started our damp trip back down the hollow.

June 27   I should like to note the importance to the human spirit of two recent trips to Gregory. One was up the fast-healing forest from Deals Gap over a trail I had not traversed for seventeen years.

I had remembered it as hot and uninteresting. But the years have brought young undergrowth and humus to the soil, and I enjoyed the trip as I had not thought I could. We passed giant cinnamon ferns and an ant hill which we chanced to upset into a seething flurry of activity. Although there was some lost motion, the intent seemed to have been to drag fat pupas down ant-spouting holes. One of the boys said:

"There doesn't seem to be much plan to it."

"Did you ever look down on a street from a high building?" I replied. "The activities of human beings on a sidewalk seem, at best, as planless."

On top we saw simultaneously a half dozen rainstorms. Boiling mist brought a few scattering drops to us, but no real rain. The clear air threw the mountains into unaccustomed relief, and the great saucer-like valley across the deep-cut gorge of the Little Tennessee River resembled a forested crater. Such clarity was unusual.

A week later, toughened by two hikes in three weeks, Anne and I went again to Gregory Bald from Cades Cove. I cannot stress too much what that toughening meant. We climbed to the shelter in two and a half hours and with little discomfort.

We moved onto the bald through striking clumps of azalea, irregularly and informally spaced. The sun was red and low across the grassy arc of the summit. For our campsite we picked a sheltered spot in the lee of a small intruding pine. A dead chestnut down on the edge of the forest yielded crooked tent poles. Our tent was tiny indeed on that vast rounded sward.

In the night there was some wind and a patter of rain; and out of measureless space came the oft-repeated, softly pulsing hooting of a lone owl. No matter what ill fortune a year can bring, for Anne and me it can always be overbalanced if we hear just once a winter wren, a veery, and the hooting of a great owl. Out of that lovely breeze-swept night on the grass of Gregory the balance dropped sharply in our favor.

I rested with my head out of the tent. The brilliance of the stars was dulled by a quarter moon. I woke to flooding light, and saw three blanketed figures who had come up from the shelter of the woods to see the sunrise. Perhaps on our grassy bed we slept more soundly, for the sun was minutes high as I craned my neck around the slope of the tent.

The day enhanced the gorgeous color of the azaleas, and the air was vibrant with the song of the veery.

The same area could hardly have been more different on those two weekends. On the first, the surrounding mountains looked clear, green, and sharp; on this one, faded, blue, and haunting. Our feet dragged as we turned from the bald to the trail and went down by the shelter to the Moore Spring. Perhaps not as cold as the McGee Spring, nevertheless it boils out of the ground with spirit, and few there are who can forget the experience of filling their canteens from the "bubble" at the Moore Spring.

There was peace on the bald. We experienced a different peace as on the descent we rounded a bend of the trail and picked up the roar of the stream below. Then we descended into a belt of great tulips and hemlocks into whose shade we passed. Moving from open woods into their gloom was like closing the diaphragm of a camera. Even the sun could not penetrate that leafy canopy. Here again was the peace of majestic, centuries-old, virgin woods.

This harmony of man and nature was blasted after we took to the road. There was a congestion of cars; people stood excitedly about. Two youths were throwing stones violently at something on the ground. Such uncurbed ferocity could mean only one thing—a rattle-snake. I was sickened by this savage violence toward one of the creatures of this great forest. Why can't we observe, rather than destroy, even this baleful thing?

August 4 Sunday I went to Ramsay Falls with the Hiking Club. Fresh from reading in Reginald Cook's *Passage to Walden,* I think I had a deeper awareness of sights and sounds and odors. There was one odor of ambrosia which twice drifted through the air near the Cherry Orchard. It was pleasing and exotic, and I haven't the slightest notion of its source. There were musky odors, perhaps the scent of shrews and others of that family, which foxes snap at and kill along the trails and quickly drop as inedible. And there were ineffable scents of dampness and growth where water and green life crowded together and seemed to share the same space.

On the cliff alongside the falls were broad bands of gray and mauve, and faint mustard stains which the seepage had carried down across the face of the rock in a somber spectrum of colors. Then came the straightdownness of a summer shower in the Smokies, exploding goose pimples of water on the surface of the pools. Rains higher on the mountain filled the creek bed, and there was an out-jetting of white water at the head of the falls.

Down at the forks, I ventured out on the Eagle Rocks footbridge, now without rails. It bridged the tawny flood pouring down from Old Black, Laurel Top, and Woolly Tops. It was a tremendous spectacle. From the disintegrating logs I looked down fifteen feet into the tossing yellow-white surgings of that flood-mad creek. My head swam with the restless motion and the prodigious power. What a setting: great hemlocks and birches and rhododendron massing in a wall of green, and this great stream beating against solid boulders in a roaring violence of sight and sound.

August 23 On the last weekend we had another harshly memorable trip to the mountains. We had had a succession of hot days. About Thursday a cold front moved in and the weatherman predicted a cool dry weekend. I was enthusiastic. I envisaged sleeping out on the cool grass of Hooper Bald under an open sky. But something went wrong. About midafternoon on Friday I looked out the window at the office and saw the sky overcast. Saturday morning there was rain. I still hoped that the clouds would break and that the original prediction would hold.

We left town under an overcast, and as we neared the mountains they were truncated by fog. Driving up the gorge of the Tellico River, which must be as satisfyingly beautiful as any on earth, we saw clouds clinging to the slopes just above us. Up the North Fork, we were in and out of fog.

Through open woods and deep narrow rifts in the undergrowth we climbed 500 vertical feet to Haw Knob along old and muddy stock trails. The clean sward of Haw Knob was softened by mist. A white paper, speared on a branch, refreshed my recollection that we went to the right for Hooper Bald. We were on the ridge crest, which was wide and forested and stock-trampled and poorly drained. Hideously slick stones and outcrops alternated with soupy, muddy sloughs and bits of firm trail overgrown with high-bush huckleberries. On occasion the slopes dropped off beside us, to be lost in a white ocean of fog. We seemed to be tramping a green tunnel somewhere between heaven and earth.

An occasional grassy spot raised eager hopes of the bald. Once we saw dark shapes through an avenue in the trees and heard a violent pounding of hoofs. We caught up with these creatures—a half dozen wild, sleek young mules. Then we moved into a dismal upland swamp amongst the trees, crisscrossed with trails like the water channels of a muddy delta and nearly as wet. Another opening, a few more huckleberry bushes, some with broken sprawling stems. We guessed that a bear had eaten there. Another gray opening in the trees—dampness around us dripping off the trees. We fairly breathed it and soaked it up. Occasionally the penetrating odor of pennyroyal seared the back of our nostrils.

The woods opened more, the mist thickened, a broad rounded slope was lost upward in the fog. Then we saw shapes suspended in the darkening mist, and heard voices coming from those shapes. A small tent loomed on the horizon above us and two busts—motionless and detached—hung in the gloom above it. Other voices and shapes came out of the grayness. We were the last to arrive.

We elected to pitch our tent on the rounded grassy crest near Hugh and Sarah Smathers. The spot was smooth and perfect. An old fence post made a tent pole and I exhumed two stones to anchor the tent front and back, and because of the bulk of our tent pole I guyed it with a rawhide thong to another stone. I did not want it crashing down on us in the night.

Some of the group predicted rain. Hugh and Sarah said the sun was shining when they arrived in midafternoon. But remembering the prediction for clear, dry, cold air, I still thought we were in for a good night. We had hardly set our tent when there was a patter of rain. Hugh invited us and Phyllis Inman to eat under the fly in the front of their tent. He and Sarah reclined inside. Anne and I huddled at one end. Phyllis laid her poncho over the rooftree and sat with her back under the poncho. It was a miserable, crowded, telescoped meal, with water trickling down our necks and gathering in clear puddles at our feet. There was no shelter except that which we had carried with us on our backs.

Anne and I strapped our packs tightly, placed them on a rounded rock which rose just above the grass, covered them with a poncho, and went to bed. Not expecting rain, I had ignored the need of a ditch when I pitched the tent. I removed my boots and got inside and found an inch of water at the edge. Drops streamed from a spot we had touched in the tent cloth. Mist beat through the thin cloth, and already our sleeping bags were damp. Anne announced there was water on her side, and I felt a suspicious coolness along my right side as I lay on my back. And then I felt water inside my sleeping bag around my feet, and as I turned on my side, I could measure its depth —two toes deep on my left foot. Anne hugged the field glasses to her inside the sleeping bag; and I, the bird book and flashlight inside mine.

Out of the dark there was a drone of voices above the flat rat-tat of the rain. Seno came by on tour, and we talked to her through the tent. Herrick Brown and Charlie Person went by.

The rain eased after a while, and I found that the body could warm a moderate amount of water with which it was in contact. Eventually the water seeped away and we lay in *comparative* comfort. Anne was chilly; we were both damp. But once we became wet we had a recurrence, like a reincarnation, of the feeling we had had on a few such previous occasions that a drenching is not fatal! But the night was not over. Once again the rain cannonaded down, and the water crept up on my toes and dammed up against my back as I lay on my side holding the water away from the little area of dryness between us.

I dozed fitfully. Early in the night, the darkness, toned by the mist, was so intense that the ridge of the tent not four feet above our faces was lost in the inkiness. As dawn approached, I could see the ridge and then light came through the cloth. Anne was restless and got up and went out into the fog before the rain ceased.

I was curious to know how the others had fared. I slipped into my boots, rolled the sleeping bags together, dragged the poncho from beneath them, donned my rain hat, and went out into the weather.

There was ingenuity everywhere. Enormous nylon ponchos had been stretched by some into shelters under which forms moved, or huddled, or lay prone. A fire, burning under one poncho, reminded me of Indian fires for baking tortillas in peon huts in Mexico. Jane Snyder had lent her sleeping bag and had kept a fire going all night. One blonde boy had on nothing but shorts. Pink-bodied and clean, he looked incongruous in that muddy, misty setting. Two ponchos had been pitched into a low wide tent, like a pig shelter. There were puddles all around in a kind of wallow. Slightly raised above this slough, and seemingly floating as on a raft, this group slept under their makeshift tent. Out in the fringe of the trees other forms lay under ponchos without benefit of tents.

Fred Sweeton and Phil Ewald had covered their fire with a stump, and there were still live coals beneath. I ran back and got my inspirator. We split dead firm wood, laid it on the coals, covered it over with bark to hold out the rain, and in a half hour had blown up flames which licked greedily through piled-on branches. Soon we had a hot cheerful fire. Under our rain gear we were soon warm and comfortable.

The rain let up, if the mist did not; and although we walked into droplets, they did not drench us from above. I followed the edge of the forest through acres of trees felled twelve years ago to aid the grazing, down to a hollow where I heard water and scooped up a kettleful for tea. It was good to be fit and vigorous after such a harassing night. And I knew I was glad it had turned out that way. This night ranked with Tricorner Knob, Stratton Meadow, and Wiseman's View. Another memorable camp, spent with a *monumental barometric low!*

The mist did not abate, and remembering there were some three miles of primitive road to drive over, we left the top about 11 o'clock. More sloughs and interlacing trails ran with water. We paused once for huckleberries and topped out on Haw Knob at noon. It was not then raining; the fog had burned off, and we sat down and lunched and enjoyed the warmth. Once we saw the white disk of the sun through scudding fog. Down at the cars we were met with the gibe "Soggy Mountain Hiking Club."

November 15 Sunday, in a maelstrom of fog and wind generated by a cold front, we went down to Silers. Not once did we see more than 100 yards through thick gray fog, sometimes static, sometimes whipped into waves by the up-pouring wind. There was an awesome closeness about it. The center of our world shifted through the blanketing mist as we trudged onward, but its rim was never more than a hundred yards away. We were three lonely figures hedged in by the obscuring fog.

Into that world came formless shapes of dead trees on a bleak slope, the enormous vitality of limby old spruces and of great, glistening birches. There were delightful green wild nurseries of spruce and balsam seedlings. Troughs of beech leaves collected in the open pathway between the trees, their shuffling crackle muted by the moisture. There was the soft thunder of grouse taking off, and the surprise in seeing one run across the trail and hurtle into the grayness. There were those bare moors, with long grasses parted by the winds, in which we found fresh droppings of wild turkeys.

This succession of befogged experiences, merging slowly into each other as we shifted the focus of our presence, was as deeply moving as any I have ever had. Never was the insulation from mankind more complete.

I cannot but speculate about a civilization which is heedless of such profound and moving beauty. Back at the road we found people venturing but fifteen to twenty feet from their cars. We heard the blare of radios as though even within the safe comfortable interior of their cars, they dared not face the wild profundities of nature. Do we live, as Louis Bromfield intimated in his review of *The Brave Bulls*, so that no great emotions possess us in this America, and that the best of our native literature concerns itself with frustrations and futilities and not great purposes and courages? The ethical proprietorship of land of which Leopold wrote is as far as the stars from many of our Americans.

The saving of such surging, massive beauty as the Smokies is tied up with economics and tourists and is not, even among its custodians, related to the great mysteries of life and of earthly survival. Beauty is recognized for its economic value, but not for its value in harboring the secret interworkings of living things. What do the spruce and the grouse mean to us? What of the soft mat of moss and of disintegrating needles? What of those gorgeous streams, dancing with life? What of the great trees, the turkeys, those fog worlds, the on and on and on-ness of that inviting closed-in world?

December 27   A week ago Frizzell and I were in the mountains. We proposed crossing the Road Prong four times where there were no bridges. A tremendous foaming torrent put a quietus on that plan, and we turned to our knowledge of topography to circumvent the creek. One possibility was to encircle the entire watershed—go up the Chimneys to Sugarland to Mt. Collins, down the Stateline to Mt. Mingus, and down Mingus to the point of land between the two existing footbridges. We took the first leg of this possibility and gambled on a ride back to our car.

It was a heavy, misty day. We saw no one on the road after we left Gatlinburg. When we got out of the car, Guy threw back his head and yelled. This was a yell of joy—uninhibited, exuberant. Thoreau once said he would like to meet man in the woods, to be encountered like wild caribou and moose. Perhaps if Thoreau had been there at that moment his wish would have been fulfilled. There was something extraordinarily moving in having that great, lush, and beautiful area completely to ourselves.

Lucy Templeton, writing of her two wishes for Christmas, a wood fire and a trip to the mountains, remarked:

"The commonplaces of yesterday become the luxuries of today—a wood fire, pure air and water, quiet and unjostled space."

I like that term "unjostled space." Maybe there is a certain redundancy—it wouldn't be space, or spacious, if jostled, but it carries the connotation of freedom, of unthrottled movement in pleasing surroundings.

We climbed the Chimneys by the shortest, steepest route. We had hardly got above the level of the valley trees when we saw a rainbow outlined through the drifting mist. There was wildness in the air. The mist was driven in slanting waves by a tumultuous wind. Above, a leaden cloud layer was broken by rifts through which the sun kept the rainbow alive.

The trail was muddy and steep, winding across great snake-like roots of trees and arms of rhododendron. Ledges from which the deep chocolate humus had been torn and washed furnished an occasional foothold. A sheer wall of rock 25 feet high was made climbable by scattered tree roots, which could be reached by stretching and weaving across the cliff face. The soil wash is bad toward the top. The route is in a trough between waist-high walls of humus. One wonders if on this precipitous peak climbing may not have to be limited in order to preserve the dense and unique cover of rhododendron.

On top the mist, which seemed to disappear into our clothing, did not wet us much, although we were quickly dampened when we slid across a rock face in the saddle and bellied across a bulge in reaching the higher peak. But the wind and mist, the vacillating sun, the arching mist-bow, which dipped into tree tops in the near valley, built up in us an exuberance as we clambered through "unjostled space."

On the second peak, we stopped to look down a third of a mile to the stream which had forced us to this place. It no longer seemed to have that thunderous, tossing, earthshaking violence which we felt when we stood alongside it. From this far distance there was a steady inexorableness to its tawny flow, and the pouring plunges were flattened into a sort of measured procession. The ear-filling violence had given way to a thin, insistent, breezy roar. The *thalweg* and stream were the focus of the great forested valley which lay below us; and that persisting, seemingly endless flow of water seemed to belong to eternity.

Bracing ourselves for a last prodigious shout on the exposed south face, we turned toward the Sugarland Mountain, of which the Chimneys are a spur. We donned our ponchos in the roaring wind and pressed through high-bush huckleberries into the great rhododendron trail along the spur crest. Flanking it were the boles of giant red spruces, and under our feet the earth was springy with moss and needles and ancient peaty humus.

As we pushed up through the rhododendron in an increasing rain, we slipped again and again on the greasy humus, catching the corners of our ponchos as we bent double under overhanging limbs. Coming to the Sugarland trail, we found it choked with briers which whipped stingingly at our faces. But we were in the high Smokies, where the blackberries are almost thornless. There was only the lash of the canes.

Along the trail and below us was a lush belt of virgin forest left by the loggers for high-level operations later, which never came. The Park movement intervened, and this grand mixed forest was saved. There were spruces nearly four feet in diameter, and rich green rhododendron copses. One old dead spruce had several thick, horizontally branching limbs which turned abruptly upright for half their length.

The rain increased, and in each slight hollow white water spurted. Many of these streams were diverted into the trail, which we waded through or painstakingly skirted on narrow raised hummocks alongside. There was little soil. The whole slope was a shallow, crunchy, gritty bed of small gravel and thin clay held together by moss and overlapping roots. Great trees, their side roots cut to make way for the trail, had been overturned by the wind. Their root systems presented a flat intertwining façade as high as a house. The roots of these trees could not grow downward because of the rock, and were overturning from losing the interlocking support with roots of other trees. There is little pliance in spruces, and we could see their tops rocking woodenly in the rushing wind a few cubits over our heads.

The ground cover in the high Smokies is in tenuous repose, and it was an ill-advised policy which gored out this trail. Freezes on one day alternating with driving rains on the next kick up the bare ground of the trail and then carry it relentlessly to lower slopes. In places we waded inches deep in water in the middle of the trail, and along the Stateline we looked at one point into the trough, which goes for a trail, into knee-deep water. Do the men who planned these trails on their drawing boards and who worked them in the sunny, dry days of the fall, ever visit them after these merciless freezes and equally merciless rains? No wonder the lower Road Prong which we had been unable to cross was a swarthy flood.

I was furious at the blind policy which called for the gashing of wide graded trails through forest and ground cover, where the very forest and mountain cling to each other in wavering imbalance. I challenge the technicians who initiate these trails to come out into the wild violence of a winter storm and see the effects of their improvidence. I challenge their office-chair defense that these cuttings and diggings will reach a balance. Here in the deepening V of these trails is irrefutable evidence that they are not reaching a stable condition. In the West a short-sighted predator policy does violence to the browse forest. And here in the East an equally short-sighted trail policy, based upon unassessed weather and ground conditions, is doing great harm to this ancient and magnificent coniferous forest.

NINETEEN FIFTY

January 4   The newspaper report of the annual Christmas bird census in the Smokies stated, "The largest bird observed was the wild turkey." And thus was the romance completely squeezed from its discovery.

We were awakened from our beds in the loft of the cabin by the sound below of the door squeaking on its wooden hinges. It was 6 a.m. and pitch dark. I opened the wooden shutter beside us and looked out at winking stars and a clear sky. There was the glow of a fire at the cookshed. We squirmed out of our sleeping bags and into our boots, and donning sundry sweaters and jackets likewise squeaked out the door.

We started out into the blackness, moving by feel rather than by sight along the trail and onto the fire road. There was a gentle cold in the air and we were warmly dressed. The way was downhill for a mile and a half, and I had the feeling of moving totally without effort in this unaccustomed gloom—about which there were none of the distractions of sight. It was almost as though we floated in a sort of impersonal detachment in a sweetly pleasant darkness without aim, or purpose, or desire or regret.

The shapes of trees began to be outlined against the barely lightening sky, and Bill remarked that it would be wonderful to catch the turkeys against the light, roosting. I began to glance at the trees, singling out the shapes of the young poplars, the stockier bolder outlines of the sweet gums, the fragile and delicate interpositions of the hemlocks, and the solid outlines of the maples.

To the south there was but the faintest suggestion of rose on a bank of gray. We separated and moved down along the creek watching its swirling clarity. The sun lined the streaming wisps of cloud with a fiery gold. As the sky brightened, there was a window of Caribbean blue to the east, so evanescent it seemed a breath would dissipate it.

But there were no turkeys aloft, or on the ground. We searched fruitlessly a sedgy area of young saplings between the roads and we found some old scratchings under young silverbells. But the scratched areas were beaten and black, obviously made before the last rain. Back up the truck trail we went, talking of this and that. The dawn was full bright and we could see far.

Then, across a copse, high on a young tulip, still roosting, we spied a great bird. He was a good 100 yards away and 40 feet above the ground, a large blob of a body with a long drooping tail and a long erect neck. It was a turkey cock. While waiting for the girls we inspected him through the glasses and could see distinctly the beard-like wattle growing from his chest. Then he spotted us, and the long neck darted here and there for a better view of us. Immediately he flew and lit on the ground. We saw him again momentarily.

At the skyline, the evergreens stood out like the teeth of a saw. Everywhere I looked I saw this toothed outline, irregular but distinctly notched. We used to speak of the Sawtooth area, the grouping of sharp, pyramided peaks around Charlies Bunion, but here was another sawtooth zone, the wooded evergreen belt or cap of the high eastern Smokies. It is a region apart—the *sawtooth zone* of the evergreens. This southern tip of the shield of evergreens covering eastern America, lying on the high slopes of the Smokies, gives them gorgeous distinction. The sawtooth zone!—the *sierra* land of the Smokies.

Then Anne tugged at my sleeve; and looking down at a narrow wooded bench along the stream I saw the swift-moving shapes of turkeys running along the bank. Three of them spreading their wings seemed to float into the air and across to the far bank, while in thicker woods and running again, they soon vanished. They had just disappeared when we saw another movement slightly downstream. This time it was a gobbler—perhaps the same one we had disturbed on his roost. He too bounced into the air in that curiously effortless way, crossed the stream, and was lost in the woods.

When one assesses the great size of the turkeys one realizes that they must be near the top of the "biological pyramid" of which

Leopold writes. Surely such bodies must consume prodigious quantities of berries and nuts and grubs. The four we saw must represent a large portion of the turkey population of the Greenbrier. And yet there are historic accounts of flocks of 40 and 60 and even 100. Bartram wrote 175 years ago of being "welcomed by communities of the splendid meleagris." I wonder how many of these royal birds the Smokies could support. We know of several around Gregory Bald. Four is the most I have seen at one time: once in the snow on a tributary of Long Branch, and again on this occasion along the Porters Flat Prong. Dickerman said he once saw seven.

How many acres are required to support one bird? Do they feed scatteringly in the winter, and then move into "communities" for a time at some lush feeding ground which Bartram found? These four ran from us as from the scourge. Despite their present scarcity, the first person to whom we communicated our find made a vague remark about a "twenty-two."

For us observers, it was a thrilling glimpse of a prodigal past. These great game birds run with the speed of ponies, and spread their wings wide for unbelievable flights through heavily wooded land.

January 10 The Road Prong had its way again. After one bright day without rain, I had hoped it could be crossed without too much trouble. The main stream seemed quite low where it was spread out thinly over a wide bed, and there was every reason to believe that the Road Prong, the minor fork, would be well within its channel.

When we got our first look, it appeared that this might be the case. There was no tawniness to the water—only a cold, slightly emerald green. But when we came to the first crossing, the massive graybacks lying in the creek channel were encased thinly in a coating of clear ice. Except for a slight sheen, the ice was invisible. I had started up the bank, working from ledge to ledge, and was squirming under hemlock and rhododendron, when I heard shouts and looked back to see three members of the Hiking Club, who had tried to rock-hop across the creek, sprawling on those boulders with their arms and legs waving ludicrously. One waded on across, with sopping feet. The rest of us worked our way through nearly a hundred yards of steeply pitched rhododendron before Dickerman discovered a windfall which bridged the stream.

The tree was eight inches in diameter and had lost its bark as it had swept down the stream. It was so slick we could not walk it or crawl it. We hunched across laboriously with legs astraddle. Some would raise themselves high on their hands and make eight inches at a hunch; others inched along.

Dr. Marcovitch said, "Why don't they bridge these crossings?"

Someone replied, "If they did that, we would lose the adventure of hunting for a tree and working out a mode of crossing."[4]

The second crossing was made partly by slabs of rock, and partly by a massive hemlock log. Between slabs and log was a wide raceway of water which could not be leaped because the butt of the log was slick with ice. One of the boys tossed a coat onto the ice overlay. It adhered sufficiently to enable us to fall forward with our hands, gain purchase on the coat, and bring our knees forward.

Some made the third crossing along a ledge just beneath stream level and braced themselves with the tender glistening limbs of a fallen spruce. Others fought upstream through the laurel where another hemlock had bridged the wides of the water. This was a mighty log upon which one could walk comfortably upright, despite the boiling whiteness beneath.

The fourth crossing, just above the Talking Falls, was a wide one, with shallow stretches of water into which we carried our own foot logs, consisting chiefly of the tops and butt of a mountain magnolia which had been sawn in two by a trail crew.

Below the falls was the clear green pool where I had fished 30 years ago. It is fifteen yards across and so deep that its bottom is lost in a gloom which obscures but does not rob the stream and pool of its sparkling racy clarity.

Near the top of Sugarland Mountain, I left the trail to hunt out the site where Lucien and I had camped in November 1928. I found the horizontal bench on the steep slope where we had pitched our pup tent. I fancied it was springier underfoot now because of the inches of leaves and vegetation we had piled onto it to insulate our beds from the freezing ground.

I tried to recall that second merciless night when the mercury dropped to 15° below zero and the trees cracked and popped throughout the night. There had been an awful loneliness as I stood my turn at the fire watching the ghostly trunks of the trees in the white light of a half moon. I thought of the water which froze in our canteens

[4] Footlogs now bridge the stream in several places.—A.B.

—of my oiled boots which were turned to iron stiffness by the cold—
of the apples which froze solid, and which we chopped open with
an ax the next morning. I saw the spot where we had set our cups of
coffee. The moisture, congealing on the cups, had frozen them to
the ground. It was a savage night, but one I would not mind redoing
with the right companion.

I have wondered often if modern men are physically as tough as
their forebears. Today we have more equipment for use in the outdoors—sleeping bags, ponchos, and handy tents. We carry our food
with us. Our ancestors carried less but used the country more—
cutting logs for shelter, fishing and hunting. They went into the
trackless woods as a part of a way of life. We go into woods from
heated houses and lives of comfort and security. They went with
thoughts of adventure and from necessity; we, from desire and perhaps from a studied philosophy of the need for the outdoors. Those
of us today who enter the wilds make more of an effort to do so because of soft muscles and poor conditioning, but we make up for
softness with a broader understanding of the wilderness environment.

We left the Sugarland Mountain by the spur ridge which leads to
the Chimneys. Along its crest grew the greatest of laurel and rhododendron under giant spruces and gnarled old hemlocks. The broad
leaves of the shrubs and the massed crowns of the trees made a dim
world through the gaps in which we could see the blinding outer
world of mountains in brilliant sunshine. We saw the thin blue of the
sky and the azure line of the mountains, and here and there a spruce,
draped with a feathery lichen, caught the sun like a torch of green
fire. The air was still but it had an imponderable lively quality. The
green-gold trees and the distant blue skyline fairly exploded with a
static brilliance. I have never before been so soothed by the silent
peace of the wilds, and at the same time so stirred by their splendor.

January 27   On the trip to White Rock the clouds hung awesomely
over the top. There was a roaring overhead, and in the valley I could
see the green plumes of the hemlocks bending to the wind. Near
the summit we moved into a belt of fog, and on top there was a
steady, chilling wind.

Some of the younger hikers induced me to accompany them in a
bushwhacking trip straight down from the flattened pyramid, rather
than down the trail. I studied the valley, and from the texture of the

forest surmised it was glorious open woods without rhododendron. The immediate summit pyramid was almost perpendicular, but its rocky ribs rose out of thick stands of laurel and other undergrowth.

There were ledges which foiled us for a moment or two, places where we hung to a branch and dropped to the ground, scrambling. Once as I stretched for a foothold, my left leg fouled in a rhododendron crotch and I was trapped very awkwardly. Rocks from the pillar of White Rock lay insecurely on the ledges and were a hazard to those below. Twice the advance group sought shelter while we pushed over hazardous slabs. The grinding crush as they splintered upon mother rock was a savage sound. For a quarter of a mile the thin vegetation covered a snarl of treacherously poised, sharp, and angular chunks of rock. Sometimes they teetered under us, or our legs slipped into concealed openings. It is a marvel that trees can find lodgment in such surroundings. I had the impression that their roots sew the very mountain together.

Halfway down, we ran onto an old logging trail near the creek. By then the woods were so open we could descend almost at will, and the trail offered no inducement. We saw one enormous horse chestnut and one notable mountain magnolia.

Lower down we came upon the old fields, now grown up with silverbells. There were sundry piles of stones collected and laid up by the settlers out of the way of their plows, and an old chimney or two, now hardly differentiated from the stone piles. The earth was a cushion to our feet. Pines were breaking into the old fields, and once we stretched luxuriously on their needles and savored their fragrance. In spots, finding the shade of the silverbells to their liking, there were hedges of young hemlocks, possibly the third stage in old field succession. At an elevation of 2500 feet we saw one husky young spruce out of place among the hemlocks.

The first stage following abandonment of the old fields is depressing to me. Gaunt, sagging cabins, tottering chimneys, and old fruit trees stand above the briers, like old horses turned out to die. Tangles of undergrowth override the turf.

But in the second stage, when old fields are becoming young forests, when young trees shade out old briers, when humus begins to cushion the clay—and there is still the openness of the fields between the scattering of the trees—there is something mildly exhilarating. One senses the essential healthiness of nature, and there is yet absent the terrific impact of its power. It is like the pleasantness of twilight before the blackness of the night; or like the promise of the dawn before the potency of the day. Half-woods say things that whole woods cannot. They are the natural sherds of civilizations—the seeding grounds of wilderness. Half-woods are bilingual, speaking the language of man and shouting the call of the wilds.

February 7 Sunday we went up the west side of Porters Creek along much the same route pursued on the Horseshoe Mountain trip eighteen months ago. There was the winter's openness in the woods, but among the rhododendron we were hemmed in almost as effectively as in summer.

We visited the campsite we used on the Horseshoe Mountain trip. I like to visit old campsites. The changes measure the speed of decay and the onrush of new life. The black of the campfires was completely erased by one summer and two autumns. Perhaps had we stirred in the two pits in the ground where we had had fires, we might have found charcoal. But superficially there was no sign of our fires. A warty old buckeye nearly four feet in diameter, slabs from which we had used as seats around the fire, had an overhang at one end. Some of us had placed a few sticks of firewood against the log under this overhang. They were clean and sharp and dry with little sign of weathering or of decay.

March 6 Yesterday we hiked in the Maddron Bald area. It is a heath bald, not a grassy bald as I had erroneously supposed. After parking at the foot of the fire road, we went through green lush second growth, which demonstrated the great recuperative power of these woods under responsible, sympathetic administration.

Although the fire road and the absence of human activity had altered the landscape I looked for evidences of the country homes, now abandoned, which I had known twenty years before. I picked out the Jenkins place where Charley Gibson and I whiled away an afternoon with some natives in August 1931. It was there that we heard an old man say:

"There was a time when I could stand on my front porch and see the smoke from eight stills."

We were traveling up the east bank of Indian Camp Creek. After a mile or so we saw a skiff of snow on the west bank and felt a sharp tingle in the air. That momentary sharpness became permanent, as we switched at the crossing of the Maddron Bald trail. Here the ground was covered with an inch of snow which was hard and unyielding under foot, and it became exhaustingly slippery and steep.

At about 5000 feet the north-facing gorge became steeper. The ice had built up in a great thick blanket of pallid crystal over the rocks and stream. It was a spectacle austerely beautiful under the rhododendron and conifers. No one attempted to mount those glistening ice falls, and we bore to the right into the woods. Our boots slipped and our muscles clotted, as we clawed for footing. Every twig which reached out to us we grasped for the ounce of "pull" it would afford. Once the branch of a fragile old windfall collapsed in my hand and I plunged resoundingly into a mat of rotting boughs and snow. On those sharp slopes, at that elevation, it seemed that we rested more than we climbed (as when I climbed Popo). As I looked upward at the leaders, they seemed always to be stopped and relaxed and engaged in conversation!

But we did make progress, and a gleam of light finally showed through the screen of spruces and firs above us. We were nearing the top. But so confusing were the stream forkings and ridges that this "top" turned out to be only a bench on an approach ridge. We were still beneath the Stateline divide. Looking back through the rhododendron, far below and across the narrow gorge we had been ascending, we could see the treeless laurel slopes of Maddron Bald. Surely we could not be too far from the summit! A steep jungle of rhododendron with crisscrossing windfalls of fallen spruce confronted us. We had gone too far west. We were on the giant Pinnacle Lead near its summit peak—Old Black. We started edging to the east toward a low place in the main divide. But the footing was so precipitous and entangled with windfalls that we turned again to the mountain. Again we saw light. Churning up those last snowy steps, we panted into the open and into blazing warm sunshine.

Here the divide ran almost east and west. The gulf of Big Creek opened to the south, and beyond it were mountains—bold peaks, forest-clad, solid, tridimensional, with subtle gradations in color. Beyond them, and so far that the eye strained to see, far ranges melted into the sky. Much of Big Creek watershed, including the summit where we rested, had burned following the logging operations three decades ago. Where the fire had been severe and the humus incinerated, the mountain slopes were angular and revealing.

Where there had been logging only, with no fire, the contours were rounded and soft, although the paths of the skidders were outlined by snowy fingers in the returning forest.

Where we rested, the ground was warm, dry, friendly. Stripped to the waist, we soaked up the sun. Fifteen feet away there was snow and a bite in the air.

A book on the Southwest is entitled *Sky Determines*. In the Smokies it might be "Sun Determines." On the north slope, the frozen cascade and the hard and snowy ground; on the south, the sun-warmed ground and beautiful blue valley. To our left, in the sun, were the shimmering slopes of Hell Ridge; and in the other direction, the whitened steeps of Old Black. Beneath us, the ridges on their sunny side were green with pines and on their shady slopes were mauve with the naked branches of hardwoods. It looked to be a trick of the eye, those sharp differentiations of color, striping the ridge crests; but as we examined the pattern of the ridges, it was plain—that the sun determined.

The sun had determined eighteen years previously, when nine of us dragged up the untrailed furnace-like summit of Hell Ridge in a blazing August sun. Dry camping, we had sought to tramp from the oasis of Low Gap to the oasis of Big Creek Gap with the water we could carry. Between lay ten scorching miles along rocky ledges which had been laid bare by the slash fires of a few years previous. Blowdowns and a matted, clawing tangle of undergrowth and endless loops of saw briers dragged at our feet. We were 36 hours on that burning crest. Even night was a kind of nightmare, as we sparingly used the water in our canteens and were tormented by the soft roar of Big Creek thousands of feet below. Two of us, now looking at the trail snaking along Hell Ridge, recalled that inferno and the cooling dampness of the virgin forest when we reached it—and how on those life-giving north slopes we had in midmorning licked the dew from the oxalis leaves to ease our craving for water.

Wherever we looked, the sun determined. Evaporation, warmth, dictated one kind of vegetation; coolness, shade, another. Under ideal conditions in the virgin country to the west of us, the determination was not so marked where the age-old forest had built up its own humus and protection against the sun—but even there, some differences were discernible.

Calling in the laggards, we became aware that the frozen slopes of Old Black threw back some startling echoes. Time after time Charlie

Person, whose icy moccasins had given him no traction on the ascent and who had climbed in his stocking feet, slipped away from the crowd and shouted across at Old Black. The mountain did not yield up low notes, but flung back screams and high notes with a sharp defiance. Sometimes two would call in unison and a chorded beat came back. Dick Burns imitated the whoo-whoo of the barred owl, but its soft pulsations were lost in the void. Charlie tried a few bars of an old hymn with fair results.

On the descent, the graded trail changed direction sharply, and we moved into the heavy gloom of spruce woods. The sun still shone and the details of the woods were plain. But there was something almost physical about it, as though a transparent shadow had fallen about us. I have *seen* this phenomenon before; here one *felt* it with the entire body. It was at one of these dim turns in the trail that a westerner in the group remarked, "Here in the Smokies I have learned to enjoy the wilds without a gun."

Down in the broad forest at the base of the mountain far from its high haunts of midsummer, we heard a winter wren. Very early in the year and very low on the mountain, there was still no mistaking those exuberant notes. As in midsummer, I caught myself wondering, "How, by what magic, can it sing on and on and on, stringing out those rollicking notes for seeming minutes without pausing for breath?"

April 5   On the cabin work trip I spent most of the day with the woodmen felling and splitting up a chestnut for firewood. The task was complicated by the fact that after the tree was severed, it lodged in some other trees. We had to batter it off the stump with a sledge, and finally had to fell a small oak to get it down. The center of the trunk was a dark cylinder of moldering wood, but the branches seemed as hard and firm as when the tree had died, perhaps twenty years earlier. An angle cut of the ax across one of these branches shone with high polish.

In the late afternoon, husbanding our tired muscles, we rested and watched the others at their tasks. I began to hear talk of the phacelias growing along Porters Creek above the bridge. I decided to walk up alone, stopping for a view of the rhododendron jungle below the trail, and for a view of multiple terraces of rock and foaming water above the bridge.

Then the phacelias—a fragile skiff of white in midair, but only a few inches above the ground and spreading for acres up the right bank of the creek. There is something wistful in this blooming of millions of fringed lacy cups of white and the barest lavender.

I sat on a boulder and looked down an avenue of white toward the setting sun. The blooms seemed slightly astir over the whole expanse. But there was no breeze! And then I saw myriads of bees swarming over the entire bed.

Aldo Leopold has likened the interrelation of living things to a pyramid, calling the pyramid a more accurate representation of those relationships than the more familiar "balance of nature." The greater, more consumptive species live upon a larger number of weaker, more prolific species down the biotic pyramid.

Here, low in the pyramid—so fragile, it seemed to me, that they could have no end but their own flowering—these lovely blooms were furnishing the first nectar of spring to the insect world. Here the massive life-pyramid was resting on a skiff of lacy blooms drifting in the air half a foot above solid earth.

April 23   One has a different feeling in the Ramsay and Buck Fork country from that experienced around the Chimneys and Sugarlands. There are no roads, no broad trails. There is the potent feeling of being on one's own.

On a trip up Ramsay yesterday, I had this feeling first about half-way to the upper cascades and Drinkwater Pool. The damage that digging a trail can do is highlighted by the fact that this old trail, which had been pressed into the duff by feet alone, could still be detected by the feet—although it was so completely overgrown that it was invisible to the eye. There was a slight firmness underfoot, which was readily apparent when one was in the trail, and instantly missing when one wandered into the uncompressed duff on either side. Even where the trail was overgrown, the undergrowth penetrating from each side would yield as we pushed along between. Only the blowdowns played havoc with the old trail. Sometimes we scrambled across them in a direct lunge. At others, where the branches were too many and too much entangled, we had to go around; and sometimes in the labyrinth beyond we did not pick up the trail again for several minutes.

In such surroundings the primeval experience is powerful and undiluted.

Drinkwater Pool has a chill clarity. From the shelving rock which slants in from the lower edge to form its bed, I looked into its depths and could easily see the bottom except where the flow of the current agitated the surface. The pool is over six feet deep at the back edge and has a darkened beauty, hung over by rhododendron, birch trees, and gray old ledges toned with green moss.

We reached the low point in the divide between Ramsay and the Buck Fork after five or ten minutes of bucking the rhododendron. The altimeter showed an ascent of 150 feet from the pool, although it seemed much less than that.

Buck Fork was low, and the level glade where we reached it was heavenly. Great overarching trees, little underbrush, and a scattering of spring flowers amid low herbaceous growth were an invitation to bask in the sun. We were at the very heart of one of the Park's great wildernesses. This area was miles from a road, and had only the most rudimentary trails. Extravagantly huge trees and limitless stands of rhododendron lay all about this dimpled spot. It had the cleanness and order of a garden. Here was natural perfection which appealed to us with double force after the tortuous scramble down through the rhododendron on the dividing ridge.

There was no evidence of a trail, but we were shortly to detect one after picking our way through a great blowdown. The trail, such as it is, is being rapidly reclaimed by nature; and even with four or five persons searching for it we had great difficulty keeping on it. Eventually it eluded us altogether. Going toward the creek, which was afar off, we found ourselves at the very center of the second greatest stand of rhododendron I know. We found impassable pools in the creek and floundered back up the gentle slope in search of the trail. Finally we clambered onto a five-foot hemlock which had fallen across another sizable windfall, and rested—wordless.

A green thicket spread around and slightly below us in every direction. It was like a sea. From that giant tree trunk I had the sensation of being afloat on it. Never have I had such a limitless perspective of rhododendron. Like Paul Bunyan going through the Blue Ox with a lantern, we had learned of this copse from the inside. Finally we hit a slough which veered toward the stream at a sharp angle. It was the key to that green sea in which we had been entangled. Ultimately we reached the Buck Fork and found clean dry rock along its edges, and we were able to follow it with some celerity as the twilight deepened.

At the Chapman Prong we picked up the half mile of majestic trail leading down the main stream to the confluence with Ramsay. In the quiet of the twilight, we noted an elusive fragrance. I was reminded that several times Thoreau remarked he became aware of a fragrance so sweet and captivating that he was afraid to trace it to its source. He never did. We, however, followed ours to an oasis of phacelia which flanked the trail like snow. And the heavy, tense, strenuous day came slowly, evenly, peacefully to an end, like the subsiding notes of a great symphony.

June 23 At every opportunity I walk among the young trees which I have planted. Some are still seedlings; some are saplings; some are mature trees. Trees are very satisfying. They stay put; they don't go out at night; they don't have dates; they are hardy and responsive to treatment; many are long-lived. In the growing season, one can see daily changes. The larger white pine has a long, limber, brilliantly green leader which must have already grown 30 inches.

Trees are more satisfactory than causes, which are often short-lived, artificially stimulated and kept alive, and which ultimately languish and die. Trees are in a sense more satisfactory than pets because they are longer-lived and are more predictable. Living less complex lives, they are not as stimulating as people, although, on the other hand, they are less disappointing than many people. They are less trite and are rooted in the earth, a fact not true of every person.

September 25 We were told that the crown of fog which hung around the Bull Head and Le Conte was thin; and that above, there was sunshine and brilliance. But we were not to get that high.

Along the trail we enjoyed the diffused reds of the black gums and sourwoods. The leaves of one sourwood had a waxy texture which made me think of Christmas candles. Leaves of the black gums were beginning to carpet the trail; and the maples were a rich combination of red and green, reminding one of corroding bronze.

I had not been on this part of the trail before. There were two cavernous overhangs of rock and several admirable outcrops. The pattern of fields and forest in the lowlands had almost been erased. Almost all was forest now—young forest set in the old, except for the ordered rows of the fruit trees at the Cherokee Orchard.

We climbed to the head of the great hollow which lies between the Bull Head and an offshoot of Balsam Top—part of the Le Conte massif. The forest in its depths was magnificent. As I looked down upon it, I wondered if it was uncut. Marcovitch answered:

"It must be. How could trees possibly have been taken from this hollow?"

November 2   The past two weekends we have had moving glimpses of the fall in its wilder aspects—two weeks ago at the Chimneys in the Smokies and last week in Bear and Barker Creeks in the Nantahala National Forest.

We were one week late on the Chimneys trip. The scarlet of the maples had rusted, although we were in time for the winking brilliance of the mountain sourwoods. With the yellow fronds of the fruits trembling against the scarlet transparence of the leaves, we were treated to a kind of living lambency breaking out amidst the somber greenery of the hemlocks and spruces.

And on the higher slopes of the Sugarlands a faintly lavender grayness, springing from the naked twigs of the deciduous trees, cast the aspect of winter.

But the Smokies have a living quality too, especially along their creeks. We stopped on the ledges below Essary's cascade in the Road Prong. Water spread over the full width of the ledges. There on the bare rocks of the creek bed, we saw the life stream of the forest coursing down the valley.

Portions of the water cycle are obscure. Moisture, we are told, is drawn from the "giant stewpot of the Gulf" (as François Matthes once described it) and is carried in miles-deep cloud-layers to the lofty Smokies. Of this we may not be aware. But we have experienced many times the drenching, pounding downpours, when water starts its cycle from sky to earth, to river, to gulf. The extensive catacombs in which trembling drops of water are hidden at the roots of the forests and which feed the trickling beginnings of the streams are lost to us. It is only when these limpid, lucent threads of water emerge into streams that the everlastingness of the process is laid bare. We stood on one ledge and, leaning lazily with our arms over another, looked upstream at the exquisite spectacle of the cascade. Framed in acres of rhododendron thickets, overhung with delicately drooping hemlocks, it was a picture of life eternal.

Silvery birches were losing their leaves. Leaf after leaf dropped erratically through the air. Some fell on still pools and were gathered in great pads on their surface, seemingly turning water into land. It was a world of magnificent, unhurried life.

November 5   The Road Prong in its lower and middle reaches is the most satisfying stream I know. Its only lack is remoteness. It is touched by the highway at its mouth and is crossed by the highway above its source at Indian Gap. The intimate, climactic, meadowed charm of Indian Gap is gone. But in between, this stream is less touched by man than it was 30, or even ten, years ago.

The trail which 30 years ago was wagon-wide is now for the most part a mere pathway through an undergrowth of rhododendron and seedling trees. The opening in the forest, which we knew as Beech Flats and which was blocked off above and below by a gate of poles to restrain cattle that browsed there, has now all but vanished in a copse of young beech trees. Indian Grave Flats, 400 yards and one stream crossing higher, where once there were two pole cabins and a two-acre clearing, has now been reclaimed by the forest. It takes a discerning eye to see that it is *young* forest which has taken over the flats.

November 29   In short minutes we emerged from the warmth and comfort of the car to a frigid world as savage and bleak as I have known in a decade. The contrast was almost terrifying. The thermometer stood at 10° above zero, and the wind cut at our cheeks like slashes from a razor. I have been in much worse cold: 20° below on Le Conte in 1928, and 15° below at Bear Pen Gap in the same year. But in describing the transition as terrifying, I don't mean that I was in fear, or danger, of freezing. Not that. Rather I felt more sharply than ever before the implacable extremes of the natural world. This crunching cold was devoid of any suggestion of man's world. Nature is not malevolent. It is indifferent. There was no tempering of the air for our benefit.

From Indian Gap we went into the heavy woods to the west. In exposed places, although the ground was white, the snow was but a heavy skiff on the surface. In sheltered places it was powdery and shinbone deep. Small balsams were draped solidly in a mantle, unbroken from crest to ground—tiny, fluffy, circular cascades of frozen whiteness. We went between solid walls of whiteness, sheathing close-growing ranks of young balsams. Where there was rhododendron, the leaves were curled in tight, drooping cylinders of white and green. There was a certain forlornness about the dormance of this ordinarily lively and flashy green shrub.

In places which were open to the wind, twigs of balsam and spruce littered the ground. In more sheltered places the litter was made up of needles both green and brown, plentifully distributed over the snow. Over the whole had fallen the barest skiff of snow—perhaps from a subsequent fall or mayhap blown from the trees. This sheer blanket was so light and transparent, the needles could be seen through it. The effect was as though a delicately tinted fabric had been laid over the ground.

Moving, our feet and hands were warm. But stopping, we felt the wind slashing at our cheeks, and in moments our noses lost feeling and seemed to congeal.

On the south side of the main ridge, there had been heavy mist. Twigs were spined with white frosty needles, and tree trunks had a prickly ghostly mottling where freezing mist had formed on the darker bark. It was a weird white world of complete stagnation. To beings who function best in a warm temperate world, there was a deathly quality to it. Without fire and warm clothing, there would have been nought but death for us.

I thought of the men in Korea, trying to sustain their own lives in colder, more desolate surroundings.

I wanted greatly to make this trip to the mountains. I did not relish the roads, coated in a glaring sheen of ice which was tricky to negotiate, but not completely paralyzing once we got the hang of it. We risked the roads because we wanted the experience in the high forest in the beautiful—inhumanly beautiful—wizardry of winter. The harsh loneliness of it cannot be communicated, but I wish all people could experience it just once. There is no substitute in man's world for its cleansing contrast. It is only in this naked, dazzling, tameless wildness that one realizes man's world has been hewn from it. He has brought the warmth of personality and comradeship into the natural world. Its aloofness and coldness inspire greatness in the individual as he confronts it. One wishes there were less of polished triviality in the world that man has secured for himself.

INETEEN FIFTY-ONE

January 5　　　　　　　　　　On the weekend just past we went, as last year, to the Greenbrier to participate in the annual winter bird count. The results were different this year; there were no turkeys, no grouse. We did see several pileated woodpeckers, two of them spectacularly close, near the springhouse at the cabin.

The higher mountains, glistening with frozen mist, were hauntingly distant. I don't know what there is about the gleaming mist encasing the serried ranks of the evergreens which engenders this untouchable quality. It is as though they are so far away they can never be reached and their heights never attained. There is a feeling that they know they will never be violated. Returning in the late afternoon along the road from the cabin to the parking place, we looked through a gap in the darkened ridge of Porters Mountain to the sun-bright summit of Woolly Tops set back in a kind of ethereal diorama, cold and unreachable. Such spectacles reach unplumbed depths of longing and yearning in our souls. Rue the day that I ever take such sights for granted.

January 10 Last Sunday the Hiking Club went to Blanket Mountain via Blanket Creek and Bear Pen Gap. When we got as far as the gap, we were in heavy fog which in the frigid air was freezing thickly on the trees. We had crossed a temperature boundary. Above it, clear and apparently pendulous raindrops had frozen to the twigs and could not be brushed off. Then the rain had turned to sleet which fell in small granules most of the day, and collecting in depressions gradually whitened the mountains. But the sleet bounced off our bodies and off the trees, not dampening us.

Here again we found old wagon roads, completely healed, and old fields completely reclaimed by broom sedge and briers. Old apple trees stood out with broken limbs and scaling bark. A standing chimney, its mortar almost washed out, was little more than a column of loose stones. There were fallen fences, made of three to five strands of barbed wire, and rotting and collapsed bridges on the higher slopes which had bridged the streams for the cable cars used in past logging operations. Along the route there was a massive rusting pulley which probably was employed to reduce the friction of the cable as it turned a bend. (These things reminded me of a day in August 1925, when in a dense fog I followed a cable car down the slopes of nearby Miry Ridge thinking I could be decapitated if the straining cable should part.)

But in the woods on this hike I saw no raw slope so much as a foot square. Nature in its own good time was covering again the entire mountainside, were it old field or old loggings. Everywhere on these upper slopes the water was clear. The great timber was not there except in a thin belt near the ridge crest. But young timber was in the initial stages of return to luxuriant forest.

This trip marked an innovation. On a hike years ago we had crossed the Little Tennessee River by ferry. But this day we crossed the Little River in a boat of our own provision. One or two of the boys waded in water knee-to-waist deep. The rest of us crossed by an inflated rubber boat, brought to the mountains for the purpose. I was much interested in the uncoordinated launching and towing effort. If one idea failed, another was quickly advanced, and the boat was finally lashed between two ropes and towed back and forth until all were across.

At the end of the day, there was a long wait at the river crossing while the slower trampers came down the mountain. The youngsters utilized the time for unscheduled horseplay with the boat. Several were thoroughly drenched. They did not seem to mind. They were of the age of those who fight our wars and who take privation, hardship, and fatigue in their stride. As I watched them, the endurance of our troops in Korea seemed more understandable.

The trail to Bunker Hill fire tower was neither long nor steep, but it was overgrown. Dodging the brush had wearied me and a sharp wind blew at my right cheek until my jaw teeth ached. We came to a little spot of sunshine under the pines. I relaxed against a tree and listened. The wind came in waves, reaching on occasion a kind of crescendo at which I expected to hear the cracking of trunks that could no longer stand the strain. A thousand pines were within ear-shot and beyond them countless others. There was nothing complex in the music, just those teasing, recurring waves of sound—rising and falling like the swells on the ocean, with the seventh swell threatening but never quite flattening the trees.

Pine music has always been to me one of the saddest, and sweetest, of sounds. It is nonearthly—inanimate, stirring far doubts, bringing a chill to one's convictions. What is this world of ours, this revolving orb, lost in the cavernous emptiness of space? As I reclined there, eyes shut, listening, all the veneer of civilization, all the cheery sociability of man's world left me. I strained to that impersonal, enigmatic, elusive flowing of sound. I seemed on the verge of touching new meanings to life—the life which lies beyond the pale of men —where singly and nakedly men face the universe, shorn of all but their intelligence and perceptive longings. I wish I could hear the wind in the pines oftener. Perhaps I could not often stand those awful lonely implications which chill me and yet somehow uplift me.

February 19 Yesterday we mounted a ridge on the southern slopes of Cove Mountain above Laurel Falls. Living poplars, straight and stately and older than the Americas, had been on that very spot before the Revolution. They had been there before John Adair in 1788 had set up his trading post in Grassy Valley in Knox County; before the English in 1752 had set up their Fort Loudoun on the Little Tennessee River. They had been there even before Columbus set out on his fateful voyage of faith 460 years ago. One could only imagine the dignity of the great forest in which these trees had spent their sapling days. These old trees had been dominated in their day, even as they now dominated the fledgling forest beneath them. I had no idea that this magnificent cove lay above the falls. Under the great tulips the clean, smooth, bowl-like curves of the earth lines, free of shrubs, brought a sense of spaciousness into my heart, into which the menace of Joe Stalin seemed but to rattle around.

March 8 I have now been to Woolly Tops five times from the north side, and once from the Stateline. I have only snatches of memories about the earlier climbs. I recall a look-off toward Le Conte on

94

the first trip and the circle we made around the entire Laurel Branch watershed. On a later trip, I recall a hilarious argument between Guy and Lucien as to who would carry the lunch pack. On that trip I recall with a grin, even yet, Guy's being wakened suddenly by a warm current of air from Dutch's inspirator, thinking that a bear was breathing down his neck. I remember the shifting snowy slopes on the third trip and the interminable wallowing through miles of rhododendron weighted down by snow. And the fourth trip was vitalized by the tinkling, disembodied music of the winter wren.

Laurel Falls

"Something inscrutable and elusive about this noisy
activity which I enjoy . . ."

This fifth venture leaves a heavy solidity in my memory. I watched youngsters walk away from me, even as I used to walk away from others. I labored. Jumping from one rock to another was not a confident, smooth movement, but a heavy, jarring progression which was interrupted while I searched for the next footing. I was out of condition for such a strenuous trip. Mind, and the will once again to climb Woolly Tops, met matter in the form of those prodigiously steep and thickety slopes. In the tussle, they came out about even.

I hardly thought I would get to the top; but after I started I knew that my longing would never let me stop. I didn't exactly revel in the climb, for it *was* tough going. My legs were not too strong, cramping on occasion, and my heart seemed taxed. But I experienced an important feeling of accomplishment. I was again pitting my powers against a very rugged mountain. I wanted to experience the progressive steepening of the slopes, the searching of both banks of the stream for the opening through the undergrowth or for the flattening of the floor of the tiny valley which made progress possible. I coveted the glimpses ahead of precipitous waterfalls through openings in the trees.

I sought again the tricky angular humus-and-moss-covered rock slabs which had never been worn by water, but which had apparently been loosened by convulsions in the earth's crust and had come to an uneasy repose in gigantic confusion on slopes almost too steep to carry them. Moss and verdure had crept across these rock slabs in a threadbare blanket, leaving pitfalls into which we occasionally fell when we misread the surface signs.

Once we wormed across a rotting buckeye six feet in diameter. Occasionally we mounted a fallen trunk for a few paces, but so choked was the valley that this was not done often with profit. A few times we crossed on solid ledges below the waterfalls, and our very muscles seemed to quicken as they responded to firm, solid footing. But the steep-pitched humus slickened by rain, the tangles of rhododendron and looping, rope-like *Aristolochia*, the insecure brush which often came loose in our hands as we pulled on it, and those gigantic jumbles of moss-blanketed rocks made each step upward a distinct accomplishment.

Looking at Woolly Tops from below I knew that it was steep. But looking back into the valley from under low-lying clouds I realized how steep it was. I had the feeling that I could give a running jump and land in the main valley into which Laurel Branch fed—and avoid the racking descent which faced me.

Once when I climbed Woolly Tops in the snow, with Bernie Frank and Dickerman, I had the feeling I was in another world. I had that feeling again as I looked out into the man-kept lowlands. I sensed that this mountain existed in a somber, and somewhat grim, world-apart.

The feeling was heightened by the first traces of a plane crash—canvas torn from its wings. The craft had hurtled through the trees and finally plummeted into the side of the mountain. There it had lain undiscovered for three years. It had lacked 300 vertical feet of clearing the mountain; but that was too much, as the scattered fabric, naked framework, and grotesquely twisted propeller and engine attested. This was a lonely place to die. The occupants were never found. The streaming winds, sifting through the spruces, softened the harshness with a kind of primordial requiem. The mountain and all the forces of nature had covered the remains decently. There was a certain majesty about it. Woolly Tops did not seem to be violated by the machine which had gashed into its side.

I ate lunch just across the top. Some of the boys went on down to the high gap and climbed a great spruce for a look to the east and to the west. On the descent of the mountain others climbed out of the Big Laurel valley over the lead into Little Laurel valley. I was too worn with the plunging, jarring descent to think of doing that. But back home, rested, and with the knifing pains gone from my muscles, I have had an unwonted sense of well-being. Perhaps it was only the threatening clouds which made Woolly Tops seem somber and somewhat grim! Perhaps mind and spirit are yet the master, and perhaps I shall climb Woolly Tops yet again.

April 8 Today we scouted a trip to Russell Field via Sugar Cove. It has been nearly twenty years since Dutch and Carl and Herbert and I camped at Forge Creek, hiked to Ekaneetlee Gap, over to Spence Field, and back by Russell Field and the Sugar Cove. I don't recall now how we happened upon that route down the Sugar Cove. Perhaps we heard of it from the man who occupied the cabin at Russell Field. It had impressed me greatly, and now I was going again.

Driving up toward Laurel Gap in murky weather, we came around a bend and there, running leisurely ahead of us, was a slim oval mounted on two legs—a wild turkey gobbler. An experience with a wild turkey is always memorable, and it is becoming encouragingly frequent. I saw four in January a year ago. This one trotted to the edge of the embankment, lifted himself across a small ravine, and ran along the side of a steep grade, his wattle bobbing.

Starting our hike, we missed the road branchings about which Mr. Cody warned us, and soon came to a creek, which was high and unbridged. The only thing to do was wade. The water was cold, but we found reasonably smooth rocks, and the crossing was not too painful.

To our disappointment, the good trail on the opposite side led to another crossing and we were forced to wade again, and shortly, a third time. Wading ceased to appall us. But at the third crossing, I recognized the old road and this we followed through several blow-downs to the pine ridge. There, the eroded gash which characterized this old sled road fifteen years ago was now soft with pine needles, and on the left bank mats of trailing arbutus were beginning to cover the overhang. The blooms were luxuriant and heavily fragrant. We unashamedly dropped to our knees to smell the shy pink blossoms. Would that all erosion could be as delightfully and effectively stayed —with pine needles and trailing arbutus!

We reached the Sugar Cove, so called because of the magnificent sugar maple trees found on the slopes above. This cove was tiny, open, and warmly brilliant in the spring sun. A pile of rocks, the remains of a chimney, was 50 feet up-slope from us, and a brook purled and splashed in the sunshine 75 feet away. We dropped to the ground to rest, and the sun was warm on our bodies.

This was the first of a chain of old fields which were strung like pearls along the thread of the stream. These "pearls" varied in size and adornment, as on a primitive necklace. Sometimes they were separated by clumps of rhododendron, or were sparked by ancient, limby apple trees. Young silverbells were growing up between, and their limbs which are prey to the spring winds crackled and snapped beneath our feet.

Here the sadness of abandonment was yielding to the excitement of growth. Wylie exclaimed again and again at the dense, green clumps of rhododendron, ten or a dozen feet in diameter, which were beginning to appear in these old fields. Had their "stools" never been grubbed clean by the mountain people who had lived here, so that these fine clumps sprang up from the roots? Or, sensitive to beauty, had the people left them to add beauty to their fields?

We left the creek and took to the slope, which was desperately steep and barricaded with chestnut windfalls. There was a semblance of a path gouged into the slope; and close examination revealed the tracks of a single deer. Old chestnut trees had rotted at the roots and fallen, exposing a snaggled root system at the base of their gleaming gray trunks. The trunks of many of the standing trees were rotten at their cores, remaining erect because of the outside cylinder of sound wood. There was little evidence that young chestnut sprouts were making any headway against the ravages of the blight.

Surmounting the slope we intercepted the old crest trail, now overhung and impeded with oak sprouts and flame azaleas. These branches whipped back as we forced our way through, and were a continual threat to our eyes. Bears also were using this trail, and there were many piles of excreta.

Luxuriant massive stands of rhododendron occupied the trail the last half mile. Somehow they seemed out of place here, belonging to the hollows or to the higher and cooler balsam and spruce ranges to the east. But here they were, and so effectively did they bar the way that stepping into the Russell Field was like passing through a door.

The field lay before us, an upland rounded meadow, deep in grass but yielding here and there to briers and young pines. Brilliant in the sun, it was chilly in the wind and we dropped into a "shell hole" out of the wind. These "shell holes" occur in the forest and usually mark the fall of a tree whose roots have pulled up yards of earth in their falling, leaving a depression.

Whether a windfall was the cause of our particular depression I couldn't judge. I recall that years ago the Russell Field was dotted with stumps at the upper end. The field had been enlarged for grazing. We wondered whether the entire bald had been artificially created, and whether this "shell hole" was the site of a great forest tree before any of the field was bald.

For a couple of miles we were never out of the sound of wind in the pines. I wondered whether there is a difference in the wind tones of the spruces and of the pines, and whether differences can be detected in the music of the various species of pines!

May 14 . . . Spring this year has outdone itself. Unseasonable warmth in March was succeeded by unseasonable coolness in April, even into May, which held back many blooming periods. The dogwoods and azaleas have been lovelier than usual. Anne spoke of the breath-taking clumps of moccasin flowers in the pine woods on the second Russell Field hike; and Wylie reports that on the slopes above Sugar Cove trilliums were blooming so profusely that one could hardly walk without trampling upon them.

The last three days have been clear—brilliant and on the cool side.

Our little beech trees have been checked by the weather, but are now coming into leaf. There is a transparent delicacy to the greenness of young beech leaves viewed against the sun. The tiny leaves have a gossamer purity, which like the scent of apple blossoms seems to erase all heavy thoughts and emotions.

The maples already have fifteen to eighteen inches of new growth, the luxuriance of which threatens to engulf our west hemlock. The atmosphere of cool greenness and soothing shade, for which we have been striving for fourteen years, has been achieved. There is an ineffable sense of well-being in thus being able to cooperate with nature's ways.

June 21 We accompanied the Hiking Club on the traditional trip to Gregory Bald at azalea time. There was rain, although we were not on top overnight when the major rainfall occurred. Those who were present on Gregory in the rain that night and on Hooper Bald in the rain in 1949 say that Hooper Bald was much the worse. There was much hilarity in telling how the sleeping bags got soaked this night on Gregory. Guy said his air pillow was the only thing which kept his head above water. He said Hugh Smathers tried to sell him an outboard motor to attach to his sleeping bag.

All agreed that the bubble on the Moore Spring was never higher.

The azaleas were retarded this year. Although some plants were gloriously in bloom, the great display is yet to come. The scattering of the bloom enabled me to concentrate on the splendor of individual plants. The deep red blooms amid the rich green leaves created a picture of hardy and abundant life. Such verdance, such scandalous lavishing of color, rendered the measured and statisticized economics of our daily lives a sterile thing indeed. On Gregory, lavishness without measure; back in the city, romance and élan pinched and squeezed dry.

Clouds were stratified. We went through two distinct layers on the ascent. On the top we were in clear air at times and could see the tremulous blue-green of the lower valleys. All the higher peaks, however, were in cloud.

The trail was "greasy" from the rain, where its surface had been planed and reworked two years ago. The vegetation has not yet taken hold and we skidded and slid unmercifully. When I could, I walked on the vegetation alongside the trail and noted how firm and tenacious was the herbaceous cover. I wonder if the Park Service people will ever understand our mountains, and cease the scalping of the trails down to the raw slippery earth.

At the Gant Lot, where I waited for Anne and Robin to catch me, I found an abundance of wild strawberries. Their mild and subtle flavor was a benediction. It seems to me that the development of new strains of fruit has often involved an elimination of character and flavor. "Plains of strawberries" met the eyes of William Bartram in the southern Appalachians in 1773. Meadows of strawberries still green the high divide of western Smoky.

There seemed to be an unusual number of galls on the azalea shrubs—light green, bulbous growths the size of small apples. The galls are almost all water, have the texture of slightly frozen apple meat, and have about the same flavor. And these sons of nature in the Hiking Club were eating them! Dr. Marcovitch said they were harmless. Long association with the mountains does not breed contempt, but does engender a kind of rapport in kindred souls. And so, we ate wild strawberries and azalea galls and lounged on the grass in a kind of high Olympian leisure.

July 4 Mt. Sterling was in fog at times and we went through two distinct belts of mist on the ascent. Soon after we hit the spruce woods, there was one spot where the tops of these great trees had shaded out much of the understory. Their trunks rose like columns, soft and obscure in the fog. It was a haunting and unforgettable scene of the kind you feel but don't really see; or seeing, don't comprehend.

The trail still carried sharp displays of azalea and of crimson-pink laurel. The purple rhododendron had come and mostly gone. We saw one giant bush holding its clusters of bloom so high they were almost lost in the fog.

Mt. Sterling is 3800 feet high. In few places can one make the transition on foot so rapidly from hardwood to evergreen. The blue-green of the new growth of the pines on top near the tower was a rich sight. So lush was its color that one wondered whether it might be a subspecies found only on Mt. Sterling.

The clouds hung low. Guyot was never uncovered. The deep notch of Low Gap showed up like a gunsight as the fog thinned. I stood in the wind of the fire tower until my teeth chattered. It is unbelievable, after weeks of steamy, semitropical weather, how quickly one can become surfeited with cold. The body has little capacity to store cold, or warmth, beyond its immediate needs.

September 1   The local papers are full of pictures and stories of a flash flood in the Gatlinburg and Elkmont regions which washed out sections of road, carried automobiles a couple of miles, and committed other depredations. We saw some of the effects on a trip to the Greenbrier today. The road between the parking area and the cabin had been overrun by the creek for half its length. Gravel was washed away and gullies were washed in. All road surface down to the clay base was carried away in many places.

A weather forecaster, visiting the Smokies from Chattanooga, told us that he saw a four-foot wall of water roll down the creek. I don't know the physics of those walls—but I suppose friction along the lower part of the wave slowed that part and allowed the smoother-running upper part to spill over itself, creating a continual cascade—the wall—as it descended. The "wall," he said, was preceded by a tremendous noise which carried above the ordinary sounds of the stream. In the gorge below Gatlinburg, we saw that a swinging bridge had been washed away.

This rain seemed to center around Mt. Le Conte—although there was a similar wall of water in Little River at Elkmont. There was no evidence in the Greenbrier that Long Branch had been up, and its waters were clear. When the facts are developed, they may show that the rain centered along the Tennessee side of the main range.

The newspapers state that four inches of rain fell in one hour on Le Conte between 5:45 and 6:45 p.m. An earlier newspaper account indicates that the crest of the flood waters receded about 8 p.m. These data, loose as they may be, indicate how quickly such a flood can travel. It was barely an hour from the beginning of the rain on Le Conte until the deluge had reached Gatlinburg. The rough evidence is that that wall of water was moving fifteen to twenty miles an hour, several times faster than a man could run. Factors affecting the movement of water would be the steepness of slope, narrowness of gorge, and width of adjoining flats. Another would be the length of the period of rain. Jack Huff's wife, who was living on Le Conte, said it rained one hour on top.

September 16   I have more data on the flood. We drove up the Newfound Gap highway and on up to Forney Ridge. The flood had cut into a section of road just below the entrance to the Chimneys campground, which was closed.

At the Chimneys parking area we went down the trail to the creek. The first footbridge across West Prong, which had stood ten feet above the water, was gone. Not a sign of it. The bridge over the Road Prong was intact. There was evidence that the Road Prong had been in flood, but not damagingly so.

Between the Chimneys and Grassy Patch parking areas, the road had been taken out in four places. The worst damage was from Trout Branch and along the Alum Cave Prong. The Walker Prong, like the Road Prong, had been up, but not seriously so. But Trout Branch had been gutted. It was an awesome sight.

The destruction in the Alum Cave Prong outdid all the rest. There was no semblance of the usual boulder-strewn creek bed. Gravel had been deposited evenly in what was the stream bed. The stream had since cut a channel about five to eight feet wide through the gravel down which it flowed as smoothly and straight as in a mill race. Gravel formed a kind of beach five to twelve feet wide on each side of the water. We could walk this beach as easily as a sidewalk.

The confusion of trunks and limbs was indescribable. A hemlock a foot in diameter and 50 feet long was left in the middle of the old channel. Birches, up to two feet in diameter, had been tossed about like toothpicks and were lodged across the stream. Rocks and boulders and water had jammed in behind these, until the flood cut a new channel for itself 100 feet to the north. The diversion and carnage were massive and frightful.

Above the Grassy Patch, one or two creeks coming off Mt. Mingus had disemboweled themselves across the highway. But for the fact that they were short and did not drain a great watershed, they too would have overflowed the highway and cut it to pieces. About a quarter of a mile below Newfound Gap, on a very steep slope above the highway, the entire forest cover had slipped, leaving a scar at bedrock twenty feet wide and 200 feet in length.

From just east of Newfound Gap, we got a broadside view of Le Conte. Three tremendous vertical scars gashed its south slope. They were new, huge, and glaring. Martin Inman said that the west one was on the Trout Branch watershed, and the other two on the Alum Cave Branch. How large they are, I can only speculate. But the weight of water in the humus and the scouring action of the additional water, which could not be absorbed, had combined in a devastating way.

Another similar scar, ten to fifteen feet wide and perhaps 600 to 800 feet long, was visible on the south side of Anakeesta Ridge near the highway.

These are only scattered data, but they convince me that this was no ordinary flood. I believe it may have disturbed the forest cover more than the flood of 1927. From all appearances Le Conte was marked two weeks ago in a way which will take decades to restore.

November 14 On the hike a week ago up Tomahawk Branch with Bob Maher, I learned I was wrong in my earlier opinion that there had been no unusual flooding up the Road Prong. Actually some of the worst gutting I have witnessed in nearly 35 years in the Smokies we found on tributaries of the Road Prong. One small creek emptying from the Mingus side had cut out a chunk of trail ten feet across. There were several great gullies where before we had hardly been aware there was a rivulet. Two shocking gashes showed on Sugarland Mountain above the Talking Falls. In the dense forest they were as raw and barren as any bulldozer track had ever been.

The climax came 200 yards up Tomahawk Branch. An area of earth and forest 200 yards long and 50 yards across had given way and slipped in awful confusion into the creek. A hundred-foot spruce tree appeared to have slipped intact from a spot a hundred yards higher up, and had simply come to rest against the slope. It appeared to be without injury. Its whole world had given way and it had moved down those yards to its new resting place. It was evidence of awesome power.

We are now basking in the afterglow of autumn. The sharp rich tints of the maples, dogwoods, and sourwoods are faded, but the woods are becoming alive again with the yellows, old leather, and dull reds of the oaks. The coloring is less spectacular, but more pervasive. There is a mottling of the entire countryside after the manner of old tapestries. Perhaps old tapestries were imitative of this aspect of the countryside. They are warm and satisfying—these hues on the uplands—as though nature, not yet yielding to winter, was taking one last whirl.

December 10 ... It was warm and rainy today as we went to the Greenbrier. Several times I felt in my face the redolent warmth of spring itself.

What a day it was, with warm rain, fresh breezes, clouds and fog.

Anne and I went as far as the big poplar, but a hike in the rain up the next slope seemed too strenuous in view of the week that lay ahead. So we turned back, reveling in the expansive shallow slopes high on the Brushy side of the Long Branch trail.

The woods were for the most part virgin, with the usual mixture of forest giants, prostrate boles, dead snags, saplings, and seedlings. We surprised a pileated woodpecker where it was working on a dead silverbell about three feet above the ground. It had cut out a deep wedge-shaped notch and must have been working completely out of the rain, although we didn't see it at work.

We were delighted with the winter vistas down irregular avenues in the forest. They were unlike the great forests of the Bogachiel in Washington State, but in their manner were as splendid. Once we stood on a ledge looking down through the open woods, spread on a gentle gradient below us. The wind was roaring in a great sustained rush of sound through the tops; and the swaying of the trees, against oppositely swaying ranks beyond, presented a curious spectacle of aliveness as though the whole forest were on the move—like crowds of people, only infinitely more deliberate and dignified.

The ear-filling sound of the wind, moving ever toward a climax which did not quite come, is a majestic sound in nature. The sound was as sustained as a great swelling chord of a symphony. There was power, under control. Trees had been snapped off all around. Momentarily we expected each sweep to bring more windfalls, but each time it contained itself in its chording of sound just short of that dissonance.

Chestnut trunks lay all around, prone, decaying, crisscrossing each other, blocking our way as we maneuvered to avoid bellying over them in the rain. Only a few gaunt skeletons towered gray and bleak through the trees. The chestnuts were giving ground completely to vigorous growths of sugar maple, poplar, oak, beech, and hemlock. What mightiness has gone from the forest with their passing! We saw a hemlock growing in the crotch of a standing chestnut, fully 60 feet above the ground. Its roots had not reached the ground. It was wholly parasitic—driving its roots into the rotting center of the chestnut for moisture and sustenance.

But the other trees are taking over. The open vistas amongst great trunks with so little undergrowth bespoke complete dedication to a giant forest. We promised ourselves to come back in the spring and camp out.

We had passed by this forest many times on the way to Brushy, but had never really seen it before. What was it Aldo Leopold said? that the last great frontier is the development of perception in the human mind!

We saw one grouse, which became startled and flew with improbable speed through thick woods; we saw one owl taking off from a perch high above the ground and moving silently like a brown wraith through the fog.

But the climax came on the way out. A great turkey gobbler walked hurriedly, but with dignity, across the road. While we watched him, another gobbler and hen stepped nervously into the road and followed him up a steep slope into the deep woods and out of sight. Our hearts were full.

December 25 At the Hiking Club cabin the last weekend, we retreated indoors at full dusk because of the chill. A cheerful fire and mince pie warmed our blood. Later in the evening, Anne, Dickerman, and I took the Porters Creek trail. There was no moon—only brilliant starlight. Remembering how Lucien and I used to walk far into the night without light, being protected against limbs and other obstacles by a kind of sixth sense, I turned off my flashlight and was delighted that I could see all that was needful.

I could see the trail beneath my feet. Dickerman was a darker and more concentrated shadow ahead of me. Even in the thickest of the woods, when the trail was most obscure, my feet seemed to do the right things. Curiously there was little sense of a third dimension.

At the creek, the pounding waters gave us an impression of vast power. The water showed as broad bands of darkness and of grayness flowing and interweaving, ending and reappearing. The trees above were sharply outlined against the stars.

But the impression I carried away was of moving along a trail in darkness. I distinguish *moving along the trail in darkness* from camping, staying put at night, or moving along the trail at night with flashlight or candle lantern. On this occasion night alone was ascendant. I would I had the opportunity to take many such trips. I would like to stay up all night and keep awake for the sake of experiencing the things of the darkness.

We had quite an argument over the location of parts of the Dipper and of the North Star. And at that hour I felt the rotation of the earth. We were looking directly at the North Star and were lined up with the axis of the earth. Many times I have camped out on some eminence, like Le Conte or Gregory, and have seen stars, as well as the moon and the sun, set. But on those trips one had the impression that the movement was in the stars or in the moon. But this night looking from the line of the earth's axis, there was an awareness, as well as the knowledge, that the earth itself was rotating.

NINETEEN FIFTY-TWO

January 7   Another shocking revelation of the flood of last Labor Day came to light yesterday. The Hiking Club's first scheduled trip of the year was toward Le Conte on the Alum Cave trail to study the effects of the flood. We could have spent a month, instead of one short day, trying to unravel what happened and the sequence of events. Alum Cave Prong revealed vast devastation. Half the trail from Grassy Patch to Arch Rock was gone, undercut, or obliterated by debris. The creek was littered with boulders, trees, branches, and twigs. There was no certainty as to its prior course. Its bed had been drastically changed, shifting in some places as much as 100 feet.

Log jams were numerous. One, opposite Arch Rock, was as large and high as two medium houses, and the logs composing it were among the largest trees found in that area. One large birch, with a curving primary and secondary trunk, spanned the creek in a perfect arch. All trees in the log jams had been uniformly stripped of their branches; and their ends were chewed and frayed like gigantic snuff sticks.

The power of the flood was unbelievable. Twigs were flung into jams with such force that massed together they furnished acceptable footing wherever one wished to step. There were walls of twigs and limbs thrown into breastworks head-high and solidly meshed. Boulders had fresh scars where they had been struck by other boulders caught up in the flood.

There was much over which to speculate. Tom Duncan and I got into a genial argument over the deposition of soil from a tributary ravine. One ravine was scraped down to bedrock, and everywhere there were vistas through the trees which had not been there prior to the flood. The stone steps in Arch Rock were unaffected, but the flood had torn across the lower opening sweeping away the footbridge and all trace of the trail. Above the rock, a section of trail was un-affected where it had hung high on the bluff. Dickerman reported that where the trail contoured the slope, between Arch Rock and Inspiration Point, the wash from every side ravine had torn out the path.

Up the main creek channel toward Huggins Hell, the disturbance of the bed was uniformly wide. There was an even deposition of rocky debris, reminding me of the first rough bulldozed grade of a new road. Dickerman reported that this slash, in mounting degrees of steepness and with occasional clots of logs, extended to a point within a half hour's climb of Myrtle Point itself.

Snow fell steadily during our climb and, lying white on the debris, highlighted the destruction. It was bitterly cold and damp and foggy. No one had a thermometer. Dick Bagwell professed to be able to tell the temperature within five degrees by the droop of rhododendron leaves. With the leaves at a 45° angle the temperature, he asserted, was about 40°. If they hung straight down it was about 20°; and if tightly curled, it was 12° to 15°. The quibblers argued heatedly as to the tightness of the curl. Phil Ewald professed to detect a loosening of the curl as we descended the mountain. Rhododendron leaves are indeed very sensitive to cold; and there is little doubt that a thermometer would have recorded 10° to 15°.

The flood had evidently released iron pyrites embedded deep in the rock. For a stretch, the stream bed and rocks which it touched were reddened by a rusty film. Several times we detected the strong odor of sulphur. All of this rustiness came from a single small tribu-tary which branched off to the east toward the Boulevard Trail.

From data now at hand, I would say that the storm probably origi-nated in the valley of Little River above Elkmont and to the west of Sugarland Mountain; that it moved across Sugarland, raising the Road Prong and tributary streams, and then lost the bulk of its moisture against the south slope of Mt. Le Conte. The Alum Cave Prong suffered most, I believe, simply because of its larger water-shed. Cole and Trout branches, for their size, discharged terrible bolts of water from their barrels. The storm did not spend itself entirely against the south slope of Le Conte but overspread it to the east and into the Porters Creek drainage in the Greenbrier, where there was some minor flooding.

April 21   Yesterday I went with the Hiking Club to Little Laurel Branch. The bridges up the Middle Prong in the Greenbrier were considered unsafe for cars, so we walked the road from the main confluence near the old hotel site. I rather enjoyed the leisurely progress up the creek, stopping often to hear comments by Royal Shanks, ecologist at the University of Tennessee, or to admire a particularly striking flower. It is futile to choose favorites, but for sheer color, dainty and unassuming perfection, the dwarf iris stands high. Among the trees, the "sarvis" bears close inspection. And for mass effects, the redbuds and dogwoods stand together.

It was a fabulous spring day, with warm sun and scintillating skies. The leaves were dry underfoot because we are in the midst of a drought, but Royal demonstrated that the woods are really not suffering. Under the loose dry insulation of last season's cover of leaves, the humus was cool and damp.

We walked near Little Laurel Branch in young second growth. Through its vistas, we saw stone piles from the days of occupation and husbandry. Amongst a natural band of great boulders, the trees were larger and more varied—ash, tulips, buckeye, hemlock, and the like. On a steep east-facing slope, growing out of a thicket of rhododendron, was a stand of young poplars, which we estimated were 30 to 40 years in age and up to fifteen inches in diameter. Ramrod straight, they rose with barely a taper as much as 80 feet to the first branch. Their columnar boles, standing in close ranks, reminded me of the stand of Douglas firs up the Bogachiel River in the Olympics.

A few hundred feet farther, the band of boulders became rougher and larger, comprising a tumbled pile of huge angular sections broken from a cliff—some of them as big as a truck body or small house. We climbed this primitive stone pile, all overlain with humus and wild flowers and sprouting trees and grapevines and the ropelike Dutchman's pipe, *Aristolochia*. Many trees were actually bowed down and misshapen from these clinging vines.

Tumbling over the rock mass was a modest cascade. Not very much water, but still lovely. From the crest of the long concave band of irregular cliffs which overhung the broken rocks below, we could look out across the valley through unleafed trees to the wall of the Pinnacle Lead.

I reveled in the feeling of easy god-like attainment afforded by these full views on a warm spring day through the winter nakedness of the trees. Everything was perfection, and the views fell in our laps.

In a warm duff-colored spot above the cliff between clumps of rhododendron and open hardwood forest, I lay on my back and looked upward. The trees were scattered but their crowns mushroomed out until a thin, unleafed canopy cut the sky. Birch crowns vied with tulips. The trees had elbow room, but not much, I observed, as they rocked and swayed in the breeze. I don't know that I had ever before lain in such surroundings, with my back to the entire earth. I ruminated on the upthrust of those trees and the spacing of their crowns. As I dropped my eyes ever so little from the perpendicular, my gaze focused upon the massive wall of the Greenbrier Pinnacle. Amidst such grandness I felt as strong as Antaeus.

I glanced at the mat of duff upon which I was lying. Leaves were flattened and pasted together by the battering of the winter rains and snow—like sheets of thinnest parchment. I was as idle as a sloth and yet my mind and soul were active as I absorbed the spell of spring. I did not realize, however, that the scene and setting lacked an element of perfection until out of the maze of forest to my left came, without warning and without repetition, one full burst of song—the tinkling, lilting rune of the winter wren.

It was a warning to me, or perhaps not so much a warning as a friendly hint, that nature unspoiled is always perfect. Multiply it, add to it, or take away any aspect, and the quotient is always the same—perfection. The clear stream, the cliffs, the matchless poplars, the weather-pressed leaves, the winds, the wren—alone, or in any combination—were perfect. Even small biters and predators did not detract. I rather enjoyed scratching my insect and spider bites.

June 10 ... Last Sunday we went up Trout Branch. The hike was announced as an exhibition of the effects of the flood of last September. Even my trips up the Road Prong and Alum Cave trail last fall prepared me for nothing quite so overpowering. Trout Branch is a small stream flowing generally south off Le Conte. It empties insignificantly into the Walker Camp Prong. At its mouth along the highway there was little indication of the starkness above. The bed opened up almost at once to widths of twenty to a hundred feet. As far as I went, only twice was it noticeably brushy—once when we passed a cliff some twenty feet high, and again where a side slip has dumped into the main valley trees which had not been carried away.

There were scars on trees fully 40 feet above the level of the stream. Everywhere rocks were scrubbed clean of lichens and moss. We were seldom in shade. The valley was as open as a road-cut and much of it similar to a new road-grade. Many of the rocks, weighing up to 200 pounds, were still unsettled and dipped under our walking. There was an occasional fleeting stench, which I first attributed to putrescent organic matter partially buried by the flood. But later I determined that the odor came from thin seams of iron ore which had been uncovered in the deluge.

Herrick Brown observed that many trees had been broken off cleanly. They were mere stubs or logs, 30 to 40 feet long, shorn of branches, tops, and roots. Of course the ends of these logs had been battered. But they were not sharpened or spear-like as they would have been had they been split off.

I saw one log, a hemlock, which was more than three feet in diameter at its largest part, from which all limbs and roots had been battered.

This is not to say that all trees were so shorn. Many still had all their limbs and roots, as though they had simply floated, or had slowly given way in the water-logged instability. There were three or four slide areas, the topography of which was so shallow it was incredible that they could have gathered enough water to loosen the vegetation. From the stream course these slide areas extended close to the tops of the ridges, presenting another puzzle.

Occasionally the burden of the flood would be blocked and a tumbled jam of trees would result. One of these jams, the largest I ever saw, appeared to be well over an acre in extent. At another spot even the timing of the flood was evident. The debris from the main stream was blocked by a right angle in the main valley. And the burden of trees from a side valley had obviously been piled on top later.

The stream bed was full of sharp, clean rock. Never have I hiked more easily. Outcrops of rock jutting into the stream course were marked and battered as though a blast had been set off against them. At such spots the solid rock of the mountain uplift was exposed. But down in the valley we found in one spot alongside the stream non-water-torn boulders of substantial size which had been deposited there in previous floods. These had been completely overlain with soil and hidden with vegetation to the depth of eight or ten feet, only to be exposed by this latest tide.

The evidence of raw power was stupefying. Several remarked they would like to have witnessed the flood. For reasons of personal safety, I am glad I was not in the vicinity. After the fact, one could perhaps divine where he would have been safe. But in the middle of such a deluge (four inches in one hour on top of Le Conte and undoubtedly much heavier in the main band of rain), one could not have perceived the boundaries or islands of safety. Slopes were wiped bare which to all appearances were as stable as the forest alongside which hung on. I have spoken of tree scars 30 and 40 feet above the stream course. Had one climbed up the steep slopes, which are loose and insecure at best, he might well have supplied the extra weight which would have started another slide.

Lionel remarked that the Hiking Club could have been caught in such a storm had it occurred on a Sunday instead of a Saturday. We have in times past, in rock-hopping excursions, climbed Trout Branch and its neighbors, Cole Branch and the Alum Cave Prong. But nothing in the club's experience would have taught its members how to cope with such a cataclysm.

They would have been warned by a cloud of unprecedented blackness and by rain almost suffocating in density. Nothing would have told them how high to go on a slope for safety, nor what type of slope would have been safe. Had the group been strung out, as they often are, the slower ones would have been lower down, where the floods were huger but more dispersed. There might have been reasonable safety a few hundred feet back from the stream on the easier slopes. But what then of those persons who were higher up, where the topography included a series of converging V-shaped troughs, each gathering the rains like a funnel, and loosening the forest cover at the most unaccountable places? They would have been in unspeakable danger.

On this hike I was so engrossed with the evidence of violence that I hardly noted the familiar and lovely and peaceful aspects of the forest. Winter wrens and nuthatches sang. But could it be that they did not sing quite so effusively, or was it I who did not give my accustomed attention? The flood damage was almost unrelieved nine months after. A few ferns, all of which I could have carried in a bushel basket, and a cluster of vines a few yards square in the middle of that giant log jam supplied all the relief. It was a sobering experience.

August 5 Sunday we were climbing up through the great forests of Ramsay Prong. As I was going through the Cherry Orchard I sat down for a short rest. After a while Anne came up and stopped. We looked out through the forest. I saw birds moving high in the crowns of the trees. A log had fallen near us and lay parallel to the trail. It was covered with moss and other verdure.

"There is a wren—could it be a winter wren?" she asked.

And it was, the tiny singer of mountain lays hopping around that log, busy, unafraid, undisturbed. It came within five feet of us and did not take flight when we spoke. Oh, what a sprite of a bird— actually not bigger than a man's thumb, with a perky tail stuck in at an angle as though by an afterthought.

August 26 Last weekend I camped on Chapman Prong with Frizzell, Dickerman, and Hines. It was the first time I had been on an overnight camping trip since last October. George and Dick left town early; Guy and I, at noon. The plan was for us to follow them up the Chapman Prong until we found the campsite. Anne remarked that she hoped we all knew which was the Chapman Prong. If we did not, in the vast temperate jungle of the upper Middle Prong our task would have been difficult although not insuperable.

Guy and I started hiking about 2 p.m. At the turn-around two miles up the fire road, we talked with Warden Elmer Ogle. He said there were plenty of fish up the closed streams of the Middle Prong, that it was one of the last retreats of the brook trout. He voiced the opinion that the fish would die out if the streams were not fished. That did not make sense to me. Was he just a frustrated angler? Native brook trout undoubtedly flourished in those streams before the days of white men.

Elmer crossed the rotting old footbridge with us at the mouth of Ramsay Prong and walked up to one of the pools of the Middle Prong in the area closed to fishing. The water swirling around the boulders glinted with light, and even at great depths we could see the darting shapes of trout.

As we left him, he to go back toward civilization, we to pass deeper into the wilderness, a heavy mist drifted above us and brushed the trees lightly. The old trail was superb, soft underfoot, unobtrusive, occasionally barred by blowdowns. We passed an immense sugar maple over four feet in diameter. Gentle slopes massed solidly with rhododendron stretched down to the river. We passed through an area of younger growth where once a mountain man had had a cabin and a field; passed a giant dead chestnut and a gateway of hemlock where a section of log had been sawed from a blowdown; and descended a steep slope to the river. From that spot on, what trails there were had been swamped by rhododendron and we took to the stream.

Its appearance eludes description. Jungle-like growth intruded to the stream edge. The bed itself was a conglomeration of rounded boulders of every size and shape. It was no placid stream, but a swirling, tumbling current, streaming through the boulders, sometimes gathering into a single torrent, sometimes breaking into several smaller flows. Everything was a somber green, relieved only by the gray of the stones and by the reflected light in the water. There had been no flood here for a quarter of a century. Moss, thin and green, clung to many of the boulders. But in the eternal gloom others, water-splashed and round, were glassy slick. When we had to leap we tried to land on a mossy stone or a dry dome which stood above the flow of the stream.

The cleanest of water, it was never the same. Churning over a ledge or a boulder it was a foamy white; plunging into a pool it carried silver bubbles of air which split and divided and took on a tinge of green as they burst to the surface. The great pools were clear at our feet as they thinned out over gravel bars; they took on a somber green as the water deepened; and at their deepest part against the ledges they were almost black. But always on their surfaces they carried the potential of light, limpid, green-black mirrors.

Up such a stream we went, threading its course from one side to another, teetering on a treacherous and moist rock, or leaping for a slab roughened by moss. Sometimes we followed stepping stones, barely awash, through a pool; or wormed up through a niche in a ledge getting splashed as we did so. Sometimes ledge and pool blocked our path and we squirmed through rhododendron on the bank. Once we left the stream to hunt out an overhanging ledge where fishermen used to camp.

But always ahead of us was the open avenue of the stream. Several times we paused on a slab and turned around slowly. The dense, closely packed forest and undergrowth had profound beauty which was blended as much of spirit as of forest.

Both of us had the thought: "As many times as we have seen this stream, we forget its utter beauty from one time to the next."

Farther and farther Guy and I went into this green world—on past the Lost Fork below which the boys had said they would camp. Had we missed them where the stream split around an island, and where we took the easier of the two forks? Twice we went back to the main stream to be sure. But finding no openness in the rhododendron, where sane men would camp, we moved on. But each time doubts assailed us we found a plant turned where they had brushed by it, or saw a single fresh footprint, where they had leaped from a rock across water to gravel.

We were not looking for a needle in the haystack of the vast labyrinth of the Middle Prong wilderness. There was logic in our every move and in theirs. In low water no man would voluntarily contend with those great tangles of rhododendron. The stream was the highway and it even dictated the side which should be followed. Once we noted two footprints headed downstream.

"Why did they do that?"

I went on two paces around a boulder as big as a room and found out. A pool and a ledge had blocked that side; they had retreated to make a crossing and to force passage up the other bank.

Wildernesses are flexible. When you are very young they are huge. As you reach your prime, they shrink in size. As you grow older, they tend to expand again. The expansion was evident as Frizzell and I moved deeper into the Chapman watershed. The elusive signs indicating that our friends had passed that way and were still ahead of us led us on.

I had thought we would detect the smoke of their campfire far downstream. Actually we caught a doubtful whiff only 200 yards away from it. I should have known better. Until the sun sets, the normal course of the air currents in the Smokies is upstream. Although the mountain tops were enveloped in cloud, they were probably sufficiently warmed to create a slight up-draft which carried the smoke upstream.

George and Dickerman heard us about the same time that we detected the smoke and stood grinning at us near a small cairn they had erected in midstream. I slipped and almost fell, as they watched.

We came up to them, and in that wilderness I thought of a more celebrated meeting in the wilds of Africa.

They were camped on a little bench about fifteen feet above the bed of a stream. Around us was a forest of great size and variety. In the fading light some of the trees seemed colossal.

We lay under stars, as the chill air of a cold front melted away the clouds. Actually the leafage above us was so dense we saw only a few of the stars. From our backs, looking up, the tree trunks and limbs were thick and mottled shadows, like paint smudges on an old canvas. Here and there, brilliantly clear, we saw tiny clusters of stars winking through.

I went down to the creek for a last drink before turning in. The sound of the stream was loud, but as the rushing water came into the range of my flashlight, I experienced a start. I have had it before under similar conditions. Somehow my subconscious tells me that streams, following the custom of men, cease to work at night. The everlasting movement, even in the night, startled and thrilled me.

While I had helped with the supper, Guy had staked down our tent just in case of rain. He had scooped a very shallow hole for my hips. We laid our sleeping bags on the collapsed tent, but could have erected it almost instantly had it rained. I slept well.

Daylight brought more high clouds. Everywhere about us were the towering limbless boles of trees of a mixed forest. The crown of a giant sugar maple flared above us. Birds could scarcely be seen as they dodged about in its leaves. Nearby was a great cherry, a sizable silverbell, a linden, an ash, a birch, tulips, and hemlocks whose trunks rose like the columns of Solomon's temple. Boundless stands of rhododendron walled our campsite. Above these tangles in primordial gloom rose the shafts of the trees. Occasionally the sun broke through, transforming the forest into a vast, airy temple. Trunks were limned in silent strength. So deep were the woods we were hardly aware of the sun, and wholly unaware of the movement of the clouds, as mystic waves of light swept through the forest picking out those giant trees. One moment there was gloom—then this wonderful, powerful light. We didn't see it come; it was suddenly there —silent, strong, pervasive.

September 11 Saturday night Anne and I slept on Willie V's cabin porch in Emerts Cove under a near-full moon. The moon moved behind branches the night through. Never did it shine directly into our eyes. We expected to be uncomfortably cool. Actually we were pleasantly warm.

In the predawn I looked out at the mountains. They were more than a bluish-black silhouette against the sky, but they lacked the rounded outlines of the day. There was a tautness as though a soft azure fabric were drawn tightly across every prominence. There were three dimensions but no perspective. One could see the topography in this wondrous, elusive blue, but one could not see *into* the valleys and ravines. The curtain of night was still laid across the stage of day. It was like the black cloth which a merchant draws over his goods at night. Only here, the cloth was fragile—haze ephemeral, and blackness a slaty, lusterless blue.

". . . something of priceless worth to the human
spirit in the existence of tracts of the primeval . . ."

December 16 Sunday Anne and I chose to hike up Long Branch in the Greenbrier. As we drove toward Pigeon Forge, the mountains were in magnificent winter outline. The weatherman had predicted "scattered cloudiness." One should always witness the winter Smokies when there is scattered cloudiness. Not only were there the familiar contours but, what is so often missing in this moist, hazy country, there was bulk. Buttressing ridges were spotlighted and there was an impression of mass and depth. Now, spotlighted by the winter sun, the gray-green outlines of the high Smokies took on an unwonted massiveness. The high levels were gray with frozen mist; and when we caught a glimpse through green trees, we realized also there was blue on the ridges.

We started hiking at a fast clip. It was cold and my ears were numb. The water in the creek was a delicate green but sparkling clear.

One sees different things on different trips. On this one, Anne called my attention to the soft gray rubbery appearance of the underside of the smilax leaves. I delighted in the texture and in the varying color and size of the leaves themselves, ruddy and green and heart-shaped. On up the trail, in the winter openness, many trunks of dead chestnut trees still punctured the skyline. They are magnificent—weathered to a subtle silvery gray. They towered over all other trees in these woods and had clearly dominated the forest when they were alive.

The snow was imprinted with small tracks: delicate bird tracks, stirrings of mice and shrews, and litter of hemlock cones left by chipmunks and squirrels. There were tiny dens under roots where some creatures had been digging. The very smallness of these operations tugged at my heart. Here was life being lived in a small way and in the only way that these creatures knew.

We saw a downy woodpecker; heard the mewing of a sapsucker; and heard the shrill, undulating calls of a charm of goldfinches. We heard the scoldings of a chickadee and saw the white tail-feathers of numerous juncos. Several dun-colored birds around the stump end of fallen trees would fly along the trunks and light on the ground, ready to dodge either way if we approached nearer. From their jerky squattings we knew they were wrens.

Through the trees we could see blue sky above the Greenbrier Pinnacle and the gray fluting of its cliffs darkened by shadows. Following with our eyes the long Pinnacle Lead toward its climax at Old Black, we noted that it was a brilliant, shimmering white. Mt. Guyot was cold and remote. The view stirred our imagination, this time by what we saw; another time, by what was hidden.

For the whole trip we were alone with the forest and its trees and creatures. There was sharpness and cold, but there were beauty and peace and unmeasured time. The piles of rock which the pioneers had laid up in the fields out of the path of their plows were now deep in second-growth forest and seemed forlorn no longer. The resurgence of the forest had overcome. There was no sadness that man had found the going too harsh and had been rooted out. Already his works—in the guise of these mounds of rock—were blending into the immense pattern of the forest. This new forest was still uniform in size. It would be scores of years before the greatness and spaciousness of the climax forest would come. The signs of man's occupancy were already gone from these slopes, and through the openings amongst the second-growth trees was framed the cold and brilliant and stirring spectacle of the sun shining on the icy white of the high conifers.

There was little wind. We heard only the far rush of the river, the near sigh of Long Branch, and the musical burble of the Fittyfied Spring boiling out from under a rock near the trail.

We came back by our cabin in Cobbles Hollow. The sky became overcast and the high mountains turned dark. But as we rounded a bend above Emerts Cove, the setting sun burst through a window in the murk and a vast horizontal band of golden haze stretched between us and the skyline. Below us the houses in the cove lay peaceful, catching by reflection some of that golden light. Middle Prong rolled noisily through the center of the cove. Anne and I exclaimed over the scene.

As we met Dewey Webb, a mountain friend, he asked, "Who wouldn't want to live here?"

And there is no answer. Civilization has provided no peace, no spectacle, no assurance to the human heart which can transcend the simple, ever-changing, matchless beauty and peace of the natural world.

December 26 A couple of weeks ago there was a conference in Knoxville by business leaders, planners, and conservationists on the subject of zoning park approach roads in order to eliminate road traps, etc., but also to eliminate "free zoos," substandard hot-dog stands, billboards, and shabby tourist accommodations. The idea is that these clutter up the roadsides and block unexcelled views of the mountains. The reason given for the conference was that they want the roads to be attractive to tourists.

But why can't we eliminate ugliness everywhere simply because it is unsightly? Why shouldn't the people who *live* here, not simply those who visit here, have the same protections against ugliness? Why isn't day-to-day living more important than the holiday?

I hold steadfastly that all environment can be beautiful, or at least that the utilitarian things like factories and power plants can be located and handled as not to cast a blight over the areas where people live and work. Why should the roadside environment be cleaned up simply because it is money in hand to do so? Why shouldn't all environments be cleaned up for the souls of the people who live there?

It is interesting to meditate upon these things in connection with a speculation of Joseph Wood Krutch in his *Twelve Seasons*—that mankind is moving further and further from the natural world and into a world of abstractions and statistics and symbols. He asks why should we think upon the theoretical spring—the vernal equinox—rather than upon the real evidences of the spring—things like the peeper chorus. Our cities become places of stones and pavements, where soil and animals and trees and plants and winds and natural waters are almost entirely absent.

He thinks men are assimilating themselves into a world of statistics. The tour de force is no longer emphasized in our sports write-ups.

Krutch speaks of the extreme improvidence of nature—how it may take 6000 eggs of the oil beetle to produce one adult. He says that nature is not ordered, but is in conflict and stalemate so far as the individual is concerned. A thousand seedlings die for the one that reaches maturity. Plants vie with each other for the same square foot of ground. The total effect is beautiful.

Of course I am aware that there is a distressing result if one pushes the analogy too far. Will a civilization be beautiful in its total effect, if individuals and natives are allowed to compete to the death? Will such results give the appearance of the apparent order in nature?

In the long run Leopold is right. The world ought to be beautiful; it can be beautiful; it can be made that way.

December 30 . . . My faith, as I told Dan Hale last spring, first of all, is in LIFE itself. I have faith in the essential goodness of life and in the essential goodness of death. Curiously, most of my anxieties hinge around competitions of an essentially man-made nature. I know there is vast, brutal, and cosmic competition in nature. But need man—the spiritual being—imitate nature in all its aspects? I think he is going to copy nature tragically, if he persists in his headlong multiplication of populations and in his headlong depletion of resources. If we continue this pace I can only see that man's ultimate fate, as Julian Huxley has predicted, will be more and bitter personal competition. Man's problem, it sems to me, is to recognize the essential clash between this competition and his own spirituality. The present turmoil may be a part of the process of gaining awareness of the problem, prior to its final mastery. It may take centuries to achieve this awareness. It need not.

One of the weaknesses of the study of history is that few folks feel its lessons and urgencies. The study of history can be simply an academic exercise, or it may point the way to the future. Today events are telescoping. Cause and effect are felt in short years. The lessons of the day, if not the long perspective of history, are rammed down our throats. It may be that the fateful reconciliations, which will advance man into a brighter, more abundant and relaxed world, are nearer than any of us would have thought a decade ago.

That also is my faith. Life is rich, varied, boundless. Many of us have found it so. Someday man's intellectuality and spirituality will find the resources to broaden infinitely the base, in individual experience, of life's essential richness.

NINETEEN FIFTY-THREE

March 7   Thinking back on the Winnesoka
hike of two weeks ago, I recall one beauteous sight along the creek.
Grass overhanging the water had been splashed in the frigid air and
the whole had congealed into a tangled skein of ice.

We worked up through old woods roads. There were several
magnificent dwelling sites, now abandoned, reverting to the wilds.
They were flat and had an ampleness about them which other mountain farms did not have. The life was rough and austere but the
setting grand. Resurgence had passed the critical point. There was
more of the forest than of man, when briers are choking out rose
bushes and pokeweeds are springing up inside the shells of cabins,
and the pang of sadness I feel when there is yet more of man than
of forest did not arise. It is extraordinary, population pressures being
what they are, that there are places on earth where it has been decreed that wildness shall prevail.

It was good again to climb steeply up a virgin slope. The openness
of the forest and the fleeting views which opened out to the north
of us created a sense of great spaciousness. We were half gods and
half earthmen, as we braced on those steep slopes. The air was sharp;
there was ice in the rivulets. My nose stung with cold. There were
cliffs which loosed their sloughings into a tangle of sharp-edged
rocks.

Above we could see a line of rhododendron, and through it, light.
It was not an illusion, nor the top of a side ridge. It was the top of
the main ridge. We worked with ease through the last belt of rho-

dodendron and leucothoë. Even before we reached the summit we could glimpse pines through the green of the rhododendron.

To the north of the crest there were broad-leafed evergreens, hemlocks, hardwoods, little undergrowth, openness. Twenty feet away were the south slopes—with snarls of pines, laurel, saw briers, and blueberry bushes. It was a different world, upon which I have remarked so often. Winter and spring; north woods and south woods close by.

We found a spot in the sun and relaxed on the forest floor in its warmth. Everywhere living things vied for a place—trailing arbutus, ground pine, wintergreen, saw briers, and blueberries. And over us waved and sighed the pines. Through a rift in the forest we could see the violet mass of Le Conte. On its north slope white fingers of ice and snow reached down the ravines. In the lower valleys thousands of hemlocks emerged from a mauve understory, so homogeneous it made me think of primordial dust. This "dust" was the winter aspect of small hardwood at a distance—beeches and birches with no leaves, nestling in the hollows under the towers of the hemlocks.

I carried away an intimate impression of that spot—the arbutus, the ground pine, the flash of Le Conte. The impression is as sharp as that I have of any room in which I have lived. It *was* a room, but without walls. There was warmth, and snugness and sweetness and peace. My ancestors had to make their homes out of such environs. I can see them; I can understand them. Out of such beauty and peace must have been born aspiration. Out of such beauty and peace I can face all problems with composure and with hope and with compassion.

March 10 We are well entered into the unfoldment of spring. Brownness, with a faint suggestion of green, swells in the elm twigs —giving the trees the appearance of a brown gauze flung into the air and held there by some magic. Willows have a brilliant greenness which, viewed against the ridges, has an appearance of transparency, floating in front of but not hiding what lies behind. Maples are blood-red clottings of growth along the twigs and are losing the elusiveness of their first blooming. Forsythias and jonquils show yellow and japonicas a gorgeous red. Spiraea begins to appear as though it had been dusted with snow.

There is arresting color in every landscape—the shifting veils of

"My eyes were on Mt. Le Conte . . ."

the willows and the ruddiness of the maples against backgrounds of green-black pines and tawny fields and rusty oaks. There are the clay-reds of newly plowed fields and bright green carpets of newly sprouted wheat. And above are pale blue arctic skies which have come down from Canada. It is that time of year when we teeter between spring and winter and back again—a period of teeming expectancy.

Why is it that men take their jobs so seriously? Why is it deemed a virtue to sit at one's desk in semiconfinement when the whole outside world is breaking its bounds and clamoring for attention?

March 22 Today Frizzell and I took our first quarterly hike together. The night had been gusty. Dawn brought a mass of heavy clouds with thinnesses through which the sun touched the ridge with yellow. As we drove toward the mountains, their summits were crowned with clouds.

I thought the mountain tops would blow clear. But when we started from Newfound Gap east on the Appalachian Trail we were in thick mist, in a gray world dripping with moisture. It was incredible: from below, the bright, brilliant world of blue mountains and gleaming fog crowns; up here, a dark closed-in world of mist and moisture shutting us in on all sides.

The great distracting views were shut out. We looked at young spruces growing on the thin edge of the root mass of a great tree upended by a storm. How did they sustain life, poised so far from solid earth? How long would they survive? We looked at young birches standing on stilts, the base of their trunks one and two feet above the earth. They had taken root on a fallen trunk; their roots had worked down and around to the ground; the log had moldered away. They would be on stilts all their lives. We looked at the colors of lichens—an apple-green mass on a trunk radiating out from a center like a target. Gray patches, with a touch of green on old gray stones and soft green masses torn from trees, as damp and pliable as sponges.

The only distraction from our intensive, circumscribed delving was the riot of wind which poured through the tree tops. With such momentum, it perforce must have come from beyond. It carried scudding fog waves across open places, or rotated them like tiny nebulae where the currents met at the divide.

Here and there we saw a small snow patch and limey droppings of wild turkey. We dropped to our knees to dissect a fox scat on the North Carolina side of the Bunion. We were a spectacle—two men with eyes streaming wet from the cold, getting out their spectacles and hovering over this dropping and cogitating as to what had happened! There were quills and stringy skin from the foot of a bird, and hip joints also undigested, crushed and hanging together by shreds of tendons. Guy thought they were grouse bones. To me they seemed much too small for grouse. Perhaps they were those of a meadow lark. We had seen one running in the drenched grass near the Bunion.

Near Dry Sluice Gap the wind whipped upward through a small gap, lifting momentarily the blanket of fog. We could see Porters Flat, Emerts Cove, and far ridges and hills indelibly blue under a gray fog mass. Then the fog poured in again, condensing on every twig and branch. There was a constant drip. Our clothes were damp. We moved out along the Sawteeth, on the slightly flattened knife-edge of the Smokies. There was a gray gulf to our left. Back of us the mighty wind tore through giant spruces. We were beyond the territory of tin cans and paper wrappers and of well-trodden trails. There was a solitariness to it which was half frightening.

It was getting late. We knew we should turn back. And we did finally, where a thick spruce had crashed across the trail. The knife-edge crest of the ridge was twenty feet above us. The spruce had caught the wind; its roots had snapped and torn loose, baring the mountain down to the living slate. How had the tree held on as long as it had? The slate was fractured, but not deeply enough to receive many roots. The trees seemed not to be individually anchored, but locked together through their roots. Any disturbance, or cutting of those roots by trail building, lessened their resistance to these crest winds. The rock was bare for the area of a large room. How many decades would it be before rootlets, creeping from young seedlings, high-bush huckleberries, and rhododendron, would join and again heal over this barrenness?

We turned back. The wind was tearing at other spruces; the fog was condensing on other twigs and drops splashed on bare rock.

May 3 We parked at Forney Ridge in a wind which blasted at us from the North Carolina side. It was not raining but the fog was thick and quickly moistened the surface of our garments. We took the lower trail, and emerged west of Clingmans.

We moved in a fog world torn by a furious wind which rushed in from the south. It never really rained. Anne used her rain gear but the others did not. The surge of the air in the spruces exhilarated us. The sound was mighty, but it was made up of a multitude of thin soughings. Even so, it filled my ear with its rush, and I missed the notes of the winter wren which Anne reported later in the day. On the open slopes we were embattled, leaning into the wind as though it were a solid thing. In the spruces the wind was muted, passing over our heads. But the fog world led on and on before us.

Anne went ahead at Double Springs. We were in the beeches— stubby, limby, and many-twigged. The wind became a wild, deep-throated roar. Back of us were the strings of the evergreens—here was the bass of the beeches. It was a place of contrasts. On the ground, spreading widely in the open parks under the sparsely growing beeches, were myriads of spring beauties. Some were in bud—awaiting sun and warmth to burst into bloom. But it was a scene subdued and contained by fog and rendered wild and violent by the wind.

At the first grassy bald we looked out into sheer, gray space. The mist tore up the left slope and sheeted across the top in wildly moving curtains. Anne appeared like a wraith at the first opening, shouting, "Hurry, hurry, before the wind dies down."

It was a scene of wild, ungoverned riot. This slender bald was bound together by long grasses which writhed restlessly under the wind's lash. Along the edges the forest of stunted beeches whipped violently; and before us, all around us, engulfing us, this fog was shredded by the wind. Whence did it come—out of what maw did it pour so ceaselessly? Whither did it go? Was all the world in storm? No amount of space, it seemed to us, could contain this great moving ocean of air.

It was not the world of man. There was no sign of him except the dark thread of the path through the grass. This was wilderness, magnificent, which penetrated the social disciplines which are so much a part of man's world. Anne took off in a wild run down the steep slope toward the woods, the wind ripping at her plastic rain-coat, until in the dimness she seemed more spirit than body. I have heard of a sunstroke, but as I watched her mad dash, I thought this is the first time I have seen a wind-stroke. Almost like a bird she was buffeted back by an up-draft and joined us on top. We shouted our excitement and our words were torn from us and lost in that great roaring.

We leaned onward into the wind, which on the knife-edge of the narrows took on a deep-toned, guttural roar. Wind and fog and forest, sound and fury, clean damp smells, heavy packs—here in a jumbled, heady swirl were the very elements of living.

At the Silers Bald shelter we found that some boys had preëmpted its use. We had brought no tents and we needed some cover. I bethought myself of the little cave which Sam Cook had used when we camped here in 1917. We left the Welch Ridge trail, climbed to a little flat, now overgrown, and turned down the slope and there was the so-called cave—an angular overhang, small and cramped, but offering some protection.

Camping offers recurring delights. The man who builds a house once makes a home but once. The camper is forever making a home —a place of his own, bending slightly the ruggedness of nature to his needs. Dickerman had caught up to us by now and we set about making camp.

A great flake of rock furnished a reflector for the fire. Another furnished a base. Twigs were stripped from fallen branches. A tiny tongue of flame appeared. With encouragement the flame took hold. We had a fire. Dick rigged up a crane. We had hot water. We cooked steaks and onions and potatoes.

A rib of ledges protruded below us. I went down to see if there was another overhang which would accommodate a sleeper. I found a spot protected by a ledge. It was on a slope, but usable. A few dried leaves had accumulated.

I looked; I rubbed my eyes. I saw a mass of bent metal. It was sprawled out as big as a bushel basket. I looked almost with horror, and poked at it gingerly with a long stick. It was a bear trap with huge springs and spiked crescent jaws. How long had it lain here rusting? Twenty-five years? Although its moving parts were corroded with rust, it was otherwise in good condition. Attached to it was three feet of chain which ended in a four-pronged hook. A trapped bear would drag this horrible contrivance, weighing perhaps 30 pounds, through the woods, catching this savage multiple hook on every sapling and rhododendron tangle. It was a grisly thing, which belonged to the pioneer world when man's dominion over nature had never been completely consolidated.

After supper we built up the fire. The four of us were cramped. Two could sit abreast on sleeping bags back in the recesses of the overhang. One could sit on the steep slope close to the fire by which we approached the shelter. One could sit astride a cheval of rock near the fire upon which drops of water dripped from fissures in the ledges above. We looked down the slope into fog-shrouded trees. Tag ends of wind found our shelter and drove smoke into our eyes. The air was damp. Vapor rose in clouds from our clothing from the heat of our bodies alone. We sang of the "Foggy, Foggy Dew."

I descended to the bear-trap ledge. Dickerman ascended to an eddy of leaves beside a big log. Anne and Doris made shift between the rock outcroppings of our main shelter. I could hear peals of laughter from them as they prepared for bed.

I moved the bear trap out, and myself in. The sheltered area was about the length of my body and about as wide, and lay on a 15° slope. There were a few leaves around the foot. I rolled in, snuggling against the damp rocks. Drops of water accumulated in the fissures at about 60-second intervals and splashed my face and soaked into the hood of my sleeping bag. Beneath my hips the ground was damp and cold—a coldness which penetrated the sleeping bag. Only my feet were really in the dry. I could look outward into a fog world which must have been penetrated partially by a nearly full moon, for there was detail in the woods under the darkness of the cliff. The wind, somewhat quieter, still swelled above me. I would lie on my back until my hip went to sleep. Then I would turn outward until my side became cold, and then inward. Three full cycles and the night was done.

I loved it—discomfort and all. I get so fed up with the frets and fevers, shibboleths and delusions of men. Here were elementary things—cleanness, dampness, freshness. Several times in the night, stars shone through fast-moving clouds. Here was promise! Once softened by distance, out of the caldron of fog and tempest, I heard the truncated call of an owl. That broken falsetto—whoo-whoo—is the wilderness articulate. Man must not drive the owls to extinction; he needs these windows of sound and sight for a look into a world other than his own. The great religions of the world were born in the wilderness. Great purposes, great faiths are kept alive in many persons today by the voices and potencies of wilderness.

Toward dawn the fog deepened. It had a dark, leaden quality. During the night I had tortured my mind into thinking that the wind had changed and that we would have a change in the weather. But I had also recalled that in 1917, in this same locale, we had had a 48-hour fog without a break. I had loved the mists of yesterday but I wanted the views for today. And then there was a lightening in the sky, and my recollection of having seen stars in the night did not seem a complete illusion. The lightening was followed by a patch of blue, and then by golden brightness, as the sun shone warmly into our shelter. We dried sleeping bags while we ate.

On top, the air glimmered under the sun and under brilliant, glistening, fast-traveling clouds. Motivated by the triune benevolence of moisture, warmth, and light, the spring beauties spread out in a gorgeous sward under the beeches, covering the ground like a frosting of pinkish snow. The yellow and maroon loveliness of the trout lily was likewise unfolding. And overhead, the fragile transparent parchment of the old beech leaves trembled in the wind and against the skies, like the most delicate of Japanese prints. Again I remind myself that these things must have come first; and that the prints which are so statically beautiful must have been patterned after such tremulous, living beauty.

Gaining elevation, we passed one of the significant continental division points. We had been in southern hardwoods, which are penetrated by a great wedge of high-level evergreens growing along the crest of the Smokies. We entered that wedge at its very tip—at the westernmost point of occurrence. It broadened rapidly until we were again in a forest that had the earmarks of north woods. Bob Marshall so commented when he and I tramped this same route nearly twenty years before. There were the same gnarled spruces and the same gorgeous avenues of green.

We left the crest at Goshen Ridge, turning north and downward. The spruces and balsams persisted, reaching gigantic size. It was cool here—the aftermath of the storm had brought swirls of cold air. We rested in a sunny spot on which the sun beamed down through the trees. And then we heard the thin riotous tinkling notes of the winter wren. We first heard about a third of the full song, but it carried the spirit and lilt of the whole. Each time the wren sang, sandwiches were dropped—conversation ceased. This tiniest of birds is the king of singers. The owls belong to the night—this sprite of a bird to the day, and to the majesty of the spruce-fir forest.

Descending, we walked long miles. We passed from the stateliness of virgin forest to the clamors of second growth. We saw signs of logging and picked up an old skidway, smoothly graded and now carpeted in grass. Innumerable small branches, broken off by the spring storms, crackled underfoot.

We rounded a bend, and stretching ahead as far as we could see was the old skidway whitened with phacelia. The flowers grew so thickly it was impossible to avoid them, as it was impossible to escape the fugitive fragrance which emanated from them. Once there was a dab of purple—a cluster of phlox; and then the clear waters of the Fish Camp Prong which turned a bubbly, greenish-blue where it plunged over ledges. And thus the riot of the storm was succeeded by the gentle beauty of the phacelia.

June 4 I have observed that often I return from hiking trips imbued with new enthusiasms and resolves. How can that be? It is useless for me to carry any reading with me when I go into real wilderness. I find I cannot concentrate on the secondhand, no matter how good, when the firsthand is thrusting itself at me through every sense. I wonder at the aplomb of those who are somehow unimpressed by their surroundings. I recall the woman at Mirror Lake in Yosemite who was apparently calmly and obliviously reading a book while that ineffable crag—Half Dome—screamed down at her to be seen.

In wilderness the scents and sounds and sights crowd in upon me. The wind, not tempered to the pleasant pace of modern-day living, strikes through many pores. One feels it, swims in it, exults in it and, if too cold, crawls from it, but it is there, all encompassing, overwhelming. It deluges the forests with music on a grand scale. Fragrances float elusively on the air. And one tastes—even as he smells—the tang of spruce forests. One speaks of total war. Here is boundless, transcendent, total experience. It would be here, if anywhere, that Thoreau would find the man whom he dared not face—the person who was completely, wholly awake.

Those daring souls who settled the vast and exhausting spaces of our hinterlands must have sensed something of the prodigality of their experience. Those explorers, voyageurs, and early settlers must have been as completely alive and bold as any men who ever lived.

We who have followed after have consolidated, canalized, and packaged experiences, until zest and enthusiasm have been uprooted. Even our sports are often doped up with wagers or glamorized with sex.

Millions are revolting against this. There is a movement toward the wilds. But many take with them much of the environment which holds them captive. They go in a car along highways which someone else has smoothed, unwittingly denying themselves the experiences of sound and feel and odor and taste. This is the curse of the highway through the primitive. It deludes the automobilist into believing that the one-dimensional experience of the view is the full, rich, and jarring experience of all the senses.

Some say we need more accommodations at Yosemite and Grand Canyon. But accommodations lay a film over experience. One accepts the tawdry for the genuine. Wind and sunset; the haunting dual notes of the varied thrush; the fugitive fragrance of the phacelia; the bite of cold; the stir and challenge of muscle against mountain; the elixir of water cold from a stream; the flavor of rain-drenched blueberries—these are the experiences which bring living into focus; and the boiling, flaming torment of the hydrogen bomb is seen for what it is, the nightmare creation of a race which has lost its moorings.

June 17 Ten days ago we went to Gregory Bald. There was a stately magnificence to the forest along the creek. There was luxuriance to the rhododendron, glinting in massive thickets under the trees. The waters, coming out of virgin woods and undergrowth, had a limpid transparency. Under the great trees there was the hushed containment of a cathedral but also a feeling of openness and expansiveness which no cathedral ever had. There was both closure and space under those enormous leafy domes supported by columns of living trees.

We walked out of the cove hardwoods, and on the ridges found dry stands of pine and façades of pink laurel. What a plant is the laurel—each blossom a tiny coronet, each grouping of blossoms a coronet. And each grouping of coronets massed in living walls of pink and white bloom.

Then there was a burst of flame fanned by the springtime—the first of the azaleas. I think there is no color more gorgeous, no red more flamingly rich. Knots of living flame, as big as one's two fists, reddened the woods everywhere. There was a glory and a spirit to it which is beyond words—as out of the deep woods unexpectedly this color glowed red.

I was ruminating upon this and upon long, unimaginative stretches of man-made trail when I heard it for the first time this season—the rich, spiraling whistle of the veery. We always hear it near Gregory; we always hear it at this time of year. It is more predictable than the weather and is richly and wildly enspiriting.

I had a peculiar sense of foreverness. Out of the valley I came—out of the south this bird came—to these woods—in this season—at this elevation—all converging in time and space. One can predict that bird call as certainly as any phenomenon on earth. On Gregory is order—beautiful, wild order. There (forever, may it be) this bird finds an environment to its liking, and it returns each year in June to sing its marvelous wild notes.

August 16 I am writing this about 11 a.m. in our cabin at Cobbles Hollow. Anne and I drove up after supper last night, arriving here about 9 p.m. We went to bed in a cool 65° temperature. I feel greatly refreshed although I did unaccustomed and vigorous work at home yesterday. There is leisure, and there are sounds of the forest about us. I am enjoying complete indolence. There is nothing pushing to be done to make this place more usable. We, like Thoreau, are knowingly resisting the beginnings of evil and will spend the day as we please, writing or soaking up the outdoors in its many and appealing forms. We have already this morning seen the slim green iridescence of a hummingbird at rest on a wild plum branch. And in the "dreen" below the window is the lambent crimson of the cardinal flower. Fall is breathing upon us.

I rejoice in the complete adjustment we have made to this place. We like trees. Although we have set out a thousand white pines, we need not have done so. This little cove of ours is like a greenhouse in which many things incubate and all things flourish. Tulip poplars are springing up by the scores around the cabin. Near the little spruce at the door, I found a tulip three inches high. On the clay slope to the east there were a dozen others. The larger ones have put on three and four feet of new growth. Dickerman's misgivings a year ago about the raw prominence of the "john" are already abated.

The old apple trees around the house and spring seem to be dying. They were probably set out at the same time and have reached senility together. Already pushing up under and through their branches are young and vigorous seedlings and saplings. The only thing we have to do is to adjust mentally to the changes which the heat and moisture and fertility of this place bring about. It is one of the hardest things men have to do—to accept nature. Many work and fret and wear themselves out trying to control and direct nature. Here at the cabin we have learned to accept it, and a rich and rewarding and relaxing leisure is born.

There are adjustments to make, other than the inner resolve to let nature have its way. When we were here a month ago, Anne spotted a snake skin about two-thirds of the way up the chimney on the outside. The chimney is constructed of flat, sharp-edged slate with deeply raked joints, and after the demonstration of climbing enacted for us last spring by the three black snakes, it did not seem impossible for one to climb outside the chimney and scrape off its old skin in the doing.

Our cabin is tight—and yet on our arrival last night we found foot-long fragments of snake skin on the floor. In my opinion, the snake could have gotten in only via the chimney; and as I looked up its smooth bore from the fireplace this morning, it did seem to me to be a remarkable feat that one should have obtained access to the cabin by that route. I have more respect for these harmless and not unfriendly creatures. Thus we have to adjust to the sharing of our cabin with friends for whom we had not planned.

August 30 This has been a hot, dry, early fall day with 94° temperature and 34 percent relative humidity.

I sat out on the front step at home in the sun. The heat was mellow and relaxing. It was on such a day fourteen years ago that the Germans invaded Poland, and the British and French sprang to arms. That was the beginning of the end of the British empire. It marked the beginning of Communist Russia's entry into world politics. It touched off new and fiendish ways of fighting wars. It was the beginning, although we were not aware of it, of the division of the world into two great armed camps, with only the frightfulness of the atomic and hydrogen bombs standing between mankind and the holocaust of another world war. Perhaps there is hope in this very frightfulness. Poison gas was never used again after World War I.

But the world has lost some of the drowsiness of fifteen years ago. Some of the change came from the intensity of the defense effort and expansion to peacetime uses of the technical developments of war. Bulldozers, earth-moving equipment, are changing the face of the earth, and there is a restlessness in the temper of men which shoots through all of society. What it portends one cannot even guess, although one trembles for its effect upon wilderness.

September 24 At its best the world, but for the demands of overpopulation, has seldom held more promise. Although it has fallen woefully behind in assimilating its accretions of knowledge, the possibilities inherent in the possession of this knowledge are boundless. Philosophy—synthesis—the writings of men like Murie and Mumford and MacKaye attain an overwhelming importance. It is such men, who have assimilated and brought more nearly into a whole the discoveries of these days, who are almost indispensable to mankind. The selfless, disciplined men who do the thinking for all men everywhere should be the guides in this new day.

In his Pacific University lectures, Olaus quoted Benton: "Wild land is an integral part of a balanced civilization, just as tilled land forms the other integral part . . . I enjoy the highlights of Broadway as also the aroma of the new-mown hayfield, and with them both the frog chorus in the damp and distant muskeg . . ."

The more time *I* spend in the wilds or in pleasing, natural country, the less I like big cities. In the last analysis, they are dependent upon tilled land and a complex of transportation and communication. The larger the city the more senseless the multiplication and duplication of functions. Are metropolises a necessary element of civilization? The horrid stenches and uglinesses of industrial cities should not receive even the most perfunctory benediction.

Aldo Leopold said once that he does not hold that the ugliness of cities—and its demands—from which people seem en masse to be trying to escape by their movement to the suburbs *is necessary*. Cities or towns should be beautiful. If the emphasis in cities were upon beauty rather than upon money, perhaps elements of the wilds would not be pushed so far from their borders. And the fight to save the wilds, to which so many of us are committed, would not be so unrelenting.

I resent the destruction of beauty in towns. The senseless exploitation of natural resources and environment at the expense of the well-being of our fellow man is a symbol of our world's ills. A reversal of this trend will not be easy. The growing number of people may make it unattainable. But processes and practices which bring vileness and ugliness into our world cannot be justified in any thinking civilization. The more colossal, noisy, and intolerable cities become, the more precarious our defense of Sun River, the Greenbrier, San Jacinto, and all the rest. The very pressures which drive men away from their cities send them swarming toward these wild lands. The greatest of these pressures are numbers, ugliness, and insecurity of mind.

November 16 I made a trip into the Charlies Bunion area from the Greenbrier, accompanying some others on their scouting trip. There were smoke in the air and oak coloring on the hills. Leaves lay in a deep shuffling layer on the trail; there were even some faded maple and sourwood leaves. But those which caught my eye were the rich tawny sycamores and the almost as tan, but not so tough, magnolias. There were still green and bright yellow leaves on the beeches. In color, this autumn has been rich as any—even though the massive displays were thinned by the drought. A tangy fragrance sprang up from the leaves, whose rustle drowned the sound of the low-flowing creek. We crossed the creek on the old trail. Rhododendron shoots were reaching out and reclaiming it, although the trail was still firm and wide underfoot. At the last crossing we took to the stream.

The creek was low and the rock was sharp and firm. We enjoyed a novelty in Smoky hiking—no underbrush, and a margin of clean rock which gripped our boots. The cushion of the duff gave place to the security of flood-scoured boulders. I had not been up this route for four years. There were evidences of the Labor Day flood of 1951 —the open stream bed, mounds of water-worn stone between the boulders, and a new log jam which overlay an older log jam.

Several of the familiar jams had been swept out, and there were places where the ravine was a gaunt undulating U of naked, slaty rock. This rock was polished and weather-worn from earlier centuries of wear. It was distinctly smooth to the touch and decidedly slippery to the boot. It contrasted sharply with the rough grip of the lower boulders and the angular edges of the strata which we climbed when we pulled to the left out of the ravine.

But reamed by two floods 25 years apart, this couloir was barren and sterile; and the mossy green, which we surmised must have existed here before the forest fire of 1925 and the flood of 1927, was replaced by a white scarf of ice. It seemed as limp as silk as it hugged the convolutions of the rock. Beneath the ice we could see fantastic shadowy shapes, twisting, squeezing, stretching, and flowing between the ice and the rock, as drops of water melted on the sunny slopes above found their way downward.

Little progress had been made in 28 years toward the restoration of the lush green benevolence of the "Mossy Spillway." How many centuries will the Charlies Bunion area remain a barren monument to man's carelessness with fire and nature's excesses with water?

We left the chill gloom of this north-facing ravine for a side rib of sunny rock off the Bunion ridge which rose to the Tennessee-North Carolina divide. On this exciting exposed ridge, with dizzy depths on either side, when every step started a musical clinking in the slate fragments or loosened a chunk to bound into the ravine and skate dizzily on the ice, we fell to discussing the folly which brought us to such a place. I listened to the others, who were jumpy and nervous and wished they were somewhere else. As we looked at the stupendous and magnificent views across the hollow, we discovered another party of hikers who had not risen to the challenge of the ridge we were on. The uneasiness of my companions was enhanced as by slow stentorian shouts we established communication with the other party. Very distinctly we heard the warning, "You are in bad shape. Up above it is slick all around."

As we rested, gathering our nerve, one of our party said, "Do bears ever come up here?" To which another answered, "Only people would be foolish enough to come here."

We inched upward, made uneasy by the shouted warning of the others. A little vegetation appeared and then a steep roof-like slope of insecure rock. Clinging in the midst of this, I glanced upward. I could not believe my eyes. There on this bare slope were the dried droppings of a bear. I could not see any bear food nearby.

We did not get down till late. Deep dusk caught us as we came out of the brush onto the open trail. There was no such thing as total darkness. First there was the twilight lingering ruddily in the west, and then the softening of all outlines as everything turned to shadow.

There is no describing it. One does not feel blinded as the darkness gathers. It is almost as though he no longer sees with his eyes—but in other ways feels and senses all that he needs to know. I did not use artificial light. I did not stumble once, even over the unevennesses in the trail. Windfalls somehow became a presence which I sensed and eased over. The leaves gave the trail a deceptive smoothness, but I never faltered.

The rhododendron thickets had an untouchable depth and the stream an indiscernible motion. The fragrance of the leaves, of the mosses, and of the fresh stream floated out and enveloped my body. My shuffling in the leaves drowned out the sound of the stream, but somehow it kept telling me it was there.

A fleeting shadow floated on the trail in front of me, and I looked up to the light of the quarter moon. This was a sensory experience of the deepest delight, which came at the end of an exciting day on the rocks and of an exhausting scramble down through the forest to the trail. Here I was, in solitude, in the muted, glorious stillness of the forest. I was thinking of the adventure of the day and was feeling the caress of the night.

NINETEEN FIFTY-FOUR

February 28   . . . I was up at six this morning for
the hike to the Chimneys. There was steady rain, and the creeks
had that swift white greenness which goes with high water. At the
first crossing we waded big-toe deep, but the rocks were clean and
our boots were tight. No mishaps. At the Beech Flats, where we
should have left the trail for the Essary route, some of the crowd
were ahead and Lewis Pollard and Fred Sweeton ran to turn them
back to the Essary draw.

We found a good route through the interlocking patches of dog
hobble to the creek. By then we were wet to the knees but that was
to be expected. The water in the creek was high and we ranged up
and down the banks trying to find a dry crossing. We squirmed
through rhododendron, which became involved in our ponchos and
snapped maddeningly back into our faces. While I was searching,
Anne ventured out in the swirling current with the aid of a stick,
followed a line of greasy slick boulders already under water, and
forced a crossing only ankle deep. The others followed.

We paused. White water was already slithering down the narrow
ravine of the Essary route. Phyllis Sweeton volunteered to wait for
Fred and the others, while I led our group up the hollow. The going
was comparatively easy. Giant buckeyes had shaded out woody undergrowth, and the shoulder-high herbaceous growth of summer had
collapsed.

Some of the folks were inadequately clad for the weather—a light,
persistent, and wetting rain. But we made good progress and had

almost reached the buckeye which grows in the very center of the
hollow and marks the turn to the west, when the others began to catch
up with us. I directed several how to work up through the rhododendron to the south ridge, advising them to keep in the open where
possible between clumps of rhododendron.

The Chimney Tops
". . . these precipitous and distinctive peaks."

Later I started on in the company of two hikers from Nashville.
They decided to take a higher route and I found myself alone, in an
unremembered tangle of rhododendron and saw briers. I floundered
on, heartily glad the others were not with me, and much discomfited
and frustrated by damp and springy limbs of rhododendron and
loops of smilax across all openings. I twisted and turned and snapped
smilax in a furious effort to reach the ridge. No skyline loomed
through the trees.

I finally struggled onto a very steep ridge with a bear trail on it.
I turned right, but there were few trees where there should have
been many trees; and as I peered through the fog, I could not see

the Chimneys. Then the mist lifted momentarily, and I could see the Alum Cave Prong far below and the water-whitened gash of Trout Branch and even the cross-over on the highway. But where were the Chimneys?

I looked above me to the left and saw bold outcroppings of rock in a location where rock had never been before. Seldom have I been so confused. Plowing through brush to an outlook, I was suddenly oriented. I found myself on the east flank of the high Chimney, instead of on its south ridge. I followed an opening, heard voices, and came out on the highest point of the south Chimney.

A roaring wind, solid as a wall, was battering the top. Charlie Person and Myrtle Brown were there. The wind whipped at our ponchos and threatened to sweep us off the mountain. Fog, rain, dampness, and those frightful gusts forced us down. As we descended, I stopped to drink from a small rectangle of clear and sweet water.

The strata of the cliff are vertical and their edges seized our boots. Usually on this descent I would balance myself airily on these edges and descend without use of my hands. I looked up. Charlie's cap was torn from his head and, sweeping in a long arc, landed a hundred feet below us. A blast caught Myrtle off balance, got under her poncho, and threatened to lift her off the cliffs. Charlie just in time grabbed a fold of her poncho and stayed her. After witnessing these two incidents, my pride left me and I held on with my hands as I went down the south cliff.

We ate in the shelter of the Essary ravine. For those who had experienced the monumental downpours at Tricorner Knob, at Stratton Meadow, and at Hooper Bald, this was a pleasant occasion with lots of banter which was climaxed by Fred Sweeton's whimsical summation, "At least there are no insects."

Descending, the Road Prong was tawny and sleek as it glided between boulders. The current was a foot higher than when we crossed in the morning. There were no more half-covered stepping stones. Everything was submerged by powerful, surging currents of angry water. We decided to wade the shallowest spots, holding to each other for support. We were quickly knee-deep in water, and it poured icily into our boots. We made the far bank with nothing more than rainy-day discomfort.

It continued to rain. The water remaining in my boots warmed perceptibly from my body as we moved through the brush to the trail. The next crossing had not concerned me, because I had noticed a fallen tree which bridged the creek just above the ford. When we got there some of those ahead of us were not using the tree but were taking to the stream again, which there was nearly waist-deep. The poncho of one girl had caught the current; she was swept off her feet and was literally carried across by Fred and Dick, who had plunged in to help her.

I urged the others to take off their ponchos and cross by the tree—a solid birch with a substantial fork about midway providing footing on one fork and handholds on the other. The last half could be safely cooned. But only Anne and I tried the tree. It was fully ten feet above the tossing waters. Although steady and strong, it may have seemed dizzily high to those left on the wrong bank. At any rate the three remaining girls tried the creek.

They were immediately in trouble. The stream swirled into their ponchos. Two of the girls were very tired. The third was the petite and indomitable Myrtle Brown. Fred Sweeton, who had been taking pictures of the tree crossing, saw their danger and scrambled to their help. I followed as soon as I could get down off the log and get untangled from my damp and clinging knapsack. Fred was ahead of me, waist-deep and firmly anchored above a boulder.

The three girls lost their footing simultaneously. From a place below a boulder where I could get secure footing I could close the gap to Fred. One girl had taken off her rain gear. I grabbed a handful of jacket and pulled her to safe footing. Fred had the other two by the hands as they were knocked off their feet and were supported in the water by their ponchos. Only he stayed them from being carried downstream. I managed to reach Myrtle and pulled her to a boulder which was barely awash. She scrambled up and announced pertly: "I am all right."

Fred and I quickly got Helen to the safety of a boulder.

This ford was on the old Thomas Road which had been constructed across the main range in the Civil War. The grades were prohibitive. There are stories that when mountain men brought wagons, lurching and straining and groaning across the ledges and boulders, they sometimes reached a point where progress was impossible. These iron-willed men would then unload and carry the contents on their backs past the obstruction, would return to the wagon, dismember it, and carry it down part by part. They would then reassemble the wagon, reload it, and lurch onward.

In our modern world we have certain technical masteries which they did not have. But they possessed a mastery of themselves which served them well.

March 12 ... Last weekend I took a conditioning hike in the event I should be able to join Mr. Justice Douglas on the long swing along the Chesapeake and Ohio Canal from Cumberland, Maryland, to Washington, D.C. Anne and I tried the roads above Elkmont, which are comparatively level and simulated to some degree, at least, the conditions which would prevail along the towpath. There was some snow. Probably two-thirds of the thirteen miles we traversed was under snow and on the bridges it was eight inches deep. I drove myself in order to toughen my heart and leg muscles and felt the toll half through the week which followed. And then one morning I awoke with a sense of great well-being.

I recalled that Ober was much impressed with Alexis Carrel's thesis in his *Man the Unknown* that the body functions better when taxed. Can it be that we can never live deeply with mind and spirit alone— that there must be a triune mingling of body, mind, and spirit?

The worst of the trip last Sunday was that in pressuring myself I had little opportunity to take in the slick, gray-green sparkle of the swollen river. What lilting, pounding turbulence!

April 18 The simplicities, the obvious goals, the deep searchings of spirit and body of the Chesapeake and Ohio Canal trip represented something clean and ennobling.

The story has been told by top-flight journalists with understanding and humor. They recognized the unusual gathering of men from over the country. They recognized the obvious simplicity and the sense of elemental accomplishment in the subjection on foot of relatively long distances of towpath. These writers were proud of their own accomplishments on foot and wrote feelingly of sleeping out under the stars.

And yet, with few exceptions, in the final summing up they surrendered to the popular view and gave lip service to the attractions of the automobile. This obeisance to the motor age is a psychological phenomenon. These men really didn't feel that way. There was such an obvious genuineness in their writing about the trip itself that this sudden about-face at the conclusion did not carry conviction. I have no real explanation for it. These were not bread-and-butter writers. They were men of intelligence, independence of mind, and integrity. Was there some subtle fear of getting out in left field with a minority?

I am not too much worried about the current craze for doing everything by gadgetry and the automobile. True, the car has for many people become a sort of extension of their personalities. But if they were forced to do without cars they would adjust quickly. Studies in the physical conditioning of modern Americans show that many of this generation may not be fit because of softening influences in their formative days. But the race is not injured basically and the next generation, if need be, can be strong again.

But what concerns me is the rejection of the past in this summary way. These folks who talk so glibly of the charms of the gold-plated Cadillacs are turning their backs, evidently without a pang and with little perception, upon their own past. They have become so entranced with the illusions of power which the automobiles and the other contrivances of modern living have bestowed upon them, that they want to dedicate themselves to such a life without thought of the consequences to themselves, their history, and the works of their own ancestry. They eschew physical strain or exertion except as performed for them by menials or by professional athletes.

A second illusion is that they can soak up beauty and natural values from an automobile in the same manner and to the same degree as on foot. Sounds and subtleties which the canoeist or foot traveler would hear and sense do not exist for the motorist. The claim that the motorist should have the same right to scenery as the walker is premised on the unspoken assumption that he can get as much out of the same sights in three hours that a walker would get in ten days or two weeks. Apart from what he would not get at all by the ear, nose, and touch, those perceptions which he did have would be too fleeting for permanence. As I look back on it, even our eight days on foot along the Canal were far too short.

June 13 Few conservationists are born. Most of them have, at some time in their lives, seen natural areas in a magnificent state of health and preservation. Then change occurs and they see the deterioration or exploitation of those areas. This they deeply resent, as though it were happening to them personally, and they become concerned with trying to preserve. Then they organize their knowledge, develop a philosophy, broaden their understanding and awareness, and become conservationists.

Conservation roots in indignation and strong feeling. But the best conservationists are those who fuse sentiment with knowledge—like Bob Marshall and Aldo Leopold. The others are often too cold to be convincing, in the one case; or too emptily emotional to be taken seriously, in the other. De Voto seems to fall in no category. He writes with great intelligence and acumen. He resents exploitation, but personally does not care for wilderness. He is an anomaly, but a very effective one.

July 5 Over the weekend we took a hiking trip along the rim of the Greenbrier. The feeling of remoteness comes more quickly in the Greenbrier than in any other locale. Newfound Gap was crawling with cars. We left it at 11:30 a.m. with Charles Mooers. We were the only ones with packs.

On our return two days later I saw people standing listlessly by their cars. What had the automobile done to them? There is infinitely more truth than satire in what Bill Voigt said—that cars have become a secondary sex characteristic for most people. They simply won't go where they can't take their cars, and they pack in cleaning tissue and sundry aids without which they cannot live. These days, personality and individuality come from without rather than from within. Perhaps it has always been so, although it is more evident in these modern times. Driving creates an illusion of thinking. Impressions taken in through the eyes pass across the brain, leaving fleetingly a sense of thought and of doing.

But to get back to our trip. We proceeded slowly eastward along the Appalachian Trail. Muscles and endurance became important to us, and we were carefully assessing our physical resources. The world we were heading for drove a slim wedge into our consciousness as we heard a bit of song from the winter wren. Laurel still bloomed in many places, and in one spot near the gap there was a gorgeous clump of azalea. Soon we saw the first of innumerable pinkish purple blossoms of the *Rhododendron nudiflorum*. There was the softest apple-green growth on the tips of the spruces and firs. There were the usual blowdowns and dead trunks, moist and inert, sinking into a spongy formlessness which would ultimately mingle with the thin layer of earth and humus that sustains the forest.

This "waste" of ripe trunks seemed to bother Charles at first. The full concept of a national park is hard to grasp. That which is un-economic or non-economic cannot be grasped in this mad world of production in which we live. And yet nowhere is the thinness of the earth's skin more evident than in the Smokies. Along the trails gravel crunched under our feet and flat slivers of slate clinked as we walked over them. On less than half the trail did we find smooth soil or soft, springy humus.

The Charlies Bunion section is a graph of both the thinness and the slim hold of the vegetation. Many of the Bunion cliffs and ridges are still devoid of life. There are spots where clumps of ferns eke out an existence on the rocks. In an occasional pocket a yellow-looking spruce sapling clung to life. There were a few green mats of sand myrtle. But by and large, the cliffs were still sickeningly bare. The tree trunks which were burned in the fire of 1925 and swept away in the flood of 1927 were still visible, gathered like kindling wood in the narrow naked ravines a thousand feet down. Young birches now cover the gentler slopes on the North Carolina side where the fire took its toll in '25. The limbs of the birches were uniform in color and height and at a distance resembled a meadow. This aspect was vastly different from the rich varied nap of the virgin forest into which they edged.

Step by step we covered that part of the trail having heaviest usage, past the tattered shelter and inconceivably messy garbage pit at Ice Water Springs (which belonging to everybody received attention from almost nobody), past the popular outlook at Charlies Bunion, past the "meadow" of young birches—and into the rich gloom of unmolested forest.

There we came to slopes as steep as those along Charlies Bunion, where the ancient and endless struggle for survival had been won. Ramparts of the purple-flowered R. *nudiflorum* formed a natural railing and we looked over it into shimmering valleys where spruce and balsam, birch and beech, mountain ash, rhododendron, viburnum, and tulip poplars vied to the very summit for a place to cling. On slopes nearly as steep there were also, and unaccountably, forests of pure spruce and fir under which the ground was open and brown with needles.

We left the trail and pushed up through the brush to an outlook on Laurel Top and then down a narrow lead through sand myrtle and high-bush huckleberries for a better look. The ravines on either side were steep. Ridge after ridge overlapped, losing depth and color to distance, until the blueness faded into azure, and sky and mountains joined imperceptibly at the horizon. Once again we had come to a place where there wasn't the slightest evidence of man.

From our perch on Laurel Top we looked across the depths to Peck's Corner, our immediate goal. The Smokies were in an inscrutable mood that created an illusion of distance in mountains which were near.

From Laurel Top we tramped ridge crests as narrow as a catwalk and wall-steep on either side. Before they had been leveled by the trail these crests were even narrower, being made up of horizontal strata of slaty rock, truncated at each end and resting crosswise like cordwood, and almost as unstable. Across these flinty corduroys we loitered, looking down from lofty heights into gaping depths. Then the main ridge became rounded and green with birches through which the trail penetrated as a grassy avenue.

Climbing the shoulder of Hughes Ridge we heard for the first time that day the fife-like notes of the veery. We were at the center of a fastness as dateless as the oceans. There was but one work of man in the whole area—an open-front log shelter which blended unobtrusively into the surrounding woods. Toward this we descended, prodded by the booming of thunder to our rear.

It had been long since I had traveled the country beyond the Bunion. There was little change—a few more ferns and seedlings on the Bunion itself, a little more erosion on certain sections of the trail, and a little more healing on others. Otherwise, it was much the same, the same outlines of near and distant ridges, the same flowerings, the same aqua-blue fading on the horizon, the same dank odors, the same soft mystery in the whispers of the air through the evergreens, the same all-pervasive cascadings of thunder just before the rain, the same solid thudding of raindrops on the ground, and the same scattered, inconclusive splat of raindrops after the storm had passed. There was the same chill, pellucid water issuing in the hollows. There were occasional fragrances as of fresh balsam growth and of the impalpable purple-fringed orchis. There were the bold piping of the veery and the thin, spirited, long-sustained arias of the winter wren, and deep in the night and deep in the valley below us, the bark of a great owl.

All of these delights I had seen and heard and felt and smelled before. Their totality was not new to me, as it was new to Charles. These experiences, which I was having once again, belonged to a world vastly different from the tense, almost frantic one we had left. Here the wilderness could work its spell and Charles quickly felt it. Here was abounding life—and with it glory, beauty, and serenity.

I thought of the prolonged and feverish orgies of work in our office. Our objectives there—so immediate and seemingly so important— seemed to supply the reason for our being. But did they really? Human life and freedom are as basic as the beauty with which we were surrounded. But was the ascendancy of a particular corporation, or were tax savings to a few individuals in the frantic integration which we call society, as important as this serenity and beauty and repose?

The pioneers, who had laid the foundations of our civilization, had each experienced these things. Then beauty was all about—and as it became tarnished, more beauty lay to the west. The pioneers always touched it. They did not know what it was to live without it—just as modern man with a few fortunate exceptions does not know what it is to live with it. For the settlers a homestead was but a slight oasis in a boundless natural world.

The first generations which settled this western world had an almost unlimited contact with the wilds. The settlers felt the richness, the boundless potency and challenge—the Daniel Boones, the voyageurs, the Marquettes and La Salles, the Lewises and Clarks. They could not help being moved by the wilderness. They had to be giants to survive.

But the wilderness is no longer everywhere, just beyond one's back door. There are few today who will ever go anywhere that someone has not preceded them. The chances even of having an experience with the primeval, such as Charles had, become slimmer. And when people have never had that experience, the task of persuading them of its importance increases.

July 28 An outing with Alvin and Jane Anne Nielsen led to a trip to the Chimney Tops, to which neither had been.

The Chimney slopes are suffering from erosion. The commonly used trail, which follows the northeast ridge, had deteriorated greatly since I was on it last November. The vegetation and humus were washing away to the bare rock, leaving an ugly slate trough as the pathway. The hollow which was used twenty years ago is choked at its mouth with stones and trees.

On the Chimneys, deterioration has not come from fire and flood, as on Charlies Bunion, but from *use*. But the results if not arrested can become as devastating as those on the Bunion. The rock and mineral layers on the Chimneys are covered by the shallowest and most tenuous of forest and shrub covers. Vegetation is abundant and beautiful but it is not secure against the tugging of climbers or the channeling of the rains. The mantle of green is underlain by a seamless web of roots and rootlets which hold it together. Shear those rootlets and the mantle begins to fray and tear. In the eons there could be complete recovery should man cease to climb the Chimneys. But there is no assurance that there will not be complete destruction if he does not cease.[5]

November 7   This autumn has belied most predictions by producing a gorgeous and massive display of color. I predicted the brilliance but was not prepared for the vast sweeps which we saw in the Sugarland valley and ridges. The delay in the frost may have contributed to the spectacle. The breakdown of the leaves came naturally without the searing and burning of a quick, sharp frost. There has never been an autumn when the hues burst more quickly or resplendently.

Every young tulip tree in the Sugarland valley has turned into a steeple of gold. It is a youthful extravaganza. Twenty-five years ago this part of the Sugarland valley was all field—a potpourri of tiny mountain farms. Then came the Smokies purchase program and the valley became a part of the Park. The old fields, cut-over lands, and roadsides began to explode with color. Young trees of many species got started where man had farmed and logged. Many, like the dogwoods and sassafras and sumac, never got very large. But they mass together with the young tulips and maples, gums, and sourwoods to saturate the landscape with color. A mature forest has splashes of color wherever a maple or tulip pokes its head above the canopy; but there is not this extravagant abandon which we find on the old fields and logged slopes.

People turn out by the thousands for these displays. They are talked about widely, and people are unashamed to drive to see them. Similarly, they go to the mountains for the subtler blendings of spring. It is only a step—but perhaps a long one—to wider, more understand-

[5] This trail was eventually abandoned and a new trail relocated in 1963. —H.B.

ing appreciation of all natural life. If that second step could be taken, following the first firm steps at the height of the autumn and spring, many of our conservation problems would solve themselves.

Bill Douglas was with us last weekend for his first hike in the Smokies. At the Ramsay Cascades, whither we hiked with Royal Shanks and Bob Howes, we were all very cold. There was snow everywhere and no place to sit down. But under the overhanging cliff alongside the falls, we found dryness and two degrees more of warmth. Royal caught 23° on his thermometer below the cascades, where the snow was four and a half inches deep on the footbridge, and 25° under the shelter of the cliff.

The falls splashed and splattered and sparkled in the light. Ice and icicles were everywhere. I crept out to the edge of the falls for a drink and slipped on the icy rocks and very meekly crept back to safety. I finally dipped water from a splatter of drops which collected from the snow at the lip of the cliff directly above us. Bill got up, began to take pictures.

"This beauty is intimate, you can take it in," he said. "The Himalayas are overwhelming."

I suggested to Royal that we go on up on top of the falls for the view. Snow and dampness covered those greasy ledges over which the water was pouring. Bill looked out at the snow-covered trees and rounded, frosty ridges.

"This is terrific," he said.

The weight of the snow had bent numerous saplings across the trail. As we ducked under them they dashed fluffy snow down our necks. Here an earlier frost had seared all the color out of the leaves. And the snow on the evergreens, the tightly curled rhododendron leaves, the frosting on every upright thing, the four-inch mantle of snow on the trail and footbridge, upon boulders and naked limbs, presented on October 30 a scene from the dead of winter.

On our side trip up the Middle Prong, I was interested that Royal immediately spotted the second growth at the "Hill Field." He inquired if there had ever been a clearing there. I told him that I recalled, and had a picture of, the remains of a cabin on that spot. Later we saw a pile of rocks which I thought may have composed the chimney. He observed at once that, if it had been a chimney, there had been "secondary piling" on top of it.

The great eastern hemlocks caught Bill's eye; and I was struck by huge red and sugar maples. When we scrambled under the last rhododendron and came out upon the boulders of Buck Fork, we were at the very edge of the primeval. The fishermen's trails above have disappeared. There was a belt of unlimited primeval, eight miles broad, between us and the Appalachian Trail at the top of the divide. I would like to work through it again, as I did many times in the 1930's and '40's. There is nothing forbidding about it, but this eastern wilderness is dense and it takes time to penetrate.

$\mathscr{N}$INETEEN FIFTY-FIVE

January 2   We observed the New Year yesterday by walking to the mouth of the Ramsay branch. The day was
mild. To 4000 feet the air was clear; above that a heavy gray mist was
clamped upon the high peaks. We ate at the confluence of two creeks.
One creek carried water from Old Black and Guyot; the other from
Tricorner, Eagle Rocks, and Laurel Top. The two streams drained
a vast wild area. The water was limpid and green in deep pools, and
white with deep-borne bubbles at the foot of a plunge. Where it
struck a half-submerged boulder it was a swirl of liquid crystal.
The streams seemed to be the voice of that great wild area. And well
might they be—for both the flow and the transparency were linked
with the condition of the forest above.

I looked at that beautiful current and at the dense and massive
forest of hemlocks, birches, magnolias, and silverbells. I looked at
the thickset understory of rhododendrons, solidly green with broad
leaves quivering in the wind. I looked at the ground itself, brown
and deep with humus. Here was vigor with serenity, immensity with
intimacy, and impersonality with infinite appeal.

January 11   Last Sunday the mountains were enshrouded in mist—
a mist so saturated that it congealed increasingly on twigs and needles
and then dripped to the ground. Occasionally there was rain. The
wind tore through the trees, wild, raucous, and deep-toned. It found
its way even into the crowded woods at the Jumpoff, and there was
no escaping it, except on the precipitous east slope below the crest.

One by one my companions retreated over the top until I was left alone, whereupon I too sought out the shelter of the east slope.

Twice there was a whitening in the gray void below the top, but the cloud layer never broke. On the return there were occasional belts of clear air. At such times I could see the mist a few feet from me being blown horizontally against the slopes, rather than upward along the slant of the mountain. It was strange also to stand there in the clear, watching the clouds scudding by, seemingly only a stone's throw away.

Snow was drifted deep and solid. Out along the Boulevard trail, where I walked joyously alone, I looked at the silvery birches and at the spines of the spruces almost lost in the fog. It was a lonely, wild scene and I was glad to be there. Friends in the Hiking Club on the scheduled trip up the Walker Prong to the trail were likewise undaunted by such loneliness and elemental violence. If they were not quite comfortable with the rain blowing down their necks, they were probably not perturbed. It was a rough day. I heard only one bird all day, a kinglet on the sheltered side of the main divide.

I stopped for a closer look at tiny spruces, hardly bigger than my hand, springing up in the duff along the trail, and for a look at the fluted transparency of a wall of ice clinging to a cliff. Through the ice I could see dark droplets of water squeezing slowly between ice and ledge. I thought of the green torrent far down the valley. It came from millions of such drops, originating behind ice barriers, among rootlets, working through rock crevices, converging slowly fanwise across the entire upper valley.

January 24   Yesterday we went to the mountains for the third time this month . . . We had not been on the trail a half hour before I realized I was taking it very easily.

Then the pattern of our day changed. We had come to a bend in the trail which took off around the nose of the mountain to the Cat Stairs. Above us, bare and challenging, was the line of cliffs which is the distinctive mark of the Greenbrier Pinnacle.

Henry Gray proposed to leave the trail for the cliffs with his two friends. Anne and I joined them, hardly expecting to keep up. We did keep pace for as long as was necessary, and in this we were lucky. Two routes seemed feasible—one up a precipitous pine ridge with ominous gray outcroppings; the other up the hollow along the left flank of the ridge which was the route of the now unused telephone line to the fire tower. We reckoned if others could lay the wire, we could follow it to the top. Our only difficulties occurred when we deviated from the wire, and these difficulties were substantial.

At first our route was conventional enough, though steep. We had to scramble from one side of the hollow to the other, dodging a bit of ice, plowing through an accumulation of snow, or kneeling gingerly into the dampness under a fallen tree.

We came to a small cliff and bore to the left away from the wire. It looked easy and we traversed it by toeholds to a small shelf. Henry got his fingers into a fissure in the rock where a laurel bush was anchored. Between us, we hoisted Anne.

Then he put his foot down for me. I got a good hold, turned loose momentarily with one hand to grasp the laurel bush, three times tried for its sturdy stem and three times got only a limber branch. I dropped back to the ledge for I had no strength for another such effort.

I crept along the shelf to a small tree, found a toehold, and bracing outwardly with my back against the tree, scrambled upward to another toehold, and reached another small shelf level with Anne and Henry.

Through very thick brush we now climbed toward the citadel cliff which guarded the top. This was another matter entirely. We were tired; there was some snow and we had no rope. Several routes offered themselves, but they allowed for no misstep on the hundred feet of gray cliff. Henry and I moved east where there seemed to be a fault in the wall of rock. This opening was perhaps 50 feet wide, and over a chockstone in its center a trickle of water filmed out into a casing of ice.

Our line of attack was against the right buttress. We gained fifteen feet up the wall by hanging on to a fallen tree. This was the key. Above were laurel and pines. If we could reach them, we were up. Henry floundered up the bulge under the edge of the right buttress where the water seeped. He stood on a sodden mass of vegetation and took Anne's hand and literally dragged her up, just as the mat of vegetation upon which he was standing started to break loose. They scrambled to safety and in doing so a jacket and a loaf of bread spurted from his pack and landed in snow 25 feet below. In the midst of it all, my eyes caught a flash of brown—a hermit thrush.

The Winters boys and I were now wary of this spot because of the loosened vegetation. We backed up and tried the ridge to our right. More bulging gray monoliths! One route looked feasible but it was fearfully exposed; one slip and the cant of the rock would throw one outward with a clear drop of 50 feet.

We started down, thinking of searching the base of the cliff for another route. But as we passed, we had another look at the passage Anne and Henry had taken. In the very groin of the rock we found a tiny, sharp protuberance. Bellying up this bulge with help, the first boy caught his foot on this point and made it. So did the second. I tossed up my pack, plastered my body to the moist stone, shoved against this jut of rock, and with their help also made it. I looked down. The pitch was 70°, and the walls on either side were nearly perpendicular. The cliff was a leaden gray. There was fearfulness in its clean, dark lines. A thousand feet below we could see the snowy flat where we had left the others.

A hundred feet above, deep in snow and embrangled with hemlocks and rhododendron, we found a ledge angling off to the right. We inched along to join Anne and Henry. From there on it was a safe but maddening scramble. Every foot upward was a double struggle against the pitch of the slope and the impediment of laurel. Scrubby pines and looping smilax vines punctured our skins. I was very tired when we reached the crest. The old trail, which skirted the crest of the cliffs, we found to be greatly overgrown.

We turned right and came to a smooth outcrop rock, flat on top but perpendicular on the valley side. The snow had melted there and it was dry. There was no wind. Three thousand feet below lay the valley, and above it Mt. Le Conte towered 5000 feet.

It was a colossal scene. Every side valley, every clearing, every cliff was white with snow. But there were dark ridges where the snow had melted. The entire landscape was in relief. I saw ridges I had never known before. The overcast was still stratified, high above the mountains, and below we could hear the hollow roar of the streams.

After lunch we decided to go down the trail, which although it had been there for twenty years I had never followed. Snow as soft as flour lay a half foot deep and my thigh muscles protested as I raised my feet to shuffle through it. On the south-facing bends the snow was nearly gone. Then more snow. Across the void of the valley in revealing snowy relief we could see the great masses of Guyot, Chapman, Eagle Rocks, Sequoyah, Hughes Ridge, and Woolly Tops.

On the trail we picked up the tracks of a fox, evenly spaced and in line as he walked leisurely along. Once he had stopped and defecated on a small stump. We went on down and at a turn in the trail proceeded through open woods over two bands of cliffs to the fire road.

May 8 A week ago, we took the scheduled trip to Russell Field which Royal Shanks and I had scouted in the snow about five weeks before.

We went out into a crisp, brilliant, polished day. The long shadows of late dawn were still on the fields. The atmosphere was perfumed and sparkling and infinitely fresh. The day was full of promise. The promise was soon fulfilled—a turkey gobbler stalked across the road, colorful and glinting metallically in the morning light.

Cades Cove stretched out flat miles to the mountain foothills. It was a pleasing sight—the wide pastures and grazing stock. But there was a subtle difference from earlier times. The cove seemed slightly more deserted; the meadows, broader. There were fewer fence rows, fewer houses. The effect—the gracious merger of sward and slope—seemed slightly more studied. The blend of husbandry and wilderness which existed so satisfyingly 30 years ago was now painted in broader, more professional, strokes. The cove no longer looked lived in.

The road was being widened a bit. The fords, where road and stream once excitingly overlapped and where one crept into the water wondering how deep it was, were now being lengthened and given a concrete base. Some of the spice and risk and inconvenience is being removed. Memories will be flattened like the ruts, and experiences will merge into a great pleasantness with no highlights, no overtones, no nip of danger or of annoyance.

This is going on throughout the entire Park system. Jeeps, rather than man power or horse power, now serve the fire towers. Everywhere administration is being streamlined and experience is being sugar-coated. The dangers, the sharp tough experiences and impressions which were memorabilia of early trips to the Park are being removed. In the light of these thoughts, I was delighted to hear a young Park naturalist say that he had urged the Service to sponsor a series of overnight hiking and camping trips to some of the far places in the Park. His suggestion was discouraged by the administrator who might have given it life.

But there was still wildness. There was first an extraordinary blooming of pink lady's-slippers—hundreds of them—springing up under a thicket of pines. We scattered out among these exquisite plants and were driven by some inner impulse from one clump to another. Like the old cow which reaches over the fence for the grass on the far side, we searched out the next clump before we had observed the exquisite colors and proportions of the first. Late in the day, as I moved tiredly down the trail, I saw a single lady's-slipper. I enjoyed its lone beauty more than all the others.

Saturation is one of the more subtle killers of human experience. The road builders, who would level all experience to V-8 uniformity, are amongst the worst of all killers. We punish him who takes a human life. We penalize one who carelessly injures a person. No punishment is visited upon those who dilute human experience to dull and vapid uniformity.

In the foothills the hike followed old woods and sled roads and crossed an unbridged creek. Across the creek the old sled road climbed steeply and evenly to the Sugar Cove. Worn deep by bygone use, its trough was now carpeted with leaves and cushions of needles. Trailing arbutus hung over the edges and azalea flamed alongside. We crossed two hollows, shady with rhododendron and moist with water. Then, at the old chimney site, we burst into the upper clearing, which was shining and glimmering in the sun. We traversed an ancient orchard, another cabin site, and passed a deep spring which was confined with a beautifully laid U-shaped rock wall.

This was the western-facing Sugar Cove, a long, fairly level spot in the main hollow. It was a sheltered spot where men once lived; plowed and put out trees; and in the early spring collected and boiled off the sap from the giant sugar trees up the ravine. Now it was deserted. The arts of men were slowly being effaced by the fecundity of the forest.

These hill people had lived in cabins made of logs. As the logs rotted out they left no ruins except the toppled chimneys and the rock-lined spring. The dying apple trees and the uniformity in the young forest growth were the residual evidence of the presence of man. The forest was creeping into the old fields and rhododendron clumps welled out into the old spaces. The man-made order and beauty of a mountain farm was yielding with cosmic gradualness to another kind of order.

On the steep slopes above the old fields we saw deer tracks, cut deeply into the crust of the humus. I saw no evidence of browsing, although there had been pawing and rooting. One of the rangers had told us that there was a herd of fifteen down below in the cove.

157

Royal punctured my delight at this news when he reminded me that the old enemies of the deer—wolves and panthers—no longer roamed these hills, and that the deer might get out of hand.

The approach to Russell Field from the west is theatrical. Its openness is obscured on the west by a rhododendron thicket through which the trail is barely passable. A half mile of bending and twisting through its mazes left us bowed and unaware of the clean line of the field just beyond its bounds. It was a surprise to everyone suddenly to break out onto the bald. It lay in the sunlight in the earliest throes of spring. Its grass was still a tawny brown. Tiny clumps of bluets met the spring sun, and the sarvises, hung with white and bronze and copper, carried the lowland spring of a month ago to this high level.

We luxuriated on the grass, moving into and out of the shade of two pines as the whim struck us. Some of us went down a few hundred yards into the gentle trough of the old fields looking for water. Herb Webster and I searched out the highest pool and found a rounded, transparent bubble where it sprang from the earth. The chill clear water was inexpressibly sweet. Here on the open mountain top was a gorgeous blending of sarvises, young pines, and grassy meadows.

July 7 It is the fad these days to speak of going behind the Iron Curtain or the Bamboo Curtain—curtains which separate widely divergent ways of living. This was going through my mind last Saturday as we followed the Ramsay Prong into the heart of the Smokies. We too were passing through a curtain—a green and living curtain, as we moved from the fevered, mechanical bustle of 20th century civilization into the stately forests of an ancient and lightly trodden wilderness. This curtain was not fabric thin or wall thick. We did not pull it aside and pass beyond it in a moment. Rather we were hours moving from what was clearly on one side until we found ourselves clearly on the other.

After we parked our car we hiked for a mile and a half along a truck road. It passed through a fine forest along a stretch of the Middle Prong with house-sized boulders and magnificent green pools at their base. But there were still the car tracks, the graveled road, the timbered bridges. At the turn-around, we left the road and took to a trail. It was a beautiful trail through trees of enormous size and loveliness, rising out of green seas of glossy rhododendron. The trail was heavily used and had worn down to the mineral soil. There were several footbridges bearing the marks of an adz, with handrails fastened together with spikes and bolts. Where the trail was steep, rock steps had been laid and there were one or two rustic benches. Along the way candy and chewing gum wrappers and other bits of waxed paper reminded us of civilization.

A footbridge crossed the stream below Ramsay Falls. It furnished a fine view of the cascading water and was in good taste—a simple log-crossing made from a spruce tree, with bark removed and the log flattened on one side. More rock steps led to the crest of the falls, a tumbled gray cliff the height of a tall tree.

The crest of the falls marked the end of the trail. No litter, no handrails, no signs. The cliff edge was polished smooth by the stream. It was made glassy by lichens. There were no parapets, no railings. With exquisite sensibility the Park Service had decreed that from that point on, the user of this stream was on his own. The dangers and discomforts to be encountered from that point were the dangers and discomforts experienced by the Daniel Boones, Davy Crock-etts, and William Bartrams.

We had finally passed through the green curtain! Once there had been an old foot trail above these falls, made by the timber cutters crossing the main divide from their homes on one side to the work-ings on the other. It was a trail of expedience, with no bridges, no smoothing, and it probably followed originally the path of a bear. Not a calf path through a pasture, but a bear path through a wilder-ness. The logging had ceased nearly three decades before and the trail had steadily deteriorated; or perhaps more appropriately, the forest had steadily reasserted itself over this thinnest evidence of civilization.

We found this old path, not with our eyes but with our feet. Duff was everywhere, covering the entire forest floor with a springy cushion. But in the old trail the duff had been packed ever so slightly. The cushion was there, but with firmness. This we stumbled upon as we pressed through a tangle of rhododendron above the falls.

The trail, so-called, at this point had been hung on a very steep slope. Blowdowns had been upended in places. Where that had occurred the trail had been carried by tree roots and trunk to lower slopes. Digging the edges of our boot soles into the slope, we skirted it only to move into the center of a spruce blowdown. It rode high on its projecting limbs, which snagged our packs.

There is nothing more tantalizing than an old trail. It is almost easier to beat the brush without regard to a trail, but not quite! So we searched for the trail through blowdowns and heaving waves of rhododendron. Several times it disappeared even as we stood in it. We made a try in this direction or that, and found it sometimes 40 or 50 feet away. Beyond the rhododendron it rested on a jumble of moss-covered rocks. The going was easier, but the firmness beneath was the firmness of solid rock. We found the subtlest of indications of the old route—a brownness in the moss, a clawed place on a tree, and once the print of a bear's paw in the humus at the edge of the rock bar.

There was a steadily deepening sense of wilderness. Below, along the road we had seen a chipmunk and later a red squirrel; then in the great aisles of the cherry orchard we had heard distantly the tinkling melody of the winter wren. Then we saw the droppings of wildcat, and finally we came to the scarred bole of a spruce tree, ripped of its bark by a bear.

The trees of this forest stood in irregularly spaced columns and held up a lofty, continuous canopy which threw thousands of acres into shade.

In such an atmosphere we passed through the curtain to the wilderness itself.

We came to another crossing of the creek—this time without benefit of log or handrail, only boulders. Here we paused. The gorge was narrow, a green confusion of rocks on the far side, endless barricades of rhododendron on the near. Great yellow birches lifted their crowns nearly a hundred feet above the stream, and gorgeous lavender orchises gave off the subtlest of fragrance. The sweet pungency of balsam needles stirred our nostrils, supplanting the slightly acid tang of the hemlocks lower down.

The transition from man's world to wilderness had been wrought step by step, foot by foot; from road to trail, from trail to trace, from trace to unmarked forest. We had moved from the struggling saplings of second growth to an oak forest; from oak forest to the varied hardwoods of tulip, hemlock, maple, buckeye, and gum; from these to the stately wild cherries; from the wild cherries to the spruces and birches; and now to a forest of spruce and balsams.

We had progressed from the hot, bloomed-out lower valleys to the gloom and moisture of the deep ravines. A pink shield of late-blooming laurel overhung a second cascade. Green slopes of rhododendron flashed with bonnets of pink and purple bloom. Boulders which were gray and clean-lined in the lower valleys gave place to boulders that were barnacled with lichens or verdant with moss. Moss that was inches thick hung on boulders like a great, green buffalo hide, and even under water clung closely, weaving tenaciously and brightly in the lucid water.

Here in this green and vibrant and achingly beautiful spot we camped. A fire was easy. Small glistening birch limbs, carrying the volatile fragrance of the wintergreen under the silver bark, blazed freely. The chance breezes of the day reached a unity in the deepening twilight, as a cool stream of air began to flow steadily down the hollow fanning our fire. Gathering in the gaps high above us at the foot of Guyot and Old Black, it flowed steadily the night through.

Supper was hugely relished, spiced by glimpses through the birch limbs of the multiple cascades above us. At one spot the water poured between boulders in a quarter circle, like the partially glimpsed quadrant of the turn of a wheel. But the full circle, concealed though it was, we knew was not completed here. The full circle went from mountain top to plain, to alluvial valley, to the sea, and back ultimately in rain clouds over the mountain top. The glistening cascades were like currents of flowing snow, their crystals separating in the dark pools.

I lay on my back on a boulder and looked up into the lacy branchings of the birches. As I lost the horizon, I seemed to be looking downward, rather than upward, suspended over a fragile net of leaves which was the only thing that stood between me and a boundless fall into outer space. It was an eerie feeling. The solidity of the boulder at my back seemed to impel me into airy space confined only by that leafy mesh high above me.

Seven years before, I had camped at this same spot at the time of the full moon. I remembered the prologue to its rising, the gray light on the tree trunks above our camp. In the deepness of the valley we had seen the moon only briefly, and I predicted this night that the near full moon would skirt closely the south ridge. When the sun had set below us in the valley, the birch limbs became black against the sky. Then the spaces between glowed and lightened. Gray light formed on the tree trunks and then came the brilliant disk of the moon, resting momentarily in the V of the valley above us. But this time also, it did not follow the southern rim. It passed across the V and almost immediately out of our sight.

I did not sleep well. The ground was both lumpy and hard, and the surroundings were stirring. As I lay with my head buried in my sleeping bag, the water of the stream splashed around the boulders with the sound of raindrops. But the skies were clear, and through the branches I could see an occasional star. At daybreak the air was moving solidly down the valley. The great round leaves of a linden sapling turned with the air and its limbs yielded and then sprang back. I looked high into the birches and found their leaves dancing in the current of air which was descending our little valley.

As we moved up the valley after breakfast we found that from our campsite on, the old trail was almost erased. It was not discernible in the boulder field, although we picked it up momentarily where it entered the rhododendron. It had not been very plain, even 30 years ago in the heyday of its use. We came to a spot where it had disappeared. Several possible openings appeared, but when we followed them out they invariably ended in a tangle. We took to the creek several hundred yards below the well-known pool called Drinkwater. Pools which crept back under overhanging rhododendron slowed down even this mode of travel, although we found rock surfaces and low ledges over which we made good time.

I spotted Drinkwater from far downstream by the casket-shaped rock on its shelving rim. The stream was high and the water filled the pool to the edge of the shelf. It was hung over with great banks of rosebay rhododendron. The pool itself was dark. Green moss clung like a fabric to all the boulders but the fall itself at the head was spotted brightly by the sun. The place had a rare, vital beauty. The stream lost its pellucence but not its clarity in the great depths of the pool. Around its edge every inch of surface was green with living things; spruces, rosebay, and viburnum mingled with the birches. Moss was inches deep on the ground, and crept onto the boulders and ledges themselves. Rock and moss, oozing with moisture, formed the beginnings of a forest.

It was not a spot for heavy use. Life was abundant but its hold was tenuous. A baby could have stripped the moss from many of the boulders, although where it grew under the water its hold was more tenacious. Batteries of human feet would quickly wear down through its springy cover to the mineral soil; and unprotected, the soil would find its way into the streams. The seeming vitality is deceptive—the barren slopes of Charlies Bunion with their bleak and slaty crags were once as lush.

On way to Mt. Guyot.

Above the pool we picked up the trail again but only for a few moments. After a mile or so it disappeared again, submerged under great beds of waist-high ferns, stinging nettles, and blowdowns. For hundreds of yards we moved along with elbows held high above the nettles which pierced even jeans and heavy trousers. The ferns were waving acres of grace and beauty. Blowdowns, the natural decay of the forest, lay willy-nilly, and we continually changed direction to avoid them but were occasionally forced to belly over one which could not be bypassed.

We were moving very slowly. On other trips I have covered the distance from Drinkwater to the crest in a couple of hours, but this time so completely had the wilderness reasserted itself that we consumed seven hours. At each step we sank deeply into humus and moss—the equivalent of three or four steps on a firm trail. But we

163

were supremely at peace. Progress was meaningless here. Each step was touched with a divine beauty and each disclosed a new richness.

Once we sat on a log and rested. At my feet a small area a half-yard square formed a kind of unity. I looked at it, focused in the sun. There I saw dead birch leaves, paper thin; a bit of bark the size of my hand with little tunnels smaller than pencil leads interlacing it. A tiny insect emerged from one tunnel, folded its wings and squeezed into another. There were balsam needles, a birch twig, the tip of a balsam twig still green, probably whipped off in a wind. There were strands of moss, an oxalis in bloom, and a balsam seedling only an inch high, its emerging needles spread like a semaphore. I pressed the area gently with my foot. It was springy and came back to shape. Layers of decay, ages-deep, soaked up moisture like a sponge. The log we sat on was hard to the touch, but close by was one so decayed that it compressed under our feet.

We had no great urge to proceed. The thin cool air, the scent of balsam, the surrounding quiet, the vistas of rosebay, the stocky birches and trim spruces interposed between us and the blue sky all merged into a perfection that reached every sense.

But man's divinity does not reside in complete repose. We moved on. The perfection, the continuous exquisite appeal to our senses, did not cease. Sensations changed, vistas shifted, the clogging life lower down gave way to sparser vegetation. But there was the same interweaving of strands. The tapestry of experience wound on and on—with no repetition of pattern or design. The sweet fragrance of the balsams was diluted by a penetrating tang of unknown origin. The tinkling roundelay of the wren was supplanted by the heavier-belled call of the raven. The bewitching, down-spiraling song of the veery was replaced by the thin queries of the nuthatches. The soft splatter of the stream became shredded into musical gurglings from the high springs.

We ate lunch on a slope covered with balsams and spruce. The heavy understory we had been traversing had yielded to a clean, close-growing ground cover of moss and oxalis. There were long inviting avenues upward. But the openness of the ground was deceptive as we sank deeply into the moss and stumbled over rotting logs. We were in a sort of basin, furrowed with tiny ravines. Water ran cold in every depression.

The whole area was a gigantic sponge which caught and retarded the fall from every rain. At the head of the valley the deep V-shaped gap, as it had appeared from our campsite, flattened out as we wallowed higher. Light began to show through the trees, spreading to the right and left. We were coming to the gap. But there was one final blowdown, and even as the slope became level we had to use force, through down-timber and thickets of young balsams, to step into the Appalachian Trail.

The trail which had been graded out to a four-foot width in CCC days was gradually closing in. In the gap, alpine grasses and dead needles had encroached until the trail was but a footpath.

Five hundred feet higher than the trail was the summit of Mt. Guyot. On the thinner soils on the side of Guyot where the shade was thicker, we found some erosion. Growth on the high Smokies is in tenuous balance. The cover is thin. The rains come in deluges. The green mantle is fragile.

Except for the very primitive trail which we followed to the top of Guyot, the final ascent after we left the Appalachian Trail was an anticlimax. I was impressed with the good sense and good taste used in locating this trail. The Park Service twice had routed it around two immense blowdowns. There was no disturbance of the soil—perhaps one or two fallen logs had been sawed out but otherwise the woods were close about us and the experience was intimate.

I had not been on Guyot since the trip of the Wilderness Society Councillors in 1951. There were changes; it now bristled with briers and new blowdowns through which I struggled shoulder deep. My hands and clothing were snagged and torn. The air was moist and the distant mountains were a pale, bluish gray. There was as always a certain exhilaration to being on top, but it was midafternoon and we had to return. Clouds were piling up to the east. The poncho with which Anne started had been tucked under a rock far below Drinkwater.

It was hardly possible to hurry. We followed our tracks back to the Appalachian Trail and decided to try to find the old native trail down Ramsay. It was impossible. So we traveled by the most open route—through moss, around blowdowns, across ravines. After awhile, partly from memory and partly through disturbance of the mossy cover, we found our up-route.

We crossed to the left bank of the creek and stayed farther from it than on our ascent. But for miles we were without a trail. There were the waving seas of ferns and nettles, then openness and moss and viburnum. The clouds darkened back of us. We did not need to rest as on the ascent, but still the uncertainty of our route and the ubiquitous barriers slowed our descent. As we neared Drinkwater we blundered upon the trail again, but were on and off it a dozen times.

At Drinkwater we paused even though we could hear the cannonading of the summer storm back of us. We wanted to enjoy again the witchery of this pool. And there was a certain inevitableness to the storm. We had had remarkable luck with the weather. Phil had said, "If it holds good until noon, I shall be satisfied." It had. The thunder came closer. Even though one always hopes the storm will go down the next valley, it didn't. We had gone 300 yards through the massive rhododendron slick below Drinkwater and had become stranded on a rib of the south slope high above the creek.

There the rain caught us. We huddled under poncho and rain gear. The rain thudded down—huge drops found every uncovered spot on our bodies. My cap became sodden. The poncho was drawn tautly between Anne and me. Cold water oozed down my back. There is nothing fatal about a wetting, but one always shrinks from its beginnings. After our initial soaking we moved on. Fog drifted in with the rain and darkened the lingering rays of twilight. We had no flashlight. We were still a half mile from camp, which was somewhere down beyond those sodden acres of rhododendron.

We gave up on the trail and decided to try the creek before darkness closed in. I went ahead. Every branch or bough I touched dropped a further deluge upon me. Though protected slightly by the poncho, my trousers became saturated, squeezing out water as they stretched across my knees. My cap drooped over my ears and cold water soaked me front and back. We no longer cared whether we bumped into water-laden undergrowth. It no longer made the slightest difference whether we crawled on the soggy humus or brushed against the rhododendron, or whether if forced to it we had to wade the creek. There was a certain release to it—we were freed from the possibility of comfort.

Curiously, when we again reached the creek and took to the boulders, they were not scummy and slick. There seemed to be a certain suction between our squashy boots and the rain-drenched boulders. We made remarkable progress down the creek, moving onto the bank when the tangle opened up and then back to the creek when it closed in. Darkness slowly settled upon us and we strained our eyes for the openings in the woods or for the open boulders. Only the frothy cascades lightened the shadows.

Then the massive birches opened above us and we knew that camp was near. "Camp" in quotes! No tent, no fire, no dry wood. It was simply the one spot on this enormous mountainside where there were a few of our things—fairly dry, we hoped. They were wrapped in a tarp and had been pushed back under a boulder before we had set out in the morning. Phil had forehandedly shoved a few dry sticks of wood under the boulder. These we retrieved and split against a damp log. Fitful drops still splashed on us from the trees.

I got out a match and with my body shielded it and the dry splinters and struck it against a metal surface which I hoped was dry. The match sputtered and fumed and then flared into flame. I touched it to the wood. And then began an hour-long struggle. The rest of our wood was as drenched as we were. We split it to the dry core, but drenched it in doing so. Bit by bit we dried it out. The solid wood took hold and the licking flames rose a little higher. I blew on the blaze until I was drunk with oxygen, and fanned it between times with a kettle lid. Each time we thought the fire was on its own, it would settle and blacken and we had to blow some more.

Meanwhile, Anne and Ruth spread a poncho on a boulder, and working in the spot of a flashlight in the blackness of the mountain night prepared our meal. Two pots we pushed close to the fire. These caught powdery debris from the firewood we had piled high over the flames to dry. From moss and ash and bark our tea water was itself as brown as weak tea. Chunks of fresh charcoal mingled with the rice, and our teeth crunched down on it when we ate.

The down-current of the night air settled into a steady breeze. It fanned the flames, but chilled us as we worked about the fire in our damp clothing. Sometimes we sought the warmth of the swirling smoke, until our eyes smarted and streamed with tears.

We had one more night of this rich and pungent experience—and then we had to return to the other side of the green curtain.

On our trip we were at this camp spot a total of twenty hours. In that time we had trampled several short paths through the vegetation, going from sleeping places to packs, to fire, going to get wood, going for personal reasons away from the camp. The water of the stream was incomparable as it swirled by our campsite. When a cup was soiled there was the temptation to step to the stream, swish it a couple of times in that gorgeous water, and step back with it clean. It was *possible* to do this because we had four miles of stream and perhaps fifteen square miles of watershed absolutely to ourselves.

Our camp might have sustained ten other people sleeping down-stream from where we were. There would have been more trampling, more wood burned, and multiplied temptation to use the stream to swish out cups and dishes.

We didn't yield, but the temptation was there. And how insidious would have been the effect on the water at the falls a mile below had we and a dozen others so used it. We carefully soaked all embers, picked up the ashes on a piece of bark, soaked them again, and then hid them in an opening between boulders. We replaced divots of moss which we had inadvertently torn from the boulders. But careful as we were our campsite will be visible the rest of this season.

Our experience demanded space—lots of it. Space in our towns, along our highways and byways, is shrinking rapidly. There are more and more people to use less and less space. It becomes, as Vogt says, an ever scarcer resource. It cannot be imported or manufactured. There is no substitute for it.

When so many of our values are measured in profits, are marked up in quotas or flaunted in graphs and indexes, we need to keep alive the need for space. People need a sense of history. They need to read Bartram, and the journals of Lewis and Clark and of Thoreau. They need to read Robert Marshall, John Muir, Aldo Leopold. They need to understand that the seemingly limitless space and game and op-portunities of 150 years ago have shrunk beyond measure. They need to be aware of the haunting appeal of space; and of the interest and excitement of streams and plains and mountains without end.

They need to know this past—and how it is flinching and shrinking under the impact of the present. They need to know that the hardly adequate spaces of the present are drawing tighter about each in-dividual, as populations flow out over all unoccupied areas. When this awareness comes, then and then only will "summit" talks become something besides a frustration and urban life something other than a vexation. Then the suburban and rural will bloom again; and the priceless influence of an undisturbed mountainside and of an un-polluted stream will be cherished as man's most precious possession.

November 29 New concepts and discoveries, new appreciations are being added almost daily to our knowledge and understanding of wilderness. It was hardly a decade ago that Aldo Leopold hailed the greatest scientific discovery of the twentieth century. He wrote not of the television or radio, but rather of the complexity of the land organism.

Not everyone who has spoken for wilderness conservation has thought of or been motivated by the complexity of the land organism. In the report of Frederick Law Olmsted, the elder, on Yosemite and the Mariposa Grove, there was little which indicated that his appreciation or interest went beyond a desire to preserve their sublime scenery. He appeared to be interested, not in a wilderness community of infinite depth and nuances, not in a multidimensional land organism, but rather in three-dimensional scenery. Even Leopold in his earlier writings seemed more concerned with space and isolation—rich, deep, and important as they are to the human soul—than in the interworkings of the land organism. Even in the early releases and broadcasts of the Wilderness Society there was much, too much, emphasis on scenery and size and too little emphasis upon an understanding and appreciation of the infinitely interlocking animal and plant worlds.

But there were voices crying out, not only in the wilderness but *for* the wilderness. Over a hundred years ago Thoreau was pleading for national reserves in which the bear and panther might still exist, and "not be civilized off the face of the earth." Here was seminal recognition which has reached its flower in the writings of Leopold, the Muries, and others.

December 5   After a night and morning of heavy rain, we went yesterday afternoon, under heavy overcast and still damp clouds, to the mountains with Bob Maher. As we entered the Park at the edge of Gatlinburg the streams were high and tumbling. The mountains were dim and gray. We could see the Chimneys against a background of dirty white and a cascade of clouds pouring down the hollow between the two tops. We drove into streaming, dripping mist at the level of the Chimneys and followed a deserted road to Indian Gap.

The mist hung all about as we drove out of the gap to the east and onto the shoulder of Mt. Mingus. Giant spruces dominated a forest of lesser spruces growing out of the clean-floored ground. The air, the ground, the shrubs, the trees dripped with moisture. There was all about us an air of nonchalant vigor, as though this forest was aware of its might, and proud that it was deserted by such lesser beings as people while it soaked up the life-giving rain. The gray density was beautiful. Gray-green frilly lichens, green loops of lichens, and sodden green moss climbed the boles of the trees. Bulky spruces, their fragile outer limbs losing themselves in the mist, towered over the balsams along the crest.

We stopped at the sight of a tiny ball of reddish fur. It bounded into action, streaked along a horizontal limb, spurted across sheer space to another limb, around a trunk, and on across another opening to another tree. The movement was so swift in the dim light that this diminutive creature seemed to run on space itself, as without any apparent acceleration it raced from tree to tree. It was a wild spectacle of agility and sure-footedness. The airy paths 30 and 40 feet above the earth were the domain of these pixie red squirrels. Sally Carrighar says that a squirrel will survey and work out all possible routes in its domain until it knows every avenue and can escape in any direction. With compassion and respect we watched this demonstration. This was no circus act; this was day-to-day living, in storm and winter. We slushed on, thoughtful, pensive, and with warmth in our hearts for this tiny russet "boomer."

INETEEN FIFTY-SIX

February 14   Last Sunday I went to White Rock (now called Mt. Cammerer). Clouds lingered over some of the mountain tops, but others were resplendent in the sun. White Rock was clear. Valleys and draws along the north side of the Pinnacle Lead and Old Smoky were dim and haunting. The sun gleamed on the hoarfrost along the crests and threw impenetrable shadows into the hollows.

We started hiking immediately. The cold air burned our lungs and foreheads. The streams were dashing, and although they originated in second growth were sparkling and transparent.

The country through which we were ascending had not been long abandoned. Old apple trees were still conspicuous in young forests of hemlock and pine, peawood, and red maple. But there was unexploited vastness upstream, and it showed in the brooks and runs.

We climbed rapidly over a cushion of needles and leaves. The old sled road which we first followed had no raw slopes and was almost completely shielded with leaves and vegetation. The trail, a simple man-way, had not been scraped or graded. Even where it was very steep, there was little erosion. There was a healing cleanness to it.

Sooner than I thought possible, we passed through the first belt of pines and edged into a band of deciduous growth. Immediately we heard the wind roaring as it rushed through the bare limbs. It was violent, sustained, deep, and powerful. The sound made me want to shout madly.

By contrast, when we climbed into a second zone of pines the wind sounds were thin and taut. From the pines we could look out onto the precipitous north slope of White Rock itself and see frosted ridges alternating with hollows of deep green. It was truly a rugged and rare winter-scape.

On the exposed rocky summit, the very air sparkled. The wind had stilled. The mountains were blue and sharp-lined. Clouds hung on the southern and western horizons in broken horizontal layers like great dingy galleons with white decks and white foam where they break the water. Occasionally a cloud would leave the formation and throw a chill and a shadow over the gray ledges where we ate. This rocky crag dominated the landscape for many miles. One became heady with a sense of easy power as he had but to turn his head to look down upon miles and miles of the human world.

After lunch there was an unplanned gathering in a sunny pocket among the rocks. We got to reminiscing, drawing on decades of memories of experiences shared together. Laugh followed laugh like waves breaking on the shore. Sun and companionship were warm— the memories dear and choice. Can life at its finest offer more than this brilliant nexus of man and mountains? Will man ever be really happy until he restores to his daily environment the unstudied beauty and divine peace of the natural world? *I have never wanted to leave the top of a mountain . . .*

March 13 Last Sunday I hiked with Frizzell up Rip Shirt Hollow to Brushy Mountain. Frizzell is entertaining and ofttimes hilarious company. But he has a serious side. And his eye and appreciation for what he sees deepen the experience of being in the woods with him. In the second growth along Long Branch, he commented on the enormous size of the old chestnuts, some standing, some prone, which had once reigned over those woods.

His climbing was noteworthy. He was in his later fifties, but was among the first ten hikers to reach the top. Of course, he and I cut corners on some of the youngsters, conserving our energy by short cuts discovered from long years of climbing.

Brushy Mountain was easy this time, but I hardly thought we would make the top. We never pressed. We went along easily, stopping often, admiring what we saw. It was not until we were perhaps twenty minutes from the top that I had any real thought we would make it.

The cliffs and benches were much alike—barnacled with lichens, or covered with a thin skin of mingled rootlets, dead leaves, and mushy black humus which afforded only the most casual foothold. When we were on the cliffs, we were never sure whether the whole skin of humus would peel away, or whether a root would break, to let us slide gracelessly to the bottom. On each cliff top there were the usual stands of rhododendron through which we wormed. And we ripped our shirts and hands on interlacing greenbriers.

Deviating from the usual route, we ran into new problems on the cliffs which never quite taxed our best powers but which always evoked extra effort. I love these little cliffs, the north-facing woods packed with rhododendron, ferns, mosses, dog hobble, laurel, lichens, and hemlocks—young and pliant, or ancient and doughty. In winter, except under the heaviest of snows, these woods are much the same. They are always verdant and seem not to yield to winter, nor to wait for spring. It is the great deciduous forests in the valleys which have their moods—starkness in winter and an ethereal softness in the spring.

On top we burst out of lush north-slope growth into the dry austerity of pine woods. The pervasive shades of the great evergreens yielded to the arid simplicity of pine-screened vistas. Under the pines the lichens were hard and claw-like rather than soft and pliant. Needles, not duff, covered the ground. The round-leafed teaberry and ground pine, the glistening leaves of coltsfoot, and the oval leaves of trailing arbutus replaced mosses and ferns of the north slopes. We were on the dry south slopes, which were bright and exhilarating with vast views of the high ridges. And on these dry slopes we rested and ate in the open, in sight of the great peaks.

As we ate, a quivering in the rhododendron would telegraph the news that other hikers had reached the top. They would press through shoulder-high growth, catch the truly remarkable view of the mountains, and invariably exclaim. One girl, probably twenty years younger than we, stretched out flat on her back and rested. After a while she joined in the conversation and banter and said, "I admire you two for getting up here." (What she really meant was, "I didn't believe you two guys would make it, and here you are ahead of me!")

It was youth's tribute to an older and tougher generation. We had been conditioned by 25 to 40 years of hiking and climbing and know-how. She grew up in the world of the automobile and of innumerable distractions. She rode, when we walked. We knew what we could do; she was not sure. We knew there was a top; she wondered.

Leaving the top of the ridge at "the hole in the wall," the going was not difficult in the rhododendron because there was a continuous understory of dog hobble. (Wherever there is dog hobble, the ground is close and travel safe and fairly easy.) We skirted several small cliffs, worked out of the area of huge tumbled rock into firm, open woods. We gloried in the tall spare trunks of the great trees, in the absence of undergrowth, and in the groves of enforested space.

Walking through one of the abandoned areas of settlement lower down the branch, Guy commented that the older we get, the more we understand what went on here and the more we sympathize with the folks who were forced to sell their land for the Park and leave this magnificent environment.

Never had the woods been more beautiful. There was a balminess in the air, which balanced on the knife edge between winter and spring. The woods were still open and revealing. The deep blue line of the Stateline bulked large through the vertical, reedy curtain of the unleafed trees. Everywhere there was the winter windfall. Gray trunks were marked with tawny scars of raw wood, where they had fractured as they fell. The trail was blocked by windfalls whose limbs clutched at us as we detoured around them.

Spring had not burst—but it was damp at the seams. We saw no great bloomings, but here and there a single yellow violet or a half dozen purple ones showed through. There was one scattered patch of hepaticas, their blooms hardly white, as they opened above dusty green-gray leaves. Beneath our feet were dead twigs, ripped off in the winter storms, which tripped us or snapped under our tread.

It was exquisite—the feel of winter and the brush of spring. It was as though we were threading some great dividing point in time: winter at our feet, winter in the revealing bareness of the trees, winter in the thin line of ice at the base of one of the cliffs; but spring in an elusive softness in the air, in scattered pinpoints of color, in those swelling javelins of growth at the ends of the branches, in the damp freshness, and in the gentle, flowing streams. There was neither the dusty dryness of summer nor the pounding, frothy torrents of winter. It was an exquisite, tingling day, and thus we trod the tremulous line between the seasons.

June 8 Where is the best place to experience the wilderness community? The community is complex—sometimes too much so to comprehend. Sally Carrighar attempted a simplification in her book *One Day on Beetle Rock.* From the skein of living things, she separated strand after strand of individual lives—those of the deer, the bear, the chickaree, the grouse. Sympathetically and understandingly she held each one up to gaze, carrying the activities of a dozen wild creatures successively through one day of activity.

After reading through three or four of these little biographies we became aware that the activity of each touched that of the others. The single strand touched and crossed and tied into, and sometimes terminated in, other strands until the web of life was apparent. In each study the life recounted was clear, single, and understandable. It is a kind of surgery whereby an organ is lifted from its bed through an incision and examined and understood a little better, and then dropped back into place and into the great unity.

The wilderness community has similarities to a human community. Each element responds both to its environment and to inner motivation. In the wilderness the soil, the exposure to the sun, height above sea level, latitude, wind, ocean, light and darkness—each has its impact. These influences may thin out the community, as at timber line; or may place a barrier to further advance, as on the northern reaches of the tundra.

In these high settings life and life communities still find play. Maybe it is only a simple plant—with no sentience, few reflexes—it only "knows" to grow where it is possible to do so. Maybe it is the chickaree, warm, dynamic, knowing hunger and pain and fear and love, with a dash of mischief and sheer love of life thrown in. Maybe each strand touches many others—maybe the pile on the fabric is thick.

In the wilderness man may or may not be present. In the wilderness a clump of arbutus or galax is not torn up to adorn some ceremony or assemblage and then discarded. There, the loon or heron is not shot simply to satisfy the lust to try out a new weapon. A beautiful meadow is not dammed, submerged, and destroyed to satisfy the clickings of the stock tapes. A limpid stream is not befouled as a convenient channel for the disposal of waste.

Modern man must treat the wilderness as he would a child. He must recognize his own strength—and, comparatively, its frailties. He must see, as he sees in the child, the potential for beauty, balance, and realization. He does not today exploit a child; he should not today exploit or destroy wilderness without great soul-searching. Because wilderness is often made up of many strands, it has more capacity than a child to rejuvenate itself.

August 7   Two days ago Herb Pomerance and I led the Hiking Club on a cross-over hike between the Middle Prong of the Little Pigeon River and Big Laurel Branch. The trip was enlivened by the presence of Park Superintendent Ed Hummel. He showed up without prearrangement, saying simply that the trip offered him the dual opportunity of seeing a part of the Park with which he was not familiar, and of meeting members of the club. It offered us a chance to see park problems through professional eyes. We exchanged views on the grandeur of the river above the Little Laurel bridge. Ed said whimsically it was the first time he had ever walked the stretch of road to the turn-around. And I suggested that a man-way along the bank of the river would enable novices to see some of the might and beauty of the river away from a road. He agreed.

We stopped quite a while at the little footbridge. We then entered upon that beautiful, winding half mile of trail beyond. The trees have a towering stateliness. They are of many varieties and they shade a ground crowded with rhododendron, moss, phacelia, partridge berry, and other low-growing herbaceous and shrubby plants. The lofty arches under the crowns of the trees have a dim and subdued beauty. One feels the vitality—the rich variety and charm of deep forest. Ed called it "The Loitering Section."

"I wish we could get the average tourist to see this, to get this feeling," he said. "If tourists merely drive up one of the roads, they think they have seen wilderness."

His comments revealed a previously unsensed personal appreciation of the Smokies, and also reflected professional perplexity in trying to bring man and wilderness closer together.

We left the trail to the west and went up a nameless hollow. After a few scrambles through rhododendron we picked up a faint bear trail, which often eluded us but which we generally rediscovered just as the going became rough. There were a few blowdowns, over some of which we scrambled and around others we circled.

The stream was small, but clear and chill. There were some tardy rhododendron blooms and banks of broad-leafed sedge. But the overwhelming impression was of magnificent forest.

The gloom of the ages was here. The sky was etched out by the great vaulting tops of the trees: poplar, buckeye, cherry, birch, hemlock, maple, silverbell—almost any tree we could name. Every trunk was ramrod straight, reaching high to the light, until the foliage mingled in a rich and complex pattern. There was nobility in the vistas between great trunks standing deep in rhododendron but supporting that arching, leafy canopy. Sometimes these glimpses would open out for several hundred yards; sometimes the great columns would be screened by a cluster of younger trees. There we hiked, slowly, leisurely, moving for once with some of the timelessness of our surroundings.

There were low rumbles of thunder, and rain fell gently. Ed, I think, acquired a new image of members of the Hiking Club when he saw some of them sitting without jackets or ponchos in the rain— as nonchalantly and unconcernedly as though it were the brightest and best of weather.

Just beyond the lunch spot we came upon as benign an area as there is on earth. The same majestic trees standing here and there irregularly—not here knee-deep in rhododendrons, but almost barefooted on the rolling earth. This spot was covered with the lustrous, creeping porter vine—nothing else. It clung in a clean waxy green to the undulations of the forest floor. What a place to camp—on the inviting beauty of this demure vine—under the high thatching of those unbelievable trees.

While we stood in the perpetual twilight of this spot, we heard, at midday, the evening song of the wood thrush. The notes were as liquid and silvery as the flow of our little stream. They were repeated thrice—unhurriedly, after long intervals. And each of us strained to listen.

December 4 I accompanied Guy and others on a scouting trip to Grotto Falls. As we approached the village of Pigeon Forge the mountains were like cut steel against a light curtain of morning fog. It was cool and overcast as we approached the Cherokee Orchard from Gatlinburg.

We took the dug trail at the gooseneck turn of the road and were in snow from the outset. It steadily deepened as, moving east, we drew closer and closer to the great bulk of Rocky Spur and Le Conte itself. We went over the first ridge, then over a shoulder of Piney Mountain. Then came Spruce Flats, a rocky area with great hem-

Grotto Falls
"Tumbling over the rock was a modest cascade."

locks and other virgin trees. Near there we tracked between gigantic silverbells, nearly four feet in diameter.

The snow was littered with seeds and cones, which the squirrels feeding high above had dropped to the ground. Their tracks were everywhere, also fox tracks. Once we flushed a grouse. A pileated woodpecker rent the air with its alarms and swooped out of sight. We saw a community of smaller birds—juncos and chickadees together—and a majestic soaring hawk. Then there appeared delicate and gracefully curving lines on the surface of the snow. A bird had run forward as it took off, the tips of its wings marking the snow in three beats before it was a-wing. Its wings had produced a snowy vignette of utter beauty in the compass of two square feet.

As we neared the Roaring Fork, we recognized its rushing sound. It was flanked by a noble forest of hemlocks, maples, tulips, silverbells, and wild cherries. There was a scattered understory of luxuriant rhododendron which became denser and thicker the nearer we came to the stream. The latter tumbled down a narrow, dusky, heavily

178

forested gorge. At this time of year, the sun hardly touched it, as the unmelted snow blanket attested. We found a tiny sunny spot on a curve of the trail beyond the falls. The sun barely surmounted the Rocky Spur. It warmed us for fifteen minutes, and then slid back of the ridge and was gone for another twenty-three and a half hours. If snow is to be found anywhere in the Smokies, it will be found in the gorge of the Roaring Fork. Elsewhere the temperature climbed to 68°F. Along that creek, out of the sun, it was barely above freezing.

Here was wildness—wintriness—aloofness. The litter and tracks on the snow were evidence of life—and also of the struggle for life. There was grim purpose in the feasting on the silverbell seeds. The forest was not as rich as it once was, for everywhere about were the silvery hulks of the noble chestnut. One less species of tree to feed prolific wildlife. The fox tracks and mice and squirrel tracks occasionally merged in tragedy, as bits of fur and thrashings in the snow gave grim evidence.

And then we looked down upon the first massive tracks of a bear. Perhaps I was not quite as stirred as when I saw my first cougar tracks in the Olympics or my first grizzly tracks under the Chinese Wall in Montana. But involuntarily I stopped to look. Bumbling as he is, there is something awesome about one of these deep-woods bears going purposefully about the business of living. We did not see him, but in the suggestion of his tracks there was something which arrested our steps and halted the course of our thoughts. He was obviously not hibernating. And in these austere and wintry woods he had to find food sufficient for his great and demanding body. The forest took on a new interest. We don't know how far the bear ranged, nor for that matter how many bears were involved in the tracks we crossed. But these woods were home to him or them.

The bears along the roadway are softened by civilization and an abundance of garbage. We preferred these winter rangers in the deep north-facing ravines of the Rocky Spur. We were brought back humorously to civilization as we stopped to examine bear droppings near the Cherokee Orchard. We had to laugh. The dung was loaded with apple peels.

And thus flowed the current of life. The seeds of the silverbell were converted into squirrel; and squirrels were converted into fox. Everything edible, from mice and chipmunks to roots and berries and apples, was converted into bear. And bear and his tracks are converted into wonder and adventure for man.

$\mathscr{N}$INETEEN FIFTY-SEVEN

February 11 We had a beautiful, satisfying time in the mountains yesterday. It came at the end of a prolonged period of rainfall. The rivers were running full, with a measure of violence. In the valleys they were a flat, turbid brown. The higher we went the greater the transparency in the smooth curve of the water sweeping over a ledge. Gradually there came a greenness, rich and healthy and shot through with bubbles. There was still too much water for full clarity. It boiled over the rocks and ledges, and tossed with foam and whitecaps. In the infrequent stretches of comparative calm, it raced with a sleek greenness. I loved it. I thought of the enormous watershed above, so rich and dense that the flood came down as through a great sieve. The soil and debris were caught in the mantle of undergrowth and held there. Here was a gorgeous demonstration of forest health.

Tonight I read in the *Tennessee Conservationist*, under a photo of a beautiful clear stream, that all streams in Tennessee would run clear and cool and be havens for fish if pollution were cleaned up and if forests and fields were properly controlled. Here was enlightenment in officialdom. All streams *could* be like that if land users generally understood and cared. That is one thing the "daffodil lovers," as a forestry dean once characterized conservationists, really want. Streams run clear when everything is in balance above. How simple the goal when so stated.

February 16 Preoccupation with possible war is coming between me and constructive activity on behalf of the exciting, marvelous world which could be. Timeless wilderness, beautiful and green fields, unpolluted streams, convenient and stimulating cities, a balance between population and resources, research, art, mental excitement, common effort, self-knowledge, and good will! If we had these things we would set the stage for the surest heaven known to men—a heaven in which men would find happiness in conserving and in challenging effort and achievement. Such a world would furnish not the moral equivalent for war—how can any equivalent of war be moral? Rather it would meet the basic human need for effort and accomplishment and stimulation. The wilderness movement is but one phase of a many-faceted conquest of life.

February 18   I once talked with Dr. Kincaid about the scarcity of descriptions of the country during the days of exploration and before the transformations springing from settlement. He had been confronted with this lack when he was writing his book *The Wilderness Road*, and had searched in vain for descriptions by those who had used the Wilderness Road.

Then came the book by John Bakeless, *The Eyes of Discovery*. He had delved prodigiously into early records and diaries, which for the most part go back to the days of the explorers themselves—De Soto, Coronado, Drake, Bartram, Lewis and Clark, et al. This is the kind of thing which Dr. Kincaid sought and didn't find. Bakeless has done an incalculable service in bringing a picture of the land before western man changed it and in incorporating into one book an excellent image of the vast dimension of the entire continent. Although the accounts were written at different times, they were all written before the white man had changed the face of the land. Though the Lewis and Clark accounts appeared nearly 300 years after the De Soto trek, both described the land as it had been for long centuries. To have all these narratives in one book in juxtaposition—as though each leader were describing his trip as a contemporary with the others—gives them vitality and reality.

Bakeless brings alive in broad strokes the oneness of the original American scene. Who can but be proud of it, and more than a little awed?

March 4   . . . Yesterday I climbed Winnesoka again. I have liked that mountain ever since we went there by the north face about three

181

years ago. The north face of Winnesoka is steep, with inviting water-falls and benches and sugar maples.

The abandoned roads were attractive in their winter nakedness. As we climbed, the mountains stood out in warm blues through the gray screen of leafless trees. Up-slope, slender trunks cast beautiful shadows on the brown earth. There was an open, up-tilted spacious-ness to these north-slope woods, in sharp contrast to the dense and thorny low-growing trees on the south slope.

Our group paused on a commanding bench while some boys ahead shouted back they had found a wall of rock.

Above the wall, rhododendron and hemlocks covered the main rib at the right. In the hollow which carried the little stream were wide-open woods. But the earth there was steep and unstable. Several times I found myself climbing with hands as well as feet for addi-tional traction. The great February rains had loaded the soil with moisture. Each crease in the earth had seeps of water and some places had been washed bare in the heavy rains.

When we started our trip in the morning, Bob Maher had pointed out a couple of sentinel-like evergreens on the crest of the mountain. He said we should aim for them. We had lunch in a little cramped opening in the south-slope vegetation. I leaned against a pine tree. A greenbrier snagged my trousers. Laurel and high-bush huckle-berries almost obscured the high outlines of Mt. Le Conte. Needles and ground pines covered the soil and were speckled with a scattered stand of fresh green teaberries whose leaves carried the exquisite flavor of wintergreen.

After lunch we squirmed along an old trail toward the west to the high point of the mountain. Limber branches whipped at our faces, and loops of saw briers tore at our clothing and skin.

I have often speculated how that trail came into existence. It was on no route to any destination that I could think of. It was too steep for logging. I have heard of mountain people picking huckleberries on Round Top, as Winnesoka was then known. But that was decades ago, and the season was so short it hardly seems possible that this activity would result in a trail. At any rate here it was, rudimentary at best, impeded by blowdowns, briers, and undergrowth. Once we came to a little outcropping of rock from which we got a partial view of Le Conte.

Another outcrop marked the high point. A stocky jack pine grew to one side. It was easily climbed and those few extra feet lifted us out of the undergrowth and opened up awesome depths and expansive views of high mountains and valley settlements. The bleached ghostly skeleton of a dead chestnut stood a few feet to the west, and some of the boys had laid a slim log as a bridge from the outcrop to a crotch of the chestnut. Several edged across this bridge to the chestnut, and at one time three or four hikers hung from its branches like ornaments on a Christmas tree.

The day reached its climax in the late afternoon. We had purposed to make a loop around the headwaters of Dudley Creek and descend another fork to our starting point. The old wagon and sled roads were fairly open and we were making good time. But as the afternoon wore on, it seemed that our passage through old fields and orchards and by old cabin sites and barns was taking longer than it should. Suddenly the creek we were following flowed into a very large stream, one that came in from the left rather than the right. Instantly it flashed on us that this was not Big Dudley Creek, but the Roaring Fork.

In the confusion of second growth and tight laurel slicks we had crossed the divide and were miles from our destination. We were first incredulous, and then as the enormity of our mistake grew on us we began to laugh. Most of all, I guess we were impressed again with the Smokies. Some of us had been hiking in them for 40 years. They still have their surprises!

March 19 I went to Porters Flat in the Greenbrier. It was a bright, crisp, mellow day—early spring by feel, late winter by calendar. Hepaticas, anemones, several kinds of violets, bloodroot, and a few phacelia and trout lilies were in bloom. There was no leafing-out of the trees. Except for a slight ruddiness where the red maples were feeling the warmth, there was little evidence of spring overhead. The effect was unreal. Here at the beginning of the spring the sun was high overhead, and without the leaves there was a bright openness to the forest. There was none of the half-light found in deep woods in summer.

One could see for hundreds of yards through the trees. The ground and the few spring flowers were brilliantly illuminated. They bloomed early as the sun burned through, warming the ground and stirring them to life before the summer gloom took over.

From a high point on the trail, I overlooked the dense greenness of a rhododendron thicket. From above, the dark glossy leaves reflected light, never seen in the summer. The streams were full and open and bright. The sun's rays penetrated the water down to the bedrock. The cascade a few hundred yards above the last bridge—high with water and whipped into foam—was luminescent in the sun. Here was spring—brilliant, revealing, promising. Its beauty had an ineffable cleanness and simplicity . . .

April 14 . . . On a day of swift-moving sunlight and shadow, Fred Beckman and I went out the Appalachian Trail beyond Dry Sluice Gap. Our objective was to take some photos of the Bunion area. The air was bright and sharp as we left Newfound Gap. Almost immediately we saw numerous juncos and a yellow-bellied sapsucker with red on its head and a blood-red patch on its throat. Through the trees we caught a telescopic glimpse of the Bunion. As I strode down the trail, I heard a beat of wings and looked up to see a ruffed grouse lunging through the trees in headlong flight. I could hear an off-beat when its feathers brushed twigs as it plowed through interstices too small to accommodate its body.

Soon the Bunion came again into view and I squirmed and twisted into a birch tree for photos. The midday sun highlighted the Bunion's rocky ribs as the ravines between lay in deep shadow. It has now been 30 years since the flood which ripped the forest cover from the Bunion area, and there is still no substantial healing. At this time of year fallen trees lie like jackstraws on the steep slopes. A little later in the season, the bare skeleton of the mountain may be softened by ferns. But not now. Those barren slopes are a raw appeal for conservation.

On this day the air was so luminous that each leaf and rock and bit of bark—each molecule—seemed like its own little sun. There was a glint and trembling scintillation in every view.

July 7 Recently we were shown through the laboratories at Oak Ridge. We saw the block of concrete housing the second oldest atomic pile in the world. Back of its unprepossessing façade—soundless and tremorless, where it would never be seen or touched or felt—was an elemental force so powerful and explosive that uncontrolled it could do vast damage.

By contrast, we went the next day to an area of infinite serenity and beauty in the Great Smokies. From the very acme of man's inventiveness and discoveries to the finest of untrammeled naturalness! We saw only two other persons. We saw deep-flowing, transparent streams. We could see the boulders and small weather-worn stones in their beds. The tiniest ripples sparkled. The deepest pools were a dim inviting emerald. The day before in Oak Ridge we had seen windows of amberglass 24 to 36 inches in thickness which revealed without distortion the interior of the hot cells. We had looked into the shimmering de-ionized waters of the swimming-pool reactor. Some said it was the clearest water they had ever seen. I wondered if they had ever seen the deep miracle of a pool in the virgin Smokies —natural, clear, and filtered through miles of undisturbed forest cover.

Our objective was Drinkwater Pool. The sky was overcast. High-altitude laurel mingling with rhododendron glowed pink from verdant banks. There was more water than usual at the Ramsay Falls. There was a labyrinth of massive rhododendron above the falls, in the mazes of which we searched for the old trail. We became entangled in a snarl of rhododendron and saw briers on a steep slope where a tree had blown over and carried the trail with it. No longer was the trail open and flat, offering detached vistas into the woods. Here it was a mere track, crowded by rhododendron. We weren't simply *in* the wilderness as we struggled through underbrush and twisted under blowdowns, or stood bewildered in a tangle from which the trail had completely disappeared; we were a *part* of the wilderness.

I found some familiar spots—the point where the trail follows a log to the end, drops off, bends to the left, and then goes under it. We found dangling twigs where we had broken green rhododendron out of our faces two years before. We came at last to a place where we fanned out, puzzled, and found not the slightest sign of human presence. Here the underbrush was less thick and we proceeded generally upstream over a tumbled surface of moss-covered rocks. Occasionally I kicked at the moss, thinking to mark our return.

We ate lunch at an old camping spot at the foot of the second cascade. The overcast became thicker. Gnats moved in. Ruth Ewald looked up and called our attention to mist wafting silently through the trees a couple of hundred feet above us. Then there were a few drops of rain. We finished eating, but no one suggested going back. Tripping over our ponchos and other rain gear, we rock-hopped the creek and started ascending the maze of boulders on the opposite bank. They were mossy and gave a false sense of security. Holes

Ramsay Cascades

"The water was . . . white with
deep-borne bubbles at the foot of a plunge."

opened between them and we had to move carefully. Our ponchos created more of a hazard than protection, and as the rain dwindled to an erratic drip, we took them off.

We moved toward the creek and bypassed the massive rhododendron thicket through which the trail once passed. The skies brightened, and taking a chance we piled our rain gear on a rock near the water, hoping we would not need it, and also hoping we would spot it on our return. Margaret's bright red rain coat and Ruth's yellow one stood out in the general green grayness of the stream bed. We made excellent progress. The banks were often open. Sometimes we followed a chain of boulders in midstream. The creek was steep. Once or twice I needed a boost to surmount a slick, perpendicular ledge. In several spots, where the creek flowed in a horseshoe, we found that the bears had cut across the neck, leaving a passable trail.

Drinkwater was but the culmination of a succession of limpid pools. It was framed by rhododendron which obscured the green darkness at the deepest point. The sun came out and I lamented having left my camera under a rock where we had eaten. This pool is most difficult to photograph and I had thought we would not reach it because of the rain. Actually we had some brief minutes of sunshine which were broken by onrushing clouds and a rumble of thunder.

We plunged headlong back down the great terraces of the stream, taking every shortcut we could, and reached our rain gear just as the shower broke. In the underbrush our ponchos provided little protection and soon we were as wet from side-swiping bushes as from the rain above us. Picking up our packs we plowed on through the brush, pausing once to admire the ethereal beauty of a purple-fringed orchis. What beneficence led it, year after year, to sprout and flower in this particular spot in the vastness of the Ramsay wilderness?

We experienced no difficulty finding the down-route, even though my glasses were so befogged and beaded with water I was often seeing three or four routes instead of one. My body was chilled as I pushed through the rain-soaked underbrush. My poncho was worse than useless—a clinging, tripping impediment which I finally stripped off. My clothing clung heavy and damp to my body.

On the previous day at Oak Ridge Anne and I had looked on the modern wonders of man from the outside, marveling but not understanding. This day we had looked upon the ancient wonders of the wilderness from the inside. With a thousand arts wilderness had reached out and touched every sense, making us a part of it. Wet, weary, and happy, and warmed by the beauty we had experienced, we returned to the familiar world of man.

A week later we went again to the wilderness. It was a wilderness of second-growth timber. There were no fire roads, no flossy trails. As soon as we left the cars, we were in the wilds. Wild things crept to the edge of the narrow footpath and the trail followed the natural contours of the slopes. Our objective was to take the Hiking Club to Slick Rock Creek, a mountain stream which marks the boundary between the states of North Carolina and Tennessee west of the Great Smokies.

This creek drained a huge watershed and we knew we had to wade. This, three of us had learned on the scouting trip a few weeks before. The most prodigious jump would never span the last swirl of water— no matter how plausible the string of boulders which appeared to point the way to a dry crossing. At a comparatively shallow spot we made our first crossing. Things looked easy and there was little we could do to help each other. But we found that Slick Rock was well named. I nearly went in, camera and all. We made it finally, wrung out our socks, and proceeded.

We came to the second crossing—the waters were more concentrated. We searched far downstream and far upstream for a better way. Always there was one stretch of water too wide for jumping, and too deep for dry-foot wading. After we had made the second passage it began to rain.

We pushed through an endless lane of young and vigorous growth along the old railroad grade, catching views of huge boulders and ledges, tumbling cascades and sleek pools. When we came to the third crossing several of the bigger fellows took positions in the creek and anchored the rest of us as we fought our way across. We then followed an arbor of blooming rhododendron to our lunch site—a huge quartz boulder which rose ten feet above the stream.

The cooling rain made us comfortable and we did not much care whether it rained or not. Debris and driftwood and the washed-out railroad grade were stark reminders that this roistering stream could become an unbridled flood. We were concerned at the massive build-up of clouds at the head of the valley. But the area was so remote, so utterly beautiful and so hard to get to, we dawdled. Some went swimming in a magnificent elongated pool. The water was inviting, and lacking bathing suits and being wet already, some went in with all their clothes on.

Then came a sharp crack of thunder which we heard even above the rush of the stream. Rain began to fall in huge drops—a mountain storm. Our concern for the crossings downstream mounted to anxiety. I rounded up as many of the crowd as I could and started back.

A small group went on ahead of us. When they came to the crossing, they could see that the water had risen a foot. It was not dingy and the stream was still in its banks. But it had become a great stream and several bypassed the first crossing, preferring to force their way down the stream through the heavy undergrowth.

I did not like the idea. The terrain was unknown; we knew there were cliffs. Although the creek presented more of a problem now, I felt it was still passable and if we could not cross again, in an emergency we could go cross-country and avoid the lower two fordings. Guy picked up a long pole to use at the swifter places. Henry Blosser went in as midstream anchor. I anchored the pole on the near side, standing ten feet into the stream from the bank.

The girls started the slippery, treacherous passage. No attempt was made to rock hop. Safety was the main factor. Midstream was hazardous but not too deep. It was waist-deep where the water swirled into the far bank. We learned to tread on gravel where it had collected below a boulder. But we could never see those unexpected potholes beside the boulders and I plunged deeply into one of them, bruising my knee as I went down.

The remainder of the crowd had now caught up with us and they too elected to cross. But we were concerned for those who had elected not to, and who might miss us lower down. Several times I walked out on a ledge which commanded vistas up and down. I saw no one. The opposite forest was dense and steep and my shouts were drowned by the noise from the stream.

One of the fellows carried the crossing-pole between the fording places. Martin Inman, huge and imperturbable, picked up a brake shoe and a piece of chain from the long-vanished logging operations to give him added weight as an anchor.

Finally we made contact with the others who had been paralleling our course across the stream. Dick Bagwell, in shorts, moustache, and felt hat, came down to the far edge. He could not hear my questions. We made signs.

The next ford was hazardous. I scouted down the creek where a screen of willows had grown in the water. The bed there seemed fairly shallow. The others came down. Martin sauntered in. Tryg and Alex followed. They found holes but they found a route. Again we anchored the pole and the water came up to the chests of some of the shorter girls. The crossing was heady and exciting. Even those who were a little afraid had smiles of excitement on their faces. I inched across hanging onto the pole—stepping into one hole—hoping my camera was still above water and finding that the current was deep and powerful under the far bank where it seemed that it should be shallow.

Finally we all stood safe and dripping on the bank, as the vanguard of the eight came in. We counted noses carefully. Only one was unaccounted for. We were fairly certain he had gone on ahead with Trygve to the lower crossing. And there we found him. The last crossing was bouldery rather than ledgy and was very treacherous. We found a longer pole and three fellows anchored it at the end. One joined Martin in the middle, who stood with his brake shoe and chain. He guided us to the bank. All got over safely, although one girl was taken off her feet by the current.

It was a memorable trip, similar to some of those we took 30 and 40 years ago. There was hazard in what we did, and the sharpest of excitement. We were in a remote area and on our own. No one knew precisely where we were; no rangers would seek us out. Danger and discomfort and excitement were shared together.

August 8 Every time I go to the mountains I tremble for their security. In April when we went up Big Laurel, we topped the low divide and came down the unforgettable Middle Prong trail. There we found denseness of growth and great space in surroundings, somehow blending into a unity. There was a wondrous amalgam of serenity and inspiration. One was both enspirited and at peace. Here was environment at its best.

A few hundred yards down the Middle Prong trail we came to that crass loop at the end of the administrative road which had penetrated thus far. A few more steps and we found drillings in the ledges of the road. These ledges were to be blasted out so those taking the nature trail hike could ride more comfortably to the beginning of their walk. What delicate beings we have become that we can't abide a little jolting even in what the Park Service denotes the atmosphere of wilderness.

On second thought, perhaps it is not the visitors the Service was afraid of jolting, but the machines in which they ride. Humans are much tougher than the machines they have made. It is the machines which groan and protest at the ledges. We pave the way not for people but for their creations.

In the process of blasting stones and ledges, much good earth, which had been eons forming and building up on these slopes, was disturbed and loosened. We happened along at the moment of the first hard rain. Ditches were already filled and the water was boiling into the roadway itself and merrily carrying away soil and loose stones from the underlying ledges. Will this new layer of exposed rock be blasted away? People who build roads and trails in mountains in dry weather should be required to walk them in rainy!

October 13 . . . When Bill Douglas and I started Sunday from Newfound Gap, although the prediction was for clearing, we set out on the Appalachian Trail in heavy, drippy fog. At Charlies Bunion the mist was thick and close and Bill took a few silhouettes against the background of the fog.

Anne went with us the first day. We came to rest at lunch time in the middle of the trail about a mile east of Dry Sluice Gap. We tarried only a half hour. Bill was getting cold, and Anne had to walk back to the car.

At the hairpin turn in the trail before reaching Laurel Top, the air suddenly became transparent and we looked hopefully through the trees. Low on the Tennessee side were glistening clouds hovering in the valleys. I hoped they would be fully broken away by the time we reached Flat Rock View and that we could see the vast expanses of the Bradley Fork. Slowly we plodded up Laurel Top. There were one or two false clearings in the mist before we reached that spot. There was quite a descent, steep and grassed over, between Laurel Top and the Bradley View where we were socked in again. But the vertical cliffs were evident.

Two hours later we made the long pull up to Hughes Ridge and reached the Hughes Ridge campsite about 5 p.m. The old Park Service shelter had been demolished in a fire.

It had not been raining, but firewood and the ground were wet. I got my ax, put my poncho over my pack, and went to work on a charred log. Bill remarked that the wood at the heart of the log would be drier. While I worked on this project, he surveyed things and suggested that he make a lean-to. He unraveled the rope that he used to tie up his sleeping bag, threaded a strand of this through my tarp, and lashed it to one of the bars used for a hitching rack. He took the ax, made stakes, and lashed the tarp to them. Then he laid his own tarp on the ground, moved in the sleeping bags and other loose ends. He remarked it would make a very satisfactory shelter if the wind did not change. The shelter opened to the west, and the wind was from the east and luckily did not veer through the entire night. Since the shelter was pitched on a slope I suggested installing a footpiece to rest our feet against in the night, and he scouted around and found a log and staked it in.

Meanwhile, with the aid of a little pitch pine and one of Bill's briquettes I had started a fire using but one match. We had cold fried chicken, hot cocoa, bread and butter, and then topped it off with pea soup.

We were in our sleeping bags by good dark. He slept restlessly. The next morning he told me the zipper on his sleeping bag had jammed and that he had slept cold. During the night the fog thinned and I could see the dim outlines of the moon. I was sure the weather was going to clear as predicted. But the moon came and went and the full clearing of the sky with pinpoint brilliance of the stars did not follow.

There was fitful dawn; the fog vanished at intervals disclosing the opposite ridge across the Bradley Fork. There was even some color in the east. But the weather was not settled.

Bill awakens all over, no drowsing, no sleepy hang-over, always a brisk "Good morning, Harvey," and the day began full steam the way I like. We had a good breakfast: oatmeal with Pream and sugar; bacon and bread and coffee, plus an apple left over from lunch. In the half sun, we tried to dry the damp spots on our tarps and sleeping bags. It was slow business and we finally despaired and packed up.

The clouds broke ranks as we neared Eagle Rocks and we looked across the wrinkled plain of the valley to the Cumberland Mountains. The near mountains were dark and clean under great blankets of snowy clouds. We rested in the sun and photographed the view which was both rich and spectacular.

Later at the conclusion of the long pull out of Copper Gap, we sat in the sun and ate lunch; but even as we ate, clouds slipped in and we proceeded in heavy mist. Somewhere on the slopes of Chapman we thought we heard a shout, but listening intently we heard only the call of a raven.

Eventually we came to the turn-off to Tricorner Knob and could see the shelter. As we mounted the terrace two birds with large red rump spots the size of a silver dollar flew up. I learned later they were probably juvenile or female crossbills. We had hardly got settled when we looked up and saw two hikers coming in under enormous packs—a doctor from South Carolina and his companion.

Bill took delight in starting a fire with one match. In starting six fires we struck only six matches. We had some persuaders—his briquettes and some rich pine I had, plus a couple of candle ends and the inspirator, which is simply a long rubber tube through which we could blow air to help the fire. About the tube he said, "That's a better invention than some of the things we grant patents for these days."

The next day on Hell Ridge we paused for a picture in the deep forest where the trail circled a knob on the Tennessee side. The hemlocks and birches were huge and ancient. Rhododendron and mosses massed along the trail.

"This is the most beautiful forest I have ever seen," Bill said.

$\mathscr{N}$INETEEN FIFTY-EIGHT

January 12   . . . the human race can surmount disaster. The human body may be soft—but it toughens quickly; and there is great inner resilience in most men. Let them see the inescapability of the challenge and men will toughen and respond. I don't know what the future holds; but in those for whom there is not quick disaster, I think there will be reasserted an unconquerable spirit. One shudders at the possible loss of accumulated cultures, of knowledge and the intricate interdependencies of a highly developed and integrated civilization; but man's spirit, assuming some of the race survives, will never be whipped. It is greater than environment, more doughty than all hardship, more resistant than death. Man's spirit is one with life—the great miracle of the earth and the universe. Where human life persists, man will remain unconquered.

There is a seeming contradiction here. The great engines can destroy individual beings and civilization. Because of their enormous potency, the engines seem greater than the natural being we know as man. But the engines exist only because of the union of great numbers of men in the enterprise of their development and construction. Thousands of men are back of one Atlas rocket—miners, chemists, physicists, metallurgists, pattern makers, mathematicians, laborers, concrete finishers, riggers, sheet metal workers, ceramists, electricians, and others. It is the product of a great common effort by individual men and their other machines. But for the work of countless men, an Atlas rocket is helpless and inert. At its best it has but one spasm of glory. Destroy that integration and the rocket is immobilized. Destroy important segments of that team of men, and those who remain immediately function as individuals.

Man with his sentience, spirit, nobility, and resoluteness is greater than all his engines. The latter may multiply his bad qualities—as they are the fruit of all his good qualities. They may also multiply his confusions and may seem to challenge order and man himself. But in challenging his order—the coherence of his civilizations—they are only challenging another of his creations. They are not, they can never be, a challenge to the indomitable will and stoutness of heart of the individual man.

If man as a species should be annihilated, all is not even then lost so long as there is life. Man over the eons evolved from something more simple. It would be possible for something as admirable, or even more so, to rise even after the destruction of civilization.

This is melancholy writing. But it is important in the face of the whirlwind to seize upon something firm and substantial. We are by no means certain that if we come to war there will not be incalculable destruction. It will level peoples, even as the wilderness leveled individuals in the early stages of civilization. War may not come. If it does not, it will be the first time in world history that preparedness for war has not ended in war. True, this will be a war of annihilation. It is also true what some farsighted folks know, as some knew when the last great war threatened, that no one could really win it.

February 12 On the weekend Anne and I went to the mountains. Because of the intense cold and the rains which preceded it I didn't know what the footing would be. We chose to climb toward Alum Cave, parking at the Grassy Patch.

Although many people were in the mountains they were not where we were. On the up-trail, by studying the tracks in the snow, we decided there was probably one couple up toward the cave.

The day was brilliant, with six to eight inches of snow. Filmy white whiskers covered the trees both in the sheltered valleys and on some of the higher peaks. I hoped for something of the sort at Alum Cave, if we should get so far.

The snow was squeaky firm. I loved to hear it protest, in musical notes, under my boots. I loved the clean stillness. It was the first time I had been on this trail since its relocation after the flood of 1951. At one spot the trail clambered onto a prostrate log and followed it for 30 feet. We have done the same thing back in some of the wilder parts of the mountains where falling trunks had crushed underbrush and limbs beneath. Here it was an effective means of bringing home some of the consequences of the flood to persons who had had no contact with that phenomenon.

We had gone about a half mile when we met a couple returning. As we talked to them we gathered that they had been to the Alum Cave, but soon we came to the place where they had turned around and there were no other tracks.

It was wonderful, to be uncrowded in such surroundings! The snow was clean, with almost none of the litter of twigs and bark and needles which accumulate so quickly after a gale or two. There was a crisp, green-toned transparency to the stream as it swirled around boulders which were encased in an inch of ice. The sky was a sharp, faded blue. And the air raked at our faces like a many-bladed knife. At first the breeze was from behind, but as we rounded a bend it bit into our faces. The rhododendron leaves were curled tightly and were drooping. Except where it had drifted, the snow was not over five or six inches deep; but on every overhang there were massive curtains of ice, wrinkled, tubular, and arrowy. The steps in the Arch Rock were partially covered with glare ice, and at the top where the snow had accumulated on the steps before the ice had formed there were no footholds. On these we dug in thumbs and heels in our scramble upward. As the trail leveled off there was a wall of ice on our right.

After we turned west across the creek, we found that the trail in a few places had drifted full of snow. There we moved with great caution, stamping for footholds into the outer crust with our heels. In places, the snow had crusted under the last thin fall and would bear our weight. In other places we broke through with each step and progress was erratic and laborious. In this area were massive red spruces straight as shipmasts and rugged old birches which softened the rigid ranks of the spruces.

We burst onto the point under an arbor of rhododendron, and the blanket of snow mercifully covered the marks of wear at this popular place. But for the broad openness of the trail, it was as clean and pristine as it was a thousand years ago. Here there was more variety than lower down. Dark ledges lying athwart the trail had soaked up enough warmth to melt the snow. We looked up the slopes to belts of white and of dusty gray. We even rested on one of the bare ledges but quickly found that a film of water was trickling down through its crevices. Looking into the main valley, we could see spotty snow under the forest. But a tiny north-facing side valley where the sun never hit was a gleaming, feathery white. There the sun had not melted the frozen fog.

Even in the sun the air was bitter. The ice walls were higher and the trail snow was knobby with great chunks of ice which had plunged from the cliffs high on our right and had become imbedded and iced in. Here we proceeded with the utmost caution. I had not been here since the Park Service had affixed cables for the benefit of nervous hikers. The snow and ice were so deep, I observed, that these cables were at the height of our knees instead of our waists.

Through the trees we could see icy stalactites hanging from the lip of the Alum Cave. These were melting loose in the sun and were plunging to the ground with sickening thuds. We had two frightening moments—as we passed directly under this jagged lip of ice into the safety of the cave, and again as we passed from under the cave at the upper end. The floor of the cave, which is usually deep with dust, was moist and hard-packed, possibly from snow which had blown in. I fancied I could taste the sharp tang of alum on my tongue. The smell of it was very plain. It was a grim and exciting place, this great deep overhang festooned with ice.

Beyond Alum Cave the ice walls spanned the overhangs from rock edge to the ground, forming chilly rooms through which one could easily pass. There was something savage about these frigid, translucent curtains of ice. We came to a north bend in the trail and looked out upon white-blue vistas of mountains through white-green frames of spruces. Here was a winter landscape of surpassing beauty.

Anne and I were happy to be alone in the cold cleanness. We looked up at the giant wall of Le Conte and realized we were perhaps the only beings on its whole south slope. We enjoyed the beauty and the glow of competence at being at home here despite the bitter cold and treacherous trail.

A few minutes later—just before turning back—we found vanes of fog a half inch broad and as thin as paper frozen onto high-bush huckleberries. Here was the most delicate and fleeting tracery of winter—or so I thought! A few minutes later, I stopped to examine a bundle of icicles under a little ledge. They formed a tiny grotto occupied by one pencil-thin cylinder of ice. Bristling out from this transparent pencil of ice were the first tiny spines of frozen fog.

It was the first time I had ever known fog to freeze onto ice. There was such witchery, such incredible fragility, I hardly dared to breathe. One stir of warmth and they would vanish into the air.

We sped down the trail in long strides, as the brittle crust broke under our weight. The sun was still striking the icicles of Alum Cave, and they were still dropping to the ground with an awesome roar. We made a cautious entry into the cave and an equally cautious exit onto the knobby ice beyond. Long shadows thrown by the sinking sun gave a new dimension of beauty to the trail and to the backdrop of mountains.

Down below Arch Rock the gloom of night was gathering, and shortly the blanket of darkness would drop softly onto the covering of whiteness which protected the living beauty of the Smokies.

February 24 We went to Rainbow Falls yesterday. The snow was deep, the rhododendron a rich green. We came rather unexpectedly upon the falls. There was the gray wall of the cliff over which it drops, and clean, white jagged icicles hung from the upper ledge.

The ice cone itself was screened by hemlocks. Then it appeared—truncated and jagged at the top, with a tremendous sprawling base of mixed ice and snow. In shape it appeared like one of those beehive ant hills in Africa. But in color it was a delicate icy blue. This color was unbelievable—almost luminescent, almost vanishing, but real enough in its subtle beauty.

It was cold; my forehead burned. There was hardly a trickle of water falling into the heart of the cone. We tried climbing the base. It was hard ice and the snow a treacherous film on top. We got over the first slope onto a kind of pedestal with better footing. Great chunks of ice had fallen from above and were strewn grotesquely on every side. One chunk, protruding at an angle from the cone, was itself covered with icicles and looked for all the world like the head of an arctic walrus.

The silvery folds of ice hanging from the south ledge had a curious, peppery appearance. We looked closely. Clinging to the ice were millions of elongated black dots—snow fleas. Some hikers who had never seen these tiny creatures before were unbelieving. But the fleas were alive, and jumped with all the agility of the better known species.

Despite all the ice and icicles and cold masses of white, there was a certain warmth to the scene. The cliff, although it was rimmed with icicles, overhung itself and was gray in color. The right slope was in warm sunshine, and although there was much snow the vertical faces of the boulders were free. In the glare from the sun there was a mottling of gray and white and tan where some of the vegetation and tree trunks stood clear.

I sat on a tree trunk from which the snow had melted. A network of twigs glinted with light and threw a twiggy cobweb between us and the rhododendron thickets on the far slope.

After lunch we worked up the foot of the cliff, slipping crazily on the melting ice, until we came to a notch where rock had chipped out and we were able to penetrate the cliff and make the top. Above the cliff deep snow prevailed and the going was treacherous in the jumble of jagged rocks. Several times I stumbled to my knees. We moved parallel to the cliff edge but well back for safety's sake. The stream, when we reached it, was almost frozen over. A few sable pools of the clearest water lay flat between rounded frames of snow. We worked slowly to the cliff edge, but dared not look over for fear the whole mass of snow would slough off, carrying us with it.

Our immediate surroundings were a frigid white; the mountains in the distance, a warm blue. Moving through screens of rhododendron deep in snow, we worked around the cliff on its shady side, lunging through drifts toward the fluted ice masses we had studied earlier. The sun by now shone boldly on the cone and the festooned ice masses clinging to the upper edge of the cliff.

The sun had softened the snow and ice on the base pedestal, but climbing on the cone was never easy. Once there seemed to be a rumble beneath us. We looked up, and wondered at the grip of the hanging icicles. It was not a safe place and we moved down the center of the stream bed, digging our heels deeply into the softening snow.

April 27 ... A group of us were gathered at Bob Maher's mountain cabin for a farewell dinner for the Ed Hummels. The discussion turned to the western balds in the Smokies, to their possible origin and to their possible future. If I interpreted Royal Shanks's remarks correctly, there *are* natural balds in the Smokies. They have been extended from time to time by man for various reasons—perhaps to enlarge the grazing area, to open up a vista for surveys, etc. Of course the grazing stock worked back into the timber and their impact may have weakened some of the fringe trees and certainly prevented the natural reproduction which would creep in at the edges. There may indeed have been some fires.

Old photos I have collected of these balds, dating from near 1900, show many stumps and some fallen tree trunks which clearly disclose that the balds were at various times much enlarged by man. It is unlikely that anyone knows their precise natural boundaries.

The astonishing thing is that grazing probably resulted in the fiery fringe of azaleas which encircles Gregory Bald. Randolph Shields says that there was no such fringe when he was a boy, and there is some evidence that it has kept pace with the withdrawal of grazing.

But the suggestion which impressed me most was Royal's thought that the balds perhaps after all represent a near timber-line condition. The theory is that in the Smokies occurs the junction of the northern conifers and the southern deciduous hardwoods. There is a constant imbalance due to weather changes. Somewhere in this area the weather becomes too warm for the conifers. They do not appear in any numbers beyond Double Springs Gap.[6] Similarly, the high crests are almost too cold or otherwise unfavorable for the spread of the hardwoods. Hence, if either conifers or hardwoods tend to occupy the no-trees-land of the balds they do so gingerly and without much conviction. If there should come a shift in temperature, it would tend to strike down or weaken the growth of the species most susceptible to that particular fluctuation. It was never really an occupation by either type, but only a patrol action which could quickly be driven back by a change in the long cycle of the weather.

Hence, natural balds occurred in this in-between zone and they may be the vivid evidence of the meeting place of two of the major temperature and growth zones on the entire continent. The concept adds an absorbing interest to all of western Smoky.

June 4 Recently I went to Le Conte, the first time, ever, that I had climbed it alone. I was not lonesome. On the other hand, I wonder whether I got as much out of the trip by going alone. Thinking is a solitary activity; but forming impressions is to some extent social.

I studied vegetational trends on the top of the mountain. Cliff Top, perhaps because it is not so well known as it was before the Park days, seems to be healing. There are now only one or two bare out-

---

[6] In 1966 a disjunct stand of spruce, numbering over 200 individual trees ranging from seedlings to several giants 34 inches, and one 38 inches, in diameter, was discovered on Miry Ridge six miles beyond Double Springs Gap.—H.B.

crops. On most of it the cliffs are now bound down with thick stands of *Rhododendron minus* and with great billowing tussocks of sand myrtle. The profuse bud and bloom of the latter lay like a faint scattering of pink and white snow. Myrtle Point is yet largely bare, although the burned area seems to have shrunk a little as the rhododendron and sand myrtle creep back.

But these places were the exception. I had hardly passed the stile at the top of the last long slope when I began to see stumps—a foot to fifteen inches in diameter. One never sees stumps in a wilderness, except in connection with a trail. These lay 50 and 100 feet and more from the trail. Up near the gap between Cliff Top and High Top, a two-wheeled vehicle had made deep ruts in the soft soil. It seemed to have been used in connection with sawing up or dragging timber from a large blowdown on the edge of High Top. The blowdowns were obviously being used for firewood and perhaps timber. There were few fallen trees. These were being cut for the lodge as soon as they fell. The result was grove-like openness to the summit which had taken from the mountain much of its former mystery.

Once it was an adventure to work one's way through the timber between Cliff Top and High Top. Now the network of wide trails through salvaged woods has punctured that delicate sense of wilderness. I remembered the dark, trailless forest, its trees in every state of vitality and decay, and the beckoning, unknown reaches of this mountain as it was 40 years ago. The stumps, the openness, the obvious trails all nicely point to the hand and previous presence of man. With these activities the mystery seemed to go out of this mountain. The shivering loneliness of a night vigil on the cliffs has been supplanted by tameness and the shelter of the cabins. Still primitive by all standards but those of 40 years ago, few of this generation can know what this mountain had lost.

However, there was some salvage in my day on the mountain— in hearing three times the song of a winter wren, and several times (once at the foot of the mountain and again on top) the spirited, spiraling call of the veery. Around Alum Cave I heard, both on the ascent and descent, the hoarse, not unmusical, croaking of three ravens. No longer, though, do the duck hawks whip around those naked cliffs. Have they gone forever, along with the unknowables of 40 years ago?

On my trip I passed trunk after trunk blown across the trail by the wind. They had been sawed through. Near Myrtle Point was a fallen balsam. It was about four and a half thumbs in diameter. The cross-section was smooth, almost polished. The tree had stood on an exposed point. It was 70 years old. Nearby, but in a more sheltered spot, was another balsam trunk, nearly seven thumbs in diameter and 70 years old. Its wood was rough and brittle, as though it had grown fast and had been wind-shaken before being wind-blown.

Down the trail were spruce stumps, one seventeen thumbs in diameter and an estimated 300 years old. I have been thinking of those 300 years. With careful counting, I could fix the exact growth ring for a particular year. What happened 300 years ago? I don't know anything much that was happening on the white man's calendar in this area. In 1658 Jamestown was just 50 years old and the Plymouth colony less than 40. This tree or at least its center core was living then. I felt a kind of awe. I wasn't living in 1658, but I was sitting beside something which had been.

This spruce had matured in a deep forest. Its tall, straight trunk (now prone) attested to that. The forest then was probably in all respects similar in size and quality. This tree could not spread—it had to grow upward. A forest was there 300 years ago—just like this, only infinitely wider. The country was too rough for deer and elk. There were a few bears which lived unknown to man, white or red. Nothing but eagles had ever flown over it. No man had ever looked down upon it, and none probably had ever looked up to it. There were no paths—no stumps—simply a blanketing, forested wilderness stretching in every direction over the rock-and-soil frame of the earth.

Two hundred years ago almost to the day—and I found the ring that marked it—the first English settlement in the area, about 50 miles away at Fort Loudoun, was being wiped out by the Indians. This tree was already a hundred years old when the massacre occurred. Fort Loudoun was not much of a settlement. With exhausting labor, men had dragged a few cannon over the ranges from Charleston and had built a palisade, some rude buildings. They had brought a few women and children, and established white ways in the vast wilderness of the red man.

They lived off the country—turkey, bear, and deer. They cut their own wood and built their log huts from the forest which stood about. The wilderness marked them more than they marked the wilderness. And yet it was a beginning. They brought the ax and the gun, and probably fashioned the wheel to roll behind their horses. Their advent was something new, hardly noticeable—only a small cloud arising out of the sea like a man's hand. Following the massacre of that year, the cloud disappeared for a time beneath the horizon. But it was always lurking beyond the horizon and next appeared in more disturbing form from the north.

My own people were molecules of that boreal cloud. John Adair came to East Tennessee in the 1780's, when that fallen tree had added 30 more rings. It was already 130 years old. He lived until 1829, and the tree survived him by 130 more years. His 40 years in the area were sandwiched between full centuries of living of this tree.

The tree was old and still undisturbed when Washington gave his farewell address. Wolves and foxes and panthers roamed unfettered through the mighty forests of which it was part.

June 23   From the turn of the trail on Fork Ridge to Gregory Bald we were hardly out of the sound of the veery. Its two-toned call had a bewitching, spirited quality. And for the first time I heard a kind of guttural tone at the end of the call, as though the glorious, strident notes were a little frayed at the end.

On top I became more interested in the ecology of the azaleas than in the colorful displays. In two years there had come a notable influx of seedling trees into the former bald area. The fringe of trees had deepened. Several times I had the experience of looking down a vista and seeing azaleas now almost lost in the trees, which I sensed must have been on the edge of the bald as I last remembered it.

Seno, with memory-provoking poesy in her write-up about the hike, said we might hear bells near the top beckoning us to come on up. It has been twenty years since I heard them on the animals which used to graze up there. Those bells possessed a quality of music and highland charm, a mingling of the primitive and the domestic.

But the bells are no more, and the animals who wore them are no more. It was they who trampled out the balds and widened their boundaries. It was they who made woodlands of the forests. And now the forests are surging back—overleaping the azaleas and spotting the bald with trees. I continue to believe that Gregory Bald may have had natural boundaries. Nobody knows just where they were. But twenty years have drawn the noose of the woods tighter around this upland meadow. Most of the galled spots are healing. Grass has crept into them, although the eroded circles are still discernible. White pines are spotted all over, and the end is not in sight.

The area around the lean-to had a littered and used appearance. Horse use has deepened the muddy trough which serves as a trail between the lean-to and the main ridge.

Just below Gant Lot—once so open, and now closed in until it is simply the crossing point of two wide trails—was a lone purple orchis. This orchis has a fragrance so fleeting Guy says you can catch it but once.

It is now considered safe to eat the green-yellow galls which form on the azalea plants. It was five years ago that I first learned this from Dr. Marcovitch. The knowledge has now got around. Prejudice has evaporated and many were eating them for moisture. Knowledge of the good qualities of the galls has spread into a former area of ignorance—almost as the trees have infiltrated the bald.

Three miles below the bald, the duff around the big tulip has been pulverized by visitors who stand by it for photographs. The duff has washed away, leaving only compacted mineral soil on its upper side. I wonder how long this great tree can survive such treatment.

October 21   The trip up Walker Prong added another page of fact about the 1951 flood. The lower creek was flat and open—possibly because of the October level of the water. We hiked easily—sometimes along a succession of stones, with water on the outer curve where the creek made a bend. Like a baseball player, stretching a two-bagger into a triple, the creek would run wide when it was high. The outer bank was its flood plain. When the water was low it kept to channel on the inner side of the bend. Thus, to move dry-shod and to avoid overhanging rhododendron we wove back and forth, leaping the water and sometimes splashing into it where a dense accumulation of leaves in a pool gave an illusion of solidness.

In one lazy pool a pattern of bubbles had formed in striking symmetry, like the movement of iron filings drawn across a blueprint to a magnet. But here the bubbles were expelled from the little cascade at the head of the pool rather than drawn to it.

This open aspect of the stream, framed in the rhododendron which has moved healingly to its two edges, abruptly changed when we came to the stream's fork. The right fork was even more closely held by the overhanging rhododendron and by green banks of dog hobble. But the left fork—our route—had disgorged great tree trunks into the junction, and beyond there was a broad bed of scoured ledges and banks which had been chiseled clean to the height of a man on either side.

It was plain from the state of decay of the old trunks and the recency of the healing that this had been caused by the celebrated 1951 cloudburst, the effects of which I have been studying over the years. Here was a new dimension.

We followed quickly up the left fork for 300 yards and then found the bed almost blocked by debris which had poured from a steep hollow to the left. Great slabs and chunks of slate had been torn out and left in chaos at its foot. Trees were piled like jackstraws in two spots. The left hollow had been too narrow for its load, which had broken over a slight rib of rock and had poured down another ravine which emptied 50 feet farther upstream. Normally streams converge as they flow downward. This one had been so loaded it broke its normal bounds and spread its burden in two-pronged chaos into the larger stream. From the evidence, this flood had accumulated fifteen feet deep in a tiny hollow no more than a half mile long. We were tempted to climb it to the crest of Anakeesta, but looking down on it from above three hours later, we saw its beginnings in sheer gray cliffs.

Beyond this violent junction the main stream was narrow and overgrown. Some of the boulders were even mossy. Again we had found one of the outer limits of the cloudburst of 1951. We followed the stream which had been spared. It was good to be climbing again in the spruce-fir zone of open, mossy woods—interlaced at intervals with tangles of viburnum and briers.

We sat on the mosses in a spot of sun on a steep forested cone and had our lunch. We speculated on the violence of the flood. The damage had started like a snow slip, sliding into the hollow where the converging waters reached a terrifying momentum—carrying out forest, undergrowth, boulders, and flakes of slate as large as a table. The roar of the water, the crunching boom of the boulders, and the paralyzing sight of a forest upended and pouring down that ravine would have been stupefying. One would have been petrified by the sight of a seething tangle of water, boulders, and trees. The very earth would have been fluid, pulling like an undertow at the feet of anyone caught on the ridge. There would have been no place to hide. The wise would be content to leave as a secret of nature the terrifying spectacle of a dissolving forest.

We are told that the eastern highlands were once twice as high as they are today. Their rounded outlines indicate age-long weathering. The forests are old, but the forest cover is periodically torn asunder and washed downward. The ravines are ground a little deeper and the debris deposited farther down the valley. Periodically, and oh so slowly, the forests spreading outward from untouched remnants creep again into those hollows and ravines, heal them over with a mantle of life, and supply the illusion of age and stability.

And we know that these phenomena of change which seem so cataclysmic in the limited span of a man's life are, on the calendar of the ages, but pulsations in the unending interplay of force and life. The forest draws back fleetingly from the terror of the flood—but irresistibly, life creeps again over the ravaged scars. And so the earth is shaped; and so, also, life has its way:

> There rolls the deep where grew the tree.
> O earth, what changes hast thou seen!
>   . . . . .
> The hills are shadows, and they flow
> From form to form, and nothing stands;
> They melt like mist, the solid lands,
> Like clouds they shape themselves and go.
> —TENNYSON, "In Memoriam," CXXIII

NINETEEN FIFTY-NINE

January 18   A couple of nights ago I wrote a little piece about the coziness of a tight house and wood fire on a bitter wintry day. Perhaps my picture was too bland. For yesterday, on one of the coldest days of the winter, 8°, we felt we had to go to the mountains. Driving involved icy roads and a very cold car. We did not suffer from either, and what we endured would have been a small price for what we saw.

There was three or four inches of snow in the woods. No one had been down the path to the stream. The sun's rays sparkled on the billows of snow. Tiny tracks threaded the surface, stitching together equally tiny burrows. What errands took these little creatures out of their cozy havens under the snow to produce these exquisite tracks? They were like the ornate stitches found on old samplers. I used to think these were the tracks of tiny birds. But the round openings, where these tracks began and ended, proved to me I was mistaken. I suppose they were made by shrews or tiny wood mice.

Of one thing we were sure. There were no human tracks. The trail lay stark and white in the slanting sun with slight unevennesses casting delicate shadows. At the Chimneys parking area we were the first to step onto the even white velvet of the footbridge. The water was rolling beneath us, not over its customary bed of boulders and gravel, but over buttresses and bolsters of green-tinted ice! A few channels had been opened where the water was swiftest, but for the most part the water slipped over a bed of ice.

The Road Prong had more ice and fewer breaks. The familiar

terraced ledges were there but they were raised and rounded by emerald ice. The rhododendron thickets were bowed with snow, their leaves rolled into tight scrolls. Cold and the snow's light magic had transformed the grandeur of the forest from a shadowy green to a lustrous white.

The air gnawed at our faces and my fingers became numb as I worked at the dials of my camera. I hung a thermometer on a rhododendron, and we stamped back and forth as the mercury slid lower and lower, to a chilling 10°F.

At the first crossing of the creek, the ice extended out in massive, thick shelves from the banks. Boulders were capped with derbies of the lightest snow. Did they conceal tight-fitting undercaps of glistening ice? I remembered this crossing on another occasion, when a transparent skin of ice covered these boulders and several hikers slipped on the ice, banging their knees and slipping into pools before they knew it. We dared not leap from boulder to boulder. We pushed up the bank through the rhododendron, dislodging a powdering of snow down our backs—snow so light and dry I could blow it off my camera.

High water and the ice bed had raised the stream. There was water where I had never seen it before. A new pool, 60 feet across, was glazed with ice. Water was flowing across it in a serpentine channel eighteen inches wide. In another pool the current bubbled up like a spring through a hole in the ice, flowed clear for about five feet, and then was sucked beneath in a slowly revolving whirlpool. I crossed on a log below the revolving pool but could not see what became of the funneled water. Snow lay on the ground, on the trees, on the twigs, on every leaf, on every bit of vegetation—light and bright in the searching sun.

I pondered the phenomenon of the bed of ice over which the water was sliding. There seems to be only one explanation. Several near-zero spells have occurred since the first of the year. The last was less than a week ago. The stream must have slowed and turned to ice. Then came a swift warming and an inch of rain. It poured off the still frozen woods onto the ice, producing these fantastic scenes. Then came a second savage freeze, when the rain turned to snow. And the brown green of the woods was again covered with the lightest of gleaming blankets.

This was living! Joseph Wood Krutch says most people cannot assimilate the Grand Canyon. They watch it for a few moments and then turn away. One must live with it for days before he achieves the slightest understanding. So, with this rareness in January, with beauty clean, pristine, and very cold. The bitter temperature that slashed our faces had also produced these fantasies in ice and snow. We turned away. We could stand just so much of the beauty and cold. But we had lived profoundly for a couple of hours in the bittersweet of a mid-January day.

May 31   Have felt grievously the need for a trip to the mountains. I have been stale and indecisive. So today I decided to go to Le Conte alone in the middle of a period of rain brought on by *Arlene*, the season's first hurricane. It was raining when I left home.

At the Wears Cove turn-off, Woolly Tops and Laurel Top and Brushy broke through the clouds, but the white curtain of a mountain rain formed between them and moved west. The clouds were in tempestuous movement below Balsam Top, and in the draw between it and Bull Head. A more awesome sight of clouds I have seldom seen. The rains had weighted the limbs of the trees along the road shoulders, and the road was an avenue through a dark tunnel of green. Few views, few prospects—just the overwhelming density of a semitropical forest.

I parked at the Grassy Patch. The shower beyond Brushy had spread across the mountain and it started to rain. The forest seemed enormous, brooding, and very damp. I had gone only a short distance when I saw a dark form hurtle through the downpour and come to rest on the vertical trunk of a birch. As it started hunching up the tree I saw a gleam of red—it was a pileated woodpecker. Then out of nowhere, out of everywhere, came the exultant, cheery, rippling song of the winter wren. The forest lost its aloofness. Again it was a place of life; rain or shine, it was home to these inimitable birds. Rain seemed to have not the slightest effect upon them. Rain seems to affect only humans.

I rounded a bend and saw across the creek a flash of magenta, the first of a wondrous display of *Rhododendron catawbiense.* As I got higher the color lay along every exposed ridge, like fingers which had been dipped in pigments. This rhododendron has none of the fiery brilliance of the azalea, but against the rich greens of the evergreens and under the subdued influence of the rain it seemed that the whole mountain had gone to bloom.

I listened to the creek—to the incessant movement—the splashing

—the crystal current swirling around the boulders and ledges. For a moment it was as though I was hearing it for the first time, as I had over 40 years ago. I was a boy again, and was hearing it again as a new sound, softly appealing and mysterious. Sometimes it pays to hike alone.

At Inspiration Point the magnificence lost all restraint. The claret buds of laurel burst wide and innocent, rain-cleansed and fresh—a blast of color against the massed fog in the valleys. Here I paused. One loses his sophistication before these lavish, fleeting canvases of beauty. I know of no one who is not stirred. We try desperately to preserve the picture in our minds and hearts, and on film, against the fading which will come. It is this impermanence—the anomaly of beauty too fragile to last—which makes spring so poignantly sweet. It invites us to the table like an old friend; and yet, as we watch, the feast shrivels and fades. We lose something precious and go back to the marts and shops for another year. How can one capture such beauty? Its invitation and charm are personal. No man can resist it. But it is as ephemeral and fleeting as the security man covets for himself and deludes himself into believing he has.

I climbed on up to the Alum Cave through air heavy and musty from the ivory blooms of dog hobble. I had heard the throaty cries of ravens around the cliffs and thought of the changing voices of boys turning into men.

Here I found people—a family of five coming down, and two young women also descending. The man was a hearty sort who had reduced the subtleties of this lovely climb to statistics. So many hours to go up—so many to come down. He had put the vastness and beauty and mystery of wilderness into a form he could understand. On the morrow he would no doubt boast of the time it took to hoist his family 3000 feet to the summit of the mountain and of the lesser time for the descent.

He might or might not remember to tell of the extravaganza of bloom, responding to the warming rains under an arching cover of fog and carrying the dual freshness of its new-born glory and of the tremulous raindrops. I know that he had come to see this. He charged his teen-age boys, speeding on ahead, to stop down where the flowers were. It was a bit too overwhelming to ingest. It left him, and all of us, baffled and exalted by turns. But it was too intangible for his workaday world—something desirable but something having no price.

What have the organization of man into a society and the assembling of the desiderata of existence into a conventional wisdom done to man's soul? Work he must, to exist. But slave, he need not. "Consider the lilies of the field, how they grow; they toil not, neither do they spin: and yet I say unto you, that even Solomon in all his glory was not arrayed like one of these."

And so, slightly rebuffed by the statistical heartiness, I trudged on through the dust of Alum Cave to the freshness which lay beyond. Above the cave there were no massive concentrations of color; but there were large individual shrubs here and there which livened the boskiness of the forest under the low-lying clouds. I marveled at the rain-wet perfection of each cluster of blooms. They were like the face of a beautiful girl—just coming into maturity. Here was youth and beauty, absolute. No lines of care—no tattered petals—no fading of color. Just the beauty of perfection—fresh-born.

It was in this area that the silence was shredded by the chorded, spiraling notes of the veery. The sound seems to wind about in the canopy of the trees. It belongs to the deepness of a noble forest.

Above Alum Cave I had the whole mountain to myself. The trail skirted across the Hole-in-Rock ridge—now almost indiscernible. On my first trip in the area, in early September 1922 with John Deatherage and Bill Tadlock, we had beaten our way down from the top of Le Conte armed only with a very general understanding, supplied by Wiley Oakley, of the location of Alum Cave. There was no trail above the cave. We stayed on the rib of the ridge as far as Echo Point. Below that the rib divided into three prongs. The cave was under the east one. We got onto the west one, a bare, rocky, knife-edged promontory with some sand myrtle—much like the Chimneys. We were near enough to see the Grassy Patch cabins a mile away and 1500 feet down, but hadn't the slightest notion of the location of Alum Cave. Wiley Oakley was following us with a small party. We called and called. Ultimately we could hear their voices coming weakly, out of space. We shouted, "Where is the cave?"

Faintly the answer came back, "Here—over here."

Finally we divined that Wiley's voice was coming from the far side of another bare ridge, the middle one of the three ribs.

We clawed our way back through the rhododendron and saw briers; felt rather than saw the pitch of the intervening ridge; tore our way to the top of it and saw a heartbreaking cliff beneath us. We started inching down, hanging on to small shrubs. One of these gave way and I skidded completely out of control before slamming against some rhododendron. (This ridge we had crossed so precariously is now known as Hole-in-Rock ridge.) We fought our way down through enormous rhododendron to the center of the hollow and found the well-defined Alum Cave trail coming up from Grassy Patch.

We were so famished for water we turned down this trail to the creek, rather than up to the cave, and took it in great, leaping strides. Suddenly a huge prostrate tree trunk loomed across the trail. There was no time to stop. I leaped into the air, hurdling the tree completely, and luckily landed on my feet below. We caught up with Wiley and his party at the creek. In those days of pre-1927 and 1951 floods and of undug trails, the spot where the path came down to the creek was the most beautiful I had ever seen. After drinking quantities of water and after a bit of lunch we went back up the trail to Alum Cave. It was only after we had visited this shrine that we continued our great circle down the stream, down past the upper settlements around the west end of Le Conte and back up from the Sugarlands to Cherokee Orchard.

The present trail to Le Conte via Alum Cave bypasses the steep climb to Echo Point. The great laurel along the bypass is huge, and the ridge for a short stretch is level, providing a number of pleasant places to recline and relax.

I have the distinct recollection of discussing with Uncle Henry ("Prof") Essary the possibilities of converting the then privately owned Smokies into a national park. I recall that he was pessimistic. On that descent of Le Conte with John and Bill, I related my conversation with Essary as we rested in the great laurel. Well, Uncle Henry was wrong, and how glad he would be that he was!

By coincidence I met Marcovitch on the street today and he recalled the trip to Le Conte with "Prof" Essary in 1922. He remembered that when we worked our way out to what is now known as Myrtle Point, the top of Le Conte was so untrailed that we had to nick blazes into the trees to find our way back to Cliff Top.

"That was the best trip I ever had," he said.

He remarked about the changes that have taken place—the roads, the lodge on Le Conte—and finished, "It'll never be like that again."

November 16 We awoke about 7 a.m. It was damp and cold although not raining. We decided to shake off our five months' preoccupation and hike. We dressed warmly. It was overcast all the way to Cades Cove although we noticed a momentary brightening as we drove up Laurel Creek. I predicted we would hike into the clear. And we did.

We were thinking of our last trip up Anthony Creek. There was the bridge where we had posed once in rain gear—the slope which was white with trilliums—the old house site where I found a ground tapestry of violets and dead grass—the old tree which had fallen across the trail from which I trimmed a limb—the slopes of galax and arbutus and the open copse near the white pine where we had eaten. It was almost as though we were reliving our earlier trip. But not quite. *Then* we were moved by the beginnings of spring. *This day* we were faced by the threat of winter.

But it was only the prospect of winter—not its cold-fingered reality. I removed my jacket, my gloves, my hat. I felt the warm embrace of the sun and relaxed. The air was fragrant with the smell of damp leaves. At one of our stops, my eyes rested on the ground and I tried to visualize the forest about me by studying the litter at my feet. There were the curious single-winged hooks of the tulip seeds, and the four-finned cylinder of the silverbell. I wondered why they were finned so evenly along their length. I tossed one into the air several times in order to observe its fall. I could come to no conclusion. Normally wings and devices of this sort aid in the dispersal of the seeds. The spinning of the tulip seeds carries them away from the tree. But the longitudinal wings on the nut-like fruit of the silverbell tended to bring it into a vertical path. Perhaps if I saw one fall from its tree, I would see it differently.

We edged on, coming upon a curiously open and very pleasing woods which was free of both laurel and rhododendron. Though steep, one could tramp it at will in any direction. It was there that the trail was littered with the brown leather of the mountain magnolia leaves and the great, round, heavily veined, and almost transparent leaves of the linden. I have always admired the marvelous title of one of Burroughs's books—*Locusts and Wild Honey*—and I wondered if there were names which could be gleaned from our forests which would have the same appeal. To myself I tried out such euphonies as *Sarvis and Red Maple*, thinking how the cold white fire of the one and the red flame of the other kindle the colors of spring. I thought of *Sarvis and Green Laurel; Silverbells and Wild Grapes; Lindens and Mountain Magnolias; Arbutus and Shiny Galax; Veeries and Winter Wrens*. I rolled these over my tongue and listened to their inaudible melody. Did any have the charm of *Locusts and Wild Honey*? I thought not.

We shuffled on into the area of trailing arbutus and galax. Some of the mountain people call the galax "coltsfoot," in a vivid reference to the shape of its leaves.

By now we were near the crest of Bote Mountain and we could look down upon the world we had left behind. Down along the straight barrel of the valley we had climbed, we could see the yellow-brown of the floor of Cades Cove bright with sun. But beyond the blue range of Rich Mountain we could see the white blanket of clouds which had flowed through the Chilhowees at Walland Gap and had spread widely into Tuckaleechee Cove. There was the cold front! We could see its front line and its extent. It had clearly been slowed by the Cumberland range, but it was inching forward and would catch us before the day was out.

The gentle warmth and balmy languor of the day were autumn's outpost and would be overwhelmed by the legions of winter before we could return. As we topped the crest and looked over toward Wears Cove and Round Top, we saw more fleecy cloud layers spreading silently among the ridges. The winds which were booming through the naked forest would sweep in the winter. But while winter was advancing we sat on grass under the shelter of a laurel bush and enjoyed autumn's last stand. The sun was warm, the sky brilliant, the high clouds light and ephemeral. Only the wind and those silent cloud masses seeping into the broad valleys below were a threat.

We climbed on steeply and with some fatigue. But eventually the massed laurel thinned out and broke into clumps. Broad sods of grass appeared and we emerged upon Spence Field, which I had first trod through an impenetrable fog on the Easter weekend 37 years before.

There was a time when Spence Field was as close-clipped as a lawn and when its fringe of trees was well defined. Then there were galled spots where the grazing animals had eaten too closely and the rains had gullied through the turf leaving bare patches of mineral soil. Today these gullies and bare patches are healed except in some of the trails, which are poorly drained. The sod is long, tough, and matted. Off the trail one sinks into it and it is so long one trips on overlapping tendrils of creeping vines. Small saplings and laurel clumps are edging in. We noticed two small white pines. I cannot even hazard a guess whether the trees will take over or whether some ecological quirk will keep open these grassy balds for an indefinite time.

That day Spence Field itself bore the aspect of winter. Trees were bare and the grass was brown and lifeless. But the skies were intermittently clear and there were moments of warm sunshine. Then the clouds would whip in and blot out the high slopes of Rocky Top and Thunderhead. What a gray, impervious mass they were. Just as quickly they would blow clear and the blackness would give way to sunshine.

We sat out of the wind in deep grass just below the rounded crest, and watched the play of color and shadow on the Tennessee side. The streaming clouds, which had overflowed the lower valleys and which from our vantage resembled the waters of a lake, had not increased. We surmised that the cold wave had not been able to top the Cumberland range in any volume.

We had rather expected to see Lionel Edney and Dickerman on top. They had left earlier and were ascending by a longer route. We assumed they had already reached Spence Field and had probably moved on to Thunderhead. In the intervals when that mountain was clear, I would call out. My voice would bounce back with almost explosive impact from the first steep slope beyond the field. But my own voice and the mounting rush of the wind from the south was all that I heard. It was almost frighteningly lonely up there on that vast mountain—where there were no voices but ours and where our shouts were quickly ripped into silence by violent gusts. And yet, that heightened feeling of aloneness, of being the only persons on the mountain, sharpened our senses and deepened the experience. We had come for this brush of wildness on the high mountains and we had a feeling of ancient contentment.

$\mathscr{N}$INETEEN SIXTY

March 9   This has been a winter of surprises and extremes. Another heavy snow, the heaviest of the winter and one of the heaviest in local history, fell last night and this morning. It measured twelve inches on the level, up to fifteen inches on old snow, and eighteen inches in small drifts. We had not seen the last of the ice from the freezing rain of a week ago, when this fresh blow fell. Our poor hemlock at the entrance has for six days been manacled to the ground by ice. Yesterday Anne loosened its bindings, and today it was down again. It sprang up a little when I knocked the snow off a few minutes ago. But it is still deeply bowed.

We had visitors today, driven in by the snow. Most exciting was a fox sparrow with a rufous tail and brick-red side markings and dark gray patches on the head.

March 12   January ended with a slight excess in the average temperature for the month. Since then the excess has disappeared and the accumulated deficit 40 days later is $303°$. Today also the temperature has been below the average.

It is only as man has been able to overcome the rigors of the natural world that he has been able to develop a wide culture. The experiences of the last ten days emphasize the tenuousness of our dominance over the earth. It would not take many more days like the last few to set us back on our heels.

And so, a rough winter, inordinately extended as this one has been, becomes a personal malevolence. It upsets our accustomed manner of living, and we resent it. Perhaps we should welcome it. For it demonstrates that living, the boon of life, is the all-important thing; and that manners and customs, important as they may seem, are secondary. Life alone is paramount. This we see as the birds swarm in to the feeding trays—little oases of life—when winter covers the earth and shuts off the life lines of food.

May 10 Sunday afternoon Anne and I went to Andrews Bald. The day had dawned clear, but it didn't last. Clouds lightly touched the top of Le Conte. At Collins Gap I noticed a peculiar grayness in the trees and became aware that trees near the gap were encased in ice. Freezing rain on May 8! At Forney Ridge a gale was blowing.

It was dead winter on the trail along an exposed ridge section flanked with small trees and old blackberry briers. We saw two species of hobble bush in bloom, quite a few violas, a small patch of bluets and one trout lily. Several trilliums were either in bud or had had their buds frozen. Birds were scarce. There were a few juncos, a grouse, and the tune-up of a winter wren.

I had forgotten the tight growth of the evergreens down at the gap where the trail diverges to Forney Creek. There was gloom in the air and the trail was covered with twigs of spruce and fir which had been snapped off in a recent gale. My ears tingled and my chin smarted and I walked with my hands tucked up into my mittens. I dreaded the bleak openness of the bald, and when we reached it we huddled on the grass in the lee of a young spruce and ate sausage and rye bread.

This trip amidst such austerity emphasized again the essential loneliness of man's circumstance on this planet. Tiny creatures crawling over an isolated orb in limitless space! Whitman grandly confronted these shows of day and night. But the average of us could hardly bear to do so, alone. Only the warmth somehow generated by mankind's collective response to his environment relieves this numbing loneliness. Hunger and cold drive man into a pattern of activity which relieves the fright in his soul. Only the philosophers and persons pondering the great mysteries in the twilight of their lives see the sparseness of human existence.

On the return, tiny pellets of snow rattled against our clothing. One by one they fell to the earth. One by one they filled the voids between the leaves. Little by little the woods turned from brown to gray, and from gray to white. Each first pellet could scarcely be seen. Their numbers increased and the woods seemed to change into something they had not been before.

Society and the rules which men enact to govern their contacts with their fellows are often engrossing and seem to represent the end of living. But under this structure of living is the thin-skinned earth, and beyond its surface the hollowness of space. Sympathy and cooperation generate warmth—something which few remember as man forges his weapons and spies on his fellows.

May 15 ... On the last weekend Dickerman, Chaffin, and I went over a portion of the Cherokee Forest with Supervisor Gil Stradt and his ranger, L. C. Nix. There was richness in the dense and lovely vegetation and in the clear water. We had sweeping views which unrolled from the vantage of two fire towers. Here was the promised land in the soft greenness of spring and in the faded blues of distance. From the grassy cone of the Hemlock Lookout, which I had last visited nineteen years ago, the prospect was one of unbounded forest. Only toward the northwest did we see the faint yellowing and striping of the fields of men. Otherwise the richness of unbroken forest was draped over the frame of the earth, and it seemed good and inviting and full of promise. We saw the art of the foresters where they had sought to heal the scars of logging and road building. Raw slopes were grassed in, and there were greenness and health over the land. But even this goodness did not destroy the record of a richness that was gone.

Out of the square miles that we toured, there was a single primeval island (a quarter of a mile square), a remnant of the original forest which had been clipped from the slopes 40 years ago. The trees in this island were 300, 400, 500, probably 600 years old. There were wild cherries over three feet in diameter; hemlocks nearly five feet; silverbells 24 inches across; and sugar maples, birches, an ash, tulips, buckeyes, and a linden.

This enclave of the primeval may be the last tatter outside the Smokies of the great southern hardwood forest. There was more rich variety in these few acres than I have seen in an area of equal size anywhere in America. There were towering trees which drew the cover of their crowns over deep spaces beneath. Rhododendron and leucothoë grew lushly. There were more bluets than I had ever seen— breath-taking lavender carpets. There were violets, phlox, dogwoods in high-level profusion, and the white and bronze redness of the sarvises. The earth was velvety soft with humus a foot or more deep.

We stopped the car and walked across the boundary from the tautness and competition in the young woods into the stately calm of these ancient trees. It was a tiny island of 160 acres, left from the boundless forests of the Cherokees.

We looked at a two-foot stump which stood beside the road. On it were growing bluets, violets, moss, a fern, a rhododendron, dog hobble, a small hemlock, a seedling birch, and a silverbell two feet high. Such a demonstration could occur only here, where parent stock of so many species flourished nearby. Their seed carpeted the earth. The richness of the surroundings was highlighted by this stump. Here was the forest in miniature on six square feet of stump.

Reverently we walked through and looked up at the trees from beneath. We ascended a ridge, and from a cliff looked down on them from above. There was no mistaking it. There was subtle variety in the crowns, contrasting sharply with the obvious uniformity of a younger forest. There was an unevenness and softness of texture in this patrician remnant of the great forest. Here was life in all its variety and in all its stages, from the tiny seedlings we had seen below to the hoary old giants upon which we were now looking down.

All the thoughtful husbandry of man could not duplicate this rich remnant forest of the untutored trees. Leopold said the outstanding discovery of the twentieth century is not television or radio but rather the complexity of the land organism. We think we are progressive because we try to assuage the excesses of our immediate past, by grassing raw slopes and "managing" our forests. Only those who know the most, said Leopold, know how little we know about the intricate complexities of a healthy forest. A walk through this gorgeous protraction of the past left a hollowness in my soul; and the justification of "multiple use" for the great road which will divide it seemed but a hollow incantation.

June 14 After 60 or more trips to Le Conte, I sensed again, as though for the first time, the exhilaration which goes with the thin air a mile and a quarter up and the grand mystery of wind ripping through a concealing fog on top of the mountain.

I have never wanted to leave Mt. Le Conte. There is a pointedness to every experience. The world of business and of tense endeavor is absent. The mountains are dominant.

This was the second weekend of June. It is the best weekend for the sand myrtle. What an overwhelming sight it is—this rich pink and white blanket of blooms draped over the dizzying slopes of Cliff Top. What a juncture of stoutness and beauty—all held close, often in a pervasive fog. What expectation for the thinning in the mist which never came!

One of Harvey's famous hiking hats, affectionately
called *disreputable* by some hiking friends.

There are more big stumps on Le Conte. Maybe the trees had died or were forced out of plumb by the winter snows and storms. But there were more new stumps, and the grove-like appearance extends farther and farther from the camp. What is their removal doing to the mountain? The camp has now been there over 30 years. Around the "basin" there is a subtle taming.

On the other hand, around Cliff Top and the old camping area the mountain is wilder. Although Myrtle Point was burned to its rock ledges three decades past, the sand myrtle already encroaches into the path which leads to the point. It once seemed to be a very slow-growing shrub, but it is actually obliterating the wear and tear of hundreds of people walking that trail to Myrtle Point. This channeling of people helps to maintain natural conditions off the trails.

On Le Conte, there was a phenomenon which fascinated everyone. Recent rains had produced abundant ground water. In a tiny ravine it was running over a mossy ledge in several fine streams. Moss has a way of dividing water into silvery components, and several crystal columns the size of a large knitting needle dropped so evenly there was not the slightest evidence of motion. Each shaft resembled a tiny rod of glass, of unbelievable clarity. We knew each was flowing water, but each of us was tempted to, and did, run his finger through the column for assurance that it was indeed water and not some exotic crystal substance brought into being by the alchemy of the wilds. If the water dropped more than eight or ten inches it tended to break into droplets and to reveal its motion. But a slim pencil no more than four or five inches long was as motionless to the eye as a crystal rod.

I suppose the moss in these ravines is a kind of saturated carpet and the flow to these drop-off points is continuous and steady. But why is it that a flow of more than five or six inches begins to flicker? Can it be caused by the friction of the air on the surface of the column? The outside slows up, the center plunges on—ultimately dismembering it into separate drops.

November 11   Last Sunday Bob Maher and I went to Winnesoka via Big Dudley Creek. We climbed and lunched in bright sun. In the late afternoon the skies began to haze over.

On the approach we followed the old road and then up the steep trace which may have provided access to home sites, but more likely was the route for the selective logging which had been done in the area. "Selective" may not be the word. At the lower elevations there was little which had not been passed over, although the replacement forest had both variety and size. The first virgin trees we noticed were sugar maples. I can not understand why they were left unless they were above the cutting line. There the forest was spare and open and the maples may well have been the dominant species with very few competitors. The first big ones we noticed were on the broad shelf just below the great cliff.

The cliff impressed me as before. It was massive and angular, as if it had been formed by an earth-slip of fairly recent origin. There were occasional cracks where the wall had been under additional stress. One of these formed a narrow shelf which inclined inwardly and opened a safe route to the top. The woods were wet and as we toiled up the earth slope to the edge of the wall we slipped and fell many times. I dug in the edges of my Bean boots and clung to every shrub and bit of vegetation. Sometimes an additional pound or two of pull made the difference between progress and slipping down that slick surface. Bob looked up at the narrow rock shelf which had collected a bit of soil and demurred at risking ourselves on it because of the treacherous footing. But I pointed out that the shelf was itself a part of an enormous overhang and was dry and almost dusty.

At the upper end of this shelf was a vertical cleft in the rock choked with rhododendron. The roots had dug deep and we were able to worm up through its branches with complete safety. Our place of ascent projected from the main wall like the prow of a ship and was the extension of a well-defined ridge which we followed to the top of Winnesoka. In a depression to the east was a small stream which we had seen from below as a cascade, slipping down the wall in a film and staining it almost black.

The ridge itself was precipitous and I thought, "But for the rhododendron and smilax and laurel (which because of their denseness provided their own problem) this would be a rock slope which would require considerable care to ascend." This would be true of many of the north faces of the Smokies, of which the Charlies Bunion area is a prime example. On the ridge, I climbed as much with my arms as with my legs, hanging onto long pipe-like rhododendron roots or a laurel branch, or to the niches in a minor cliff. Later in the day, on the descent, I found myself slowing a too precipitate movement by a lunge at a long loop of wild grapevine.

We rested several times amid the dense thickets of this ascendant ridge and through openings could see vastnesses in the valley below. We found ourselves looking out into the crowns of trees which found their roost far below. Some of these crowns were blotches of pure crimson and gold—red and sugar maples and birches and beeches. These were spotted all about us—just far enough apart to provoke fresh excitement as we glimpsed them through the screen of rhododendron.

A long ridge called Grapeyard, the eastern rim of Big Dudley Creek, ended in a high point on the main ridge of Winnesoka. It was covered with the lush forest of a north slope—great hemlocks, maples, birch, linden, cherry, buckeyes, and others. Each contributed its own glory to the rich tapestry of the forest. There is no brilliance I know quite so unrepressed as that of the southern hardwoods in the autumn. Rich greens, crimsons, reds, scarlets, flames, coppers, bronze, yellows, light greens—dyeing the slopes in a tumult of color.

After each such saturnalia of indulgence, we would lose ourselves again in the green depths of the thickets. We wormed and crawled and at times fought our way upward. We began to encounter rich carpets of galax which thrive on the drier, sunnier south slopes; and, although we could not see the top, we knew we were nearing it. We pressed through a last tangle of briers, pines, and thickety laurel and emerged into the warmth and comfort of bright sunshine.

From that point we pushed westward along the summit ridge, following a rudimentary trail which had been little used except by wild creatures. We were thwarted by pine trees which thrust stubby, rough-barked branches into the trail, by clumps of head-high laurel, and by ubiquitous loops of smilax which lacerated us time and again with its thorns. After a quarter of a mile of this we came to a bulging rock from which we got tantalizing views of the wall of Le Conte, the summit of which loomed 2000 feet above us.

After lunch I climbed a short, limby pine and thrust my head above its topmost leader. From it I had an unobstructed view of Le Conte and flanking mountains. Unobstructed, yes, but remote under a cloak of haze which lay loosely over their contours. Even as I looked a chill crept into the air, as the haze deepened between us and the sun.

We were scouting our December hike. Three years ago we had planned to descend by Little Dudley Creek—but in the maze of ridges and undergrowth had borne to the west and had ended up to our embarrassment on the Roaring Fork near Gatlinburg, five miles from our starting point. We were determined not to make that mistake again. On a low outcrop, I climbed an old chestnut and saw the cluster of houses around Gatlinburg. We steered our course away from them as from the plague. From below, Little Dudley seemed to head up into a bullhead-shaped prominence off the northwest ridge of Winnesoka.

We eased off the main ridge. On its side slopes we moved in a forest of gigantic sugar maples. The side slopes were dreadfully steep and I never let myself go without a tree below me against which I could jolt if I went too fast. This was exciting—the awesome trees, the cruel slope, and loose footing of black loam over an underfooting of hidden talus. Sometimes we rested against a tree and swept our gaze through the golden crowns of the maples. Once we saw a fire cherry 25 inches in diameter.

Our route was obscure. We stayed on the east exposure but worked horizontally to the north across a succession of rolling ridges. Surely this would take us into Little Dudley Creek. At length thickets and briers forced us to descend. We came to a creek, sluggish and boggy. Over a flat savanna we moved, past an old cabin site to a livelier creek and an old roadbed. Bob said at once, "We are back on *Big Dudley*."

We had missed again! We were convulsed with mirth and frustration.

INETEEN SIXTY-ONE

January 25   I went to the Chimney Tops yesterday with Lloyd and Joey Lundin. It was a gray, damp day with occasional periods of light rain. Temperature was in the fifties. The mountains were almost deserted—no cars were at the parking area above the tunnel, and no one at all on the mountain.

The trail had been dry for nearly two weeks and the light rain barely dampened our jackets. There was just enough ice on the steeper places to make us watch where we stepped. One tree was working loose on the vertical cliff where it was our custom to climb by tree roots. Elsewhere the slate was clean and sharp and there was little slipping.

As we neared the point where the trail takes to the ridge spine, Joey remarked that a current of air was coming from a fissure in the rock. Here the ridge was not over 40 feet thick and the wind, blowing furiously from the opposite side, was driving a stream of air clear through the mountain.

The woods were open. From the top we could look down into the little valley threaded by the "Essary Route" and could see only scattered snow. We returned by this route and ate at the foot of a big tree about halfway from the ridge to the valley.

One thing I had not anticipated. On these north-facing slopes the ground was frozen hard and we kept in the stream course for safety. There were at least two new blowdowns, both hemlocks and both huge. The great buckeyes in the lower valley were particularly arresting in their clean winter lines.

It was beginning to rain and our clothing became damp as we floundered through the rhododendron at the foot of the ravine. However, the main creek was low and by shattering a crust of ice on one boulder we were able to cross without wetting our feet. But we absorbed a soaking as we fought through the rhododendron and dog hobble to the trail.

(I recalled my first trip to the Chimneys. It was in 1920—in August. On top there was a belt of mist and the weather was hot.)

Beech Flats, along the Road Prong, once so open and once grazed, is closing in with young beeches and spindly hemlocks. The soil must have been compacted by the grazing, because hemlocks would normally be much sturdier. The old wagon way, unused for 60 years, is shrinking to a path. The wagons and stock had dug out the soil, and little growth has taken place in the old roadway even in the 40 years since it was last used.

The giant forest in this area antedates the white man and seems to know it. It has a spare and gracious ruggedness found in aristocracy. Except for the trail, the area known as Beech Flats and Indian Grave Flats is a pocket of virgin forest as fine as any I know. Here one can glimpse the heritage America has almost destroyed—half a continent of unbroken forest which met the gaze 200 years ago. And I have lived almost a third of that time span.

January 31   On Friday we learned that the Hiking Club trip to Le Conte had not been called off despite the frigid weather. The predicted low of 9° for Knoxville presaged very cold weather on top. We determined to go. Our decision would have been easier had I not had 40 years of winter experience with Mt. Le Conte. I recalled a sudden numbing drop in temperature to 20° below zero; and another time when our gloves froze stiff on our hands and we rattled the fingers of one glove back and forth across the fingers of the other with a sound like a stick on a picket fence. I knew too much. I could think of too many possibilities—wet clothing, wet socks, the need for ample dry clothing on top. So we assembled warm clothing and looked forward to the trip with a feeling of high and somewhat uneasy adventure.

This feeling was not eased by the 5° temperature to which we awoke on Saturday morning. But the weather was otherwise good and there was the promise of a dry climb, although there was a prediction for snow on top. We left home, bravely, about 8 a.m. to meet the others.

As we approached Pigeon Forge there was a thick haze ahead and no sign of the high mountains. Gatlinburg streets, deserted, were clear of snow and of cars.

The test was upon us. Would the road to the Cherokee Orchard be deep with snow or would it be so slick we could get no traction? As we followed Phil Ewald's car I was happy to see that the snow had been compacted and that our only problem would be slickness. Phil moved well for a while. As we rounded a bend we saw that he was blocked by a car, headed down. It had slithered over the road and couldn't get traction. Phil took the packs of the hikers from that car, and I took Ken Warren in the back seat of our Volkswagen. Then Phil's car became snowbound. He dropped back of me to get a running start while I drove ahead easily the three miles to the foot of the trail.

Ken went back to help with the other cars, and Anne and I decided to start hiking alone. Just as we were ready to leave, I heard a telephone ring and answered the Le Conte Lodge field phone in the barn. Herrick Brown was calling from the lodge on top.

"Bright sun here, trail good except above 6000 feet—two and a half feet of snow on top."

By this time several more hikers had arrived and I passed Herrick's message on to them.

Anne was far ahead on her snowshoes but they did not pack the snow, which was deep and loose.

The cold was bitter and as I passed into the shade of the forest along the creek, the frigid air engulfed me almost like a sinister presence. I felt it clamping my ears and body. I had daubed my face liberally with cold cream, and two knit caps kept my ears warm. But my nose was cold, and as I gasped for my first wind I tried to keep my mouth closed against the biting temperature. With sleeping bag, camera, lunch, and extra clothes, I was carrying perhaps 30 pounds.

The snow was deep; and I had learned it was deeper on top. The trail we were to follow cut through switchbacks, and above Rainbow Falls it went straight up the hollow. I had not carried a pack up such a slope, for such a distance, for a decade or more. It would be a grueling climb.

I began to feel the pull on my muscles. The snow was very dry, but where it had been compressed by those who had gone up on Friday it had melted slightly and supplied firm footing. All trees—all limbs—were white and I looked upward to a sky which was a wondrous blue. A haze floated around Bull Head, which was both brilliant with frozen fog and black with evergreens. Such contrast, such wintry clarity!

This has been a dry winter. There was a minimum of water in Le Conte Creek. The snow partook of the dryness of the winter and, except where it had been tracked, was as loose as powder. In the maze of fractured rock just above the falls we would sway on uneven surfaces, lose our balance, and run our arms to the elbow into the snow. But our gloves remained dry and our hands warm. Once I tumbled and fell flat. There was a momentary tingle as my face hit the snow.

Between sunshine and rime the air sparkled. But the sun raised a transparent pallor from the forest which floated between us and the peaks. Their outlines remained, but the deep blues and blacks and greens were diffused by this formless veil. It was this inscrutable curtain which had obscured the mountains from us at Pigeon Forge and which masked the base from Herrick on top. It had color and an elusive substance and yet along our climb obscured nothing.

Thinking back over 40 years of experience with Le Conte I recall

"... the land as it had been for long centuries."

its many moods. In 1918 I walked back and forth across the Watson Orchard in dawn and twilight in full view of the mountain. There was a bit more settlement in the valley then than today, but less of civilization. There was a road, so-called, to the site of the Cherokee Orchard. It had been gashed and cut by flood and wheel tracks. One struggled even on foot merely to reach the base of Le Conte. Its serene and distant summit seemed untouchable as well as unknowable. And the mists and fogs which drifted about, the driving rains, and the promise of the rainbows and the revelations under bright sun brought diversity to the experience.

In 1918 I did not think about the gross differences in elevation between Gatlinburg and the summit, or of currents of air which floated up the hollow almost like a chimney as the sun touched the summit with its warmth; nor of the weight of cold air which sank down the ravine in evening as the sun dropped to the horizon. I did not know, then, that the great bulk of these mountains was a barrier to the oceans of air flowing in from the Gulf; or that the mountain chilled the moisture-laden air, precipitating those lashing rains which struck us so often on summer afternoons. I did not know, then, of transpiration and of ecology. I did not know that the trees themselves were a source of moisture when the air was not, and that this formless and almost invisible haze may have arisen from them.

In winter there is added mystery and elusiveness and untouchability. As I slogged up through the snow, this inviolate and impalpable vapor was forming seemingly out of nothingness to mock the brilliance of the day. And so although some of the mystery had been unmasked over the years, still as I began my sixtieth trip to Mt. Le Conte the lure of this mountain was as strong as ever.

I had not for perhaps a decade hit the brush with an overnight pack on a mountain whose summit was the better part of a mile above me; and I wondered how I would acquit myself through the added impediment of deep snow. I am sure the snow, the elevation, the weight of my pack, the uncertain footing, the steepness, and my nearly six decades took the edge off my sensibilities. But even so, the memories are rare and precious and stirring.

I have been in deeper snow on Le Conte, but not often. I don't believe I have ever been there in such stillness. The customary debris, twigs, bits of bark and lichen and needles and dust—the litter of the winter winds—were absent. The snow was spotless. Amid the grime and smoke of the cities, one never sees clean snow; but in the wilds, under the restless stir of the winds snow is often strewn with litter. This time it was not. The cleanness and thinness of the air were matched by the immaculateness of the snow.

In the winter woods, with the leaves on the ground and not between us and the sky, there was an aspect of openness and light. Most of my previous trips had been under the canopy of summer, and many of the winter trips had been in fog and darkness. But today was clear and the summer foliage was absent. In the summer one can see the round dome of the Bull Head only from the open, naked cliffs of Rainbow Falls. On this trip we could see this summit over much of the way and could measure our progress upward by the extent to which the Bull Head sank beneath us.

Looking out, I realized that this little valley of Le Conte Creek is not so steep as valleys go. There were only one or two waterfalls other than the great leap of the cliffs at Rainbow Falls. Compared to the dark and precipitous slopes of Balsam Top on the west and of Rocky Spur on the east, we were ascending a pleasant incline through open woods. The spruces, balsams, and hemlocks hung black over the great spur and ranges; but the deciduous birches and buckeyes and poplars also populated this hollow and, having lost their leaves in the autumn, laid it wide open for the winter.

I do not imply that the climbing was easy. As I slipped and lost my balance in the loose snow I felt my strength ebbing. My instep cramped, and losing traction on a high step the muscles in my legs knotted in protest. The younger hikers were constantly overtaking me or politely staying at my heels until I invited them to pass. My breath was not short and my heart did not pound, but somehow strength did not reach my legs. I would move upward a few paces until the will to move was drained. Then I would stop, double over to give my lungs added capacity, breathe deeply for a few moments, and enter upon another lift upward.

Above me through the trees I would see mirages of brightness where the sun soaring above the ridges would shoot a few beams into this north-facing valley. I hoped to reach one of these spots of warmth, there to warm my muscles as I ate my lunch. But those havens of warmth eluded me and I finally tramped a little flat place in the snow beneath a small cliff and ate of cold steak. I was not hungry; the steak seemed to catch in my throat as I tried to swallow it. After a few moments of inactivity, I started on.

I was climbing into the evergreens. This meant 5000 feet or more. To the east I could see the level summit of the Rocky Spur trail by which Anne was ascending the mountain alone on snowshoes. I was beginning to lose my bench mark of the Bull Head in the emptiness below. And I knew when I came into the evergreens, I would leave the pleasant incline of the stream and would be on the prodigious slope of the mountain itself.

In the evergreens the snow was palpably deeper and the slope cruelly steeper. When I lost my balance and missed one of the holes in the snow made by the trail breakers, my foot would plunge into a loose and bottomless pocket, and catching myself I would thrust my arm into the snow up to the shoulder. Climbing was maddeningly slow and debilitating. Herrick said the honest and direct route we were following measured about three and a quarter miles to the top. I was climbing no more than half a mile an hour, but was still well ahead of the sunset.

A group of three passed me. As I watched them ahead, they seemed always to be resting; but try as I might, I could not catch them. Climbing in the snow in midwinter is a terribly personal thing. In my weariness and general torpor I was not too much worried about Anne, who was climbing alone by a longer route. I knew there was no real danger, unless she broke a strap on her snowshoes or came to a drift in the trail which would give her no footing.

As I approached the 6000-foot level, the others pulled farther away from me and again I was climbing alone. I paused once and pushed my cap back away from my ears. The silence was so profound it was almost frightening. I was now above Le Conte Creek. There was no sound of its waters—no wind, no birds, no insects, no people. Once again in my life I was experiencing absolute silence. I blundered on and saw someone coming toward me through the trees. It was Dickerman, who had appropriated Herrick's snowshoes and was going down the trail to meet Anne.

The route was now very steep and I gained the better part of a foot with every step, when I could keep my balance. I was not near exhaustion, but I was very tired and had for the time ceased to enjoy the evergreens and silence and heavy snow. Eventually the tracks leveled off to the east, and as I looked down I could see that the thin vapor of the noontime had thickened into an impenetrable cloud mass which stretched like an ocean to the horizon. Only a few higher peaks rose above it like islands. I had seen this phenomenon many times and for a few moments savored the sensation of being cut off from the world of men below.

The lodge came into sight at last. In their open setting the buildings seemed bleak and stark under their blanket of snow. I was tired and dehydrated. I clumped into the kitchen and was met by warmth and a hubbub of conversation. Nearly everyone was gathered there. And there were large pots of coffee and chocolate. Two cups of the latter, plus a small snort of mountain-ash wine, and the mountain did not seem nearly so steep as I had thought—nor the snow so deep. Anne and Dickerman came in well before dark.

In the east we could see a near full moon and overhead drifted a sleazy veil of clouds. The thermometer stood at a warm 20° and we wondered if the morrow might not bring rain rather than snow. The air seemed heavy with impending change.

Around the cabins the snow was so deep we followed little angular paths which the boys had shoveled in the snow. These paths were about fifteen inches deep and some twenty inches wide and there were important intersections. One we called "Times Square." In meeting or passing someone, we usually faced each other, took hold of each other's arms lightly, and inched by in a sort of modified square dance step.

There was something exotic and deliciously primitive about our night there. We crowded into the lodge where there was a wood fire which barely heated the hearthstone. The room was lit by one smelly kerosene lamp. Dinner was served in an unheated dining room, where by the light of the feeble lamps we could see our breath as we exhaled. The spring was dry. Such water as we had came from melting snow. No one shaved or washed. The bedrooms were unheated and we stowed our aching muscles into the sleeping bags we had lugged up the mountain.

Our aims became basic and simple. We wanted sufficient warmth and food to sustain life. We wanted rest for its continuance. Finding these, our cups of happiness were full and there were tall stories and laughter and merriment. Even those who had reached the limits of their strength in climbing the mountain were uncomplaining. Life had been reduced to its simplicities and everywhere there was an aura of good will and joy.

As the night wore through, the mist vanished; the moon shone out and the clouds dissipated from the great gulf we had ascended.

Morning dawned brilliantly, and we could see far across the valley of the Tennessee. English Mountain was in the clear but its base was swathed in haze. Some of us wallowed in the clean snow to the ridge crest and saw range after range in Carolina lying distant and obscure in a milky haze. Small spruces and balsams were submerged in snow, tiny mounds marking their existence. More mature trees had a strange slenderness as the flare of their bases was deep in snow.

I broke trail out to Cliff Top and went into snow up to my knees with each step and never touched bottom. We emerged into the openness of the cliff and gazed down into an undulant world of blue mountains. This beauty, this mastery of environment, was what we had come for; and when we retreated to the lodge it was with mingled feelings of humility and of self-respect.

I descended the mountain, via the trail, on Anne's snowshoes. I expected a rather arduous trip but it was not so. The shoes rode on top of the heavy snow. The stride is a normal one, and I had trouble only when I tried to stretch my stride and stepped on the tail of the front snowshoe, or dug in the point of one. In the first situation I went to my knees a time or two; and in the second I tripped and fell forward into the snow. Where the snow had crystallized I tried a shorter step and attempted to bring the whole webbing of the shoe flat into contact with the snow. It seemed to work.

At Rainbow Falls I removed the snowshoes and stumbled on foot amongst the big, snowy rock slabs. The cone of ice under the falls was magnificent. Its top was flat and probably four or five feet in diameter. The ice was opaque with a faint trace of blue—so delicate it seemed to come and go with variations in the light. The sun, dropping a beam near the base of the cone, drew out the faintest lavender. But that color came from without, while the misty blue clearly came from within the ice itself.

It was an exotic, almost weird sight. From the normal snowy vistas of the forest and stream bed we emerged and came upon this colossal creation in ice. It was huge, white, and motionless, and against the gray cliff it dominated the head of the valley.

April 4 A week ago when we were in Cades Cove with Justice Douglas, I visited for the first time the old Cable Mill. The mill wheel, turning with "all deliberate speed," made a comfortable, slow-rhythmed, groaning sound. Bill remarked, "That is a pleasant sound."

He then told a remarkable story. In Persia some of the tribes migrate vast distances each year taking their cattle, goats, sheep, camels, and entire families with them. The very young babies are placed in a kind of sling which is fastened to the back of a cow. These children ride for long miles without whimper or outcry. The supposition is that a child so riding can hear the measured, thumping heartbeat of the cow, so like the recollection of its own mother's heartbeat before birth that it has a sense of security and is content.

The days were divine, brilliant and shiny with a touch of warmth. The extensive vistas of the fields stretched not to the horizon, but came to an end against the foothills of the high mountains. There we experienced a beauty which was expansive but which could be comprehended. We lingered at each shimmering vista and at each pioneer restoration. The combination of a perfect setting and the richly provocative evidences of slow-paced and self-contained culture held us enthralled.

We visited three of the old churches and walked through their cemeteries. One of the cemeteries was on a forested knoll which rose above its surroundings on every side. In the emerald brightness we lingered and studied the tombstones.

"What a marvelous site!" Bill commented.

"They buried better than they lived," I said.

July 24 There was a cloudburst in the mountains Saturday. On the trip to the Chimneys I found evidences of its extent. The Walker Prong was booming, its water a murky jade green. The Road Prong was higher than normal, but crystal clear. The lower part of the rough Chimneys trail showed evidence of recent washing. On top the humus was almost dry.

The great rhododendron was in every stage of inflorescence. There were pink buds and great white bursts of bloom. Some blossoms were a waxy, greenish-white, as devoid of color as any I ever saw.

We ascended in a little over an hour and a half—Jim Reid, Michael Frome, and I. A shower hit us but ceased almost as soon as we started the heavy part of the ascent. Deep banks of clouds rolled around Le Conte and we were halfway up the mountain before we could see Myrtle Point, and much nearer the top of the Chimneys before West Peak and Cliff Top became visible.

Thunder boomed distantly. Although we could see Cove Mountain, Chilhowee Mountain farther away was obscured. We reached the top in bright sun. Mike remarked that we never got out of the sound of automobile horns.

I pointed out to him below us the boundary between the cut-over areas and the virgin woods. The even growth of the tulip trees around the Chimneys campground told the story of former occupation and open fields better than words.

We clambered over to the south peak and ate on the open point facing south. Rain clouds and fog lurked around Rich Mountain, Blanket Mountain, and Cove Mountain. Then I began to notice wisps of clouds forming in the hollow to the west.

Before we knew it there was a solid wall of fog on our right, which swept up the slope of the Chimneys but left clear the valley to our left. This upward sweep finally lost its momentum and curved downward hiding the top of Mingus in ragged wisps of mist. We rested in the clear under a vast dome of fog a half mile across. Man-made domes shrink by comparison with this colossal, circular concavity under which we sat.

A towhee sang from a bush just below us. A group of swifts circled under the great dome and sometimes swept within six feet of us. The song of a winter wren trickled in from the spaces below us. Then a bolt of lightning whisked by us and we donned rain gear and descended to the safety of the woods.

Mike liked the open bear trail along the ridge crest. Jim inquired what I thought of the idea of using that ridge as an access route from Sugarland Mountain, in case it should be decided to close the steep and gutted trail by which we had ascended.

We dropped off by the "Essary Route," working our way down through the rhododendron to the ravine. The buckeyes were never more stately and the stinging nettles never more lush and virulent. Some of them were almost as high as my head. I was stung on my hands and arms, and once through the damp fabric of my trousers.

November 11 . . . Yesterday we hiked again to the Chimneys, to a spot which in one way or another has been a part of my life for over 40 years. I believe it was 1918 that I worked for a few weeks at the Watson Orchard and took my first trip up the West Prong of the Little Pigeon River and caught my first view of the Chimneys. No one had warned me of these precipitous and distinctive peaks. I was hiking along on a fishing trip, trying to keep up with the others and glanced up.

"What are they?" I cried, astounded by their sharp points and vertical slopes.

Someone said, "The Chimney Tops."

I am sure that I resolved then and there to climb them, although it was two years before I made the opportunity. But in those two years, I hiked beneath them several times on the way to the cabin at Indian Grave Flats.

I climbed the Chimneys first with Uncle Charlie Mooers and his son George in 1920. Since those first climbs, the Chimneys, the Road Prong, the dark silent pools, the gleaming foam of the little cascades— Alum Cave, Le Conte, the Smokies—the whole general area—have become deeply involved in my life. These wonderful, beautiful mountains are as much a part of me as my blood stream, or the hand which traces out these words.

So yesterday, I re-experienced the richness of this environment. I looked again at that lovely perfect pool and tiny cascade at the mouth of the Road Prong. I looked at the dense green of the great rhododendrons lining this stream as far as I could see. I looked at the green fountains of dog hobble springing out of the damp humus. I saw the bole of a great poplar—the yellow splashes of its leaves fallen on the ground—the leathery browns of the cucumber leaves—the springy curls of the oaks. On the slopes I looked out through the giant trunks of the hemlocks into spaces covered over in living green.

"This is what it means to be *inside* a forest," I thought.

From farther up the trail, I saw the twisted channel of the stream and sensed the curiously sedate and endless flow of the water. I experienced again the sense of exhilaration and of command which is a part of looking out into space from great heights.

I saw a yellow butterfly bobbing about in that space on currents of its own making. The sun was warm. Frost had abated for a day or two, and the butterfly was using its wings perhaps for the last time. It was the only one we saw, and its loveliness late in the season was deeply poignant.

A horny, gauzy winged insect with horizontal lines, remindful of a small airplane, shot from the woods into this space in which the yellow dab of color had been bobbing. He too was on his last fling, and he went at it with such violence I wondered if he was not aware of it. The season was slowing up—it was moving almost to a stop.

But next year, and every following year—as always in the past—all forms of life would be renewing themselves. I had only to come back next year to see and immerse myself in them again. It had always been this way. It always would be.

Then I caught myself thinking about that dread thing, the bomb, and I wondered. *Will it always be?* Will I come back? Will this loveliness be destroyed? Will the eternities come to an end? How can one think and live in worlds so utterly incompatible? This is the crazy split-world in which mankind stumbles. When will it ever end? Which world will win?

NINETEEN SIXTY-TWO

March 10   In going over the proceedings of
the Seventh Biennial Wilderness Conference of the Sierra Club, I
noted a remark by Regional Forester Connaughton in connection
with the administration of wilderness. He said that one job of a
forester was to put up signs in wilderness areas. This reminded me
that Jim Reid is not only against naming mountains for living people;
he is against naming peaks at all. He, like Olaus Murie, would say
Denali (the original Indian name), in preference to Mt. McKinley.
I assume Jim would not name streams, or meadows, or other features.
Such a practice would impose a terrific curb on use. People would
not be inclined to go to places that had no names. Maps would be next
to useless except as a man applied his own tags as he passed through
an area.

The idea has terrific implications. War would become almost impossible. How could people fight a country they could not describe
or name? How could a nameless Russia be hated? How could we
travel if we couldn't say where we were going? Railroads, airlines
couldn't operate without destinations. Without names they could not
get their enterprises off the ground. The thought could be carried
further. Why name anything—ideas or otherwise? Without designa-
tions or names of that sort, we could not think. All that would really
slow development!

April 1 As I walked to the cabin this morning Woolly Tops,
emerging for a moment from dark and angry clouds, was white with

rime. The streams were full, clear, and spirited—living (and I hope everlasting) evidence of the beauty and sparkle resulting from a perfect watershed. The watershed of the Porters Flat Prong has had its vicissitudes. The early farms have now returned completely to young forest. And there was the holocaust and later deluge around Charlies Bunion nearly 40 years ago. But except for some of the dug trails, the entire watershed above the cabin is in balance. I wish Americans could see and drink from these dashing streams.

Le Conte Creek
"... filtered through undisturbed forest cover"

Is there ever any compatibility between roads and wilderness? The Forest Service prides itself on preserving a band of trees between roads and streams as a filter for the run-off from the roads. Does it really work? What would residual samplings of the stream reveal? Today, after the substantial rains of yesterday, the stream was not even dingy.

East of the Porters Creek watershed, on streams which have not in historic times known logging or fire, or the disturbance of roads and trails, I have observed spots where acres of humus and trees have become waterlogged in torrential rains and have broken loose and have "flowed" down to the nearest valley. This is natural. These phenomena have rounded the contours of the mountains and over the eons have given them shape.

Such breaks in the soil cover may seem disastrous to people who have known these mountains but a few generations. But even on the calendar of men, these slippages heal quickly and streams return to their seemingly everlasting perfection. Over a very long time, forests will even return and cover the bare places which men have clear-cut.

Much of the interruption and disruption is flagrantly unnecessary. Man robs himself, and a generation or two of his children, of the beauty found by his ancestors. In a larger sense he harms only himself. Nature carries within itself the seeds of renewal. If only we could learn what Leopold preached, that man must learn to live with the least possible disturbance of nature. Conservation is not just a word; it is the observance of a physical harmony between man's activities and the natural world.

Of course, if we should in some mad moment turn loose the incredible wild fire of the hydrogen bomb, that is something else again. Every living thing may be shriveled and destroyed. If that should eventuate, then there may *never* be a renewal. The seeds and processes of restoration may be gone forever. Perhaps in some far era other life forms would evolve. But they would never be what we, in this first half of the twentieth century, have known.

On our trip this day the life forms consisted of exquisite beds of wild violets of the deepest purple and shy bronze yellow; of tiny white serried flashes of anemone; of phalanxes of young hemlocks, swaying lightly in the breeze; of massive green copses of rhododendron and the singularly lovely openness of a grove of young poplars; of clear rivulets finding the angles of every ravine; of the waxy green-yellow of the witch-hazel blooms; and of deep ruddy nuggets spreading along the fringes of the red maples. Dare we risk effacing such glory and variety from the face of the earth?

May 19 Last Sunday we went to Devil's Hole Gorge on Piney Creek above Spring City. The gorge includes about 75 acres of virgin timber. I was elated to find a fringe tree growing there naturally, a tree I had seen only once before. It had sweeping, graceful, exotic white blooms which reminded me of the feathers of an egret. I was impressed also with the gorgeous, waxy leaves of the winter huckleberry.

The walls of the gorge were highly stratified in horizontal layers. The site of the falls was U-shaped from top to bottom as well as laterally, with frightening cantileverings of flat slabs at the top. Around the bowl the growth was green and dense. There were a few huge pines and hemlocks. A great ash stood at the edge of the bowl. Laurel was in bud, rhododendron and azalea in bloom.

It was a fine, green, prolific spot, with but one notable drawback. Its stream flowed off the Cumberland Plateau and into the gorge. Upstream grazing, cultivation, and civilization had made the water murky. Silt and mud marked the bed. The situation presented a powerful argument for wild areas large enough to incorporate and protect a complete watershed.

Poison ivy was gigantic and prolific. It was impossible to avoid it. We walked in it to our knees. It grew on ledges and brushed our arms and faces, but Anne and I escaped infection.

The rock in the Cumberlands is, of course, younger than that found in the Smokies, and we saw a few fossils of ferns and trees. One of the fossils reminded me of the pattern in a modern nonskid tire.

There were definite escarpments on both sides. We bypassed the one on the east, but met the one on the west head-on. We had a few anxious moments as we worked up through crevices and under overhangs, clinging insecurely and exposed on the face of the rock.

June 27 The Knoxville *News-Sentinel* and the Smoky Mountains Hiking Club sponsored a trip to Andrews Bald, a project which grew out of a series of sketches written by Carson Brewer last summer on the subject of possible hikes in the Smokies. What good does it do to write up the hikes, he thought, if no one takes them? So an invitation went out to the Hiking Club to provide leaders. A hundred folks drawn from the local area and a half dozen Japanese and a Thai from Oak Ridge were in the group of hikers.

The day was at first misty and cloudy but became sunny. It held both the muted charm of the woods shot through with clouds, and the more open challenge of bright flowers and distant ranges. There was no rain. Enough rhododendron and azalea were in bloom to satisfy the newcomers, but for old-timers the display seemed limited.

The participants on the hike varied from scientists to business people, from family groups with small children to older persons.

I would say that it was a successful experiment. People do like to get back into the mountains, especially when the going is not too strenuous. But will it be a once-in-a-lifetime experience for them, or will their appetites be whetted for more? If there is no such carry-over it will be a disappointment to me. People come for hundreds, and even thousands, of miles to see the Smokies, but the casual way with which so many of our local people regard them is shocking. Will these trips deepen and strengthen an awareness of the great beauty of the mountains?

It is an incongruous—even a ghastly—thought that with all our vast productive capacity in this country, we may not be able to keep the economic machine producing. The economy is a mixture of a lot of things—the chief ingredient of which is human nature. And we don't yet know how to handle human nature. If we did, there would never be another depression. If we understood it we might not have to resort to the checks and controls of what is called competition. People might then not feel compelled to work for money and might then not feel impelled to work for fame, as Kipling suggested. The human race is young just as some of its most hallowed institutions are young, and neither are permanently cast in their present mold.

But how different is the uncertainty which permeates man's institutions from the glorious certitude of life itself. Farmers have their setbacks, and householders their trials with shrubbery and lawns and trees. Maybe we can't control nature after our wishes; but if we yield to it and accept it, it will burgeon and fairly engulf us.

Here on our ridge, with mixed hope and trepidation, I set out azaleas and rhododendron and laurel. But if they fail me because of my misunderstanding of their proper environment, I need only look about for assurance at the multiplying dogwoods and tulip poplars and hickories. Life in many forms is sweeping in a wave over our two acres. The surge of new life after the disruption caused by our building venture of three years ago is swamping us. Life is rich, and when we listen and look it is contagious. Wilderness people should never be discouraged. Life undergirds and permeates all their concerns.

Sometimes as I suffer momentary discouragements, I look out into the green wall of our woods sprouting up on three sides of us. We have the boon of life all about us. It is the force back of all things.

July 4 On last weekend we went to Mt. Le Conte with Bob and Margaret Howes for the joint observance of wedding anniversaries. The climb up the Alum Cave trail was easy. We did not press. There was lightness in the air, with no rain and low humidity.

Anne pointed out the beginning and end of her lonely descent a year ago during which she had injured her knee. She was alone and crippled in one of the rugged and remote areas in the Smokies. She was lucky to get out, but it was a luck bolstered by years of experience and stamina developed in the wildest and roughest places.

The vegetation pattern changes at the point where the trail cuts back across the face of Le Conte. Up to that point, one is in an interim zone of mixed trees and heavy rhododendron. Then very suddenly there is a marked change in the air and in the growth. The heaviness ceases. The woods are more open, the rhododendron more scattered. There is moss and oxalis. The spruce lessens, and the balsam predominates. The air is thinner, the trail less steep. One begins to look straight down, and not out, to the valley. One treads easily the moderate grade and looks down onto slopes over which he has labored. There comes a lightness, an exhilaration of spirit. At a few spots the trail is notched out of solid rock and there is a bit of danger to it.

Water trickles from mossy overhangs. Here one finds the moisture and greenness of high mountains, great pillows of moss, flat carpets of oxalis leaves studded with modest blooms, glistening heart-shaped leaves of the rare Grass of Parnassus, the white blooms of thornless blackberries, and the lovely pink of the punctatums springing sparingly into being in these high woods. One sees basketry in the foliage of the mountain ash; and around a bend in the trail appear tiny clumps of sand myrtle growing out of a cleft. There are occasional great spruces.

Distantly one hears the braided, spiraling notes of the veery. And all about there is the inexpressibly spirited and involved outpourings of the winter wren. One is tempted to take this song at each end and stretch it out into a thin band of simplicity and see how far it would reach.

The scene changed again as we worked around a corner and began to skirt the foot of the great cliffs which support Cliff Top. There were puffy billows of sand myrtle rolling over the convolutions of rock. The tiny waxy leaves of this plant gave a deceptive trimness to the ruggedness of those flaring crags.

Beyond these dizzy ledges was the crest of Mt. Le Conte itself. Along the level trail to the lodge we saw hellebore, *Clintonia*, and scattered oxalis. There was a curious openness to the woods. We were in the heart of a vast blowdown which was being reoccupied, densely and solidly, by thousands and thousands of young balsams varying in size from tiny inch-high seedlings to shapely saplings ten or more feet tall. They grew in impenetrable banks on each side of the trail, creating a green wall, fragrant and lush.

My early impressions of this high basin we were traversing had been gained some 40 years ago in August 1922, when S. H. ("Prof") Essary, Simon Marcovitch, and I worked east from Cliff Top across High Top to some open knobs (later to be known as Myrtle Point). The woods were dark and thick. Ferns and moss covered the ground. We stumbled over blowdowns and cut an occasional blaze to assure our return. There was an encompassing witchery to it, as of high far places.

Now the blowdowns had opened it up. There was a new denseness from resurging growth. But the canopy was gone, and ground cover had been replaced. There had been a bad blowdown in 1926 on the east side of Cliff Top. I had struggled through it on a trip immediately after law school days. Now there were additional areas of blowdowns and of dying trees. Perhaps we were in a cycle of change. Perhaps along the crest of this exposed summit the trees never reach any great height or age. I had counted 60 rings on an average tree two years before. Perhaps life on the top of Mt. Le Conte is a succession of explosions of new growth, followed by periods of decay and death as the roots of the trees compete for water and life through the thin layer of soil to the impenetrable mother rock so close beneath. Perhaps in 40 years of climbs on this mountain I had been witness to a major arc of a long cycle of change. Perhaps in another 20 or 40 years it would again be hushed and closed in and somber and slightly awesome.

Some of these thoughts—if not all of these reflections—were going through my mind as we moved on to the lodge. We were warmly welcomed. I had known Herrick nearly 35 years. Curiously, on this perfect weekend at the beginning of summer, we four were the only guests.

The lodge is a rear outpost of a primitive era almost gone. It is spotted in north woods, in a southern clime, in the middle of a geographical area which is laced with roads and subdued and battened down by modernism. There is a bit of terracing around the lodge. The ten or twelve weather-beaten log cabins are roofed with shingles frayed and battered and falling into dust. How can these fragile shingles stave off rains as heavy as four inches in an hour?

There are two odorous outhouses. There are piles of tangy wood, split and to be split. The lamps are kerosene.

True, there is a telephone line down to the maelstrom of man a mile below. There is a pump for the very primitive water system and a small generator for occasional radio contacts. Cooking is by wood, with a drying oven in the stove. A bear takes care of the garbage and at night he is held out of the kitchen by an electric fence. There are the trails, and the thrice weekly bobtail pack string. Newspapers come a day, or two days, late—the world's doings have a delayed importance.

From Cliff Top
". . . the views fell in our laps."

From Cliff Top we saw the sun set into a bank of haze. There was no sight of man except the cramped trail leading through the north woods and the sand myrtle to the cliffs. There was no sound of man other than our own quiet conversation. What leisured sanity! No entertainment—except soft-voiced exchanges of experience, and this haze-dimmed world of mountains.

I have never gone to that cliff without exhilaration. I have never left it without regret.

The calm, the immensity, the forest with a million components—healing, covering, vitalizing every foot of the scene about, below, and before us! I have no fear for life. I fear only for man, who with his works and numbers is shutting himself away from life.

After we went to bed, I thought, "There is no sound—no sound at all."

I listened. There was no breeze, no rain, no mist dripping from the trees onto the roof, no conversation, no movement by anyone or anything, no birds singing, no insects, no motors running, no planes in the sky, no radio. No sound at all. I listened and listened. After minutes of this game, surely there would be something. But I heard no stir. Silence, stillness, and peace.

At 4:30 a.m., in a clinging mist which was open above to the sky and stars, we moved out the trail across High Top in the dew, through spider webs and reclaiming vegetation, to Myrtle Point. It is a bald headland of rock and low-growing sand myrtle facing the east. The myrtle had been burned off by an irresponsible camper 30 years ago. But it was returning. And the healing was as inexorable as when, a billion years ago, life had moved out onto the land from the sea.

The mist dissolved and re-formed. Vague shapes of mountains appeared and vanished. There were stupendous, formless depths all around us. And out there in space, somewhere, but unseen, was the sun. A mouse ran from under a ledge of rock and paused for a moment before racing into a tiny opening in the gravel. When it paused, we saw momentarily its white feet.

Looking out again, we saw slivers of color forming above the maw of mist. Then a copper disk came into sight. Through Bob's binoculars I saw it become a glowing sphere, with roundness and depth, hanging out there in space.

The awesomeness of the universe and the awful loneliness of man smote me. We had come to see beauty, but the chalky curtain of haze obscured it. We came away somewhat numbed by a sense of dreadful loneliness in measureless space. Then the spirited matins of the winter wren, whose ancestors had long since made their peace with this wondrous world into which we as well as they have been dropped, changed our mood.

Bob, Margaret, and I returned from Le Conte by the Boulevard trail. Anne returned by the Alum Cave trail in order to meet us with the car at Newfound Gap.

Except in one or two spots under Myrtle Point, where there were vertical drops of 100 feet, the trail had lost its barrenness. The myriad plant life of this alpine zone, which had crept into the trail, included wild touch-me-not, *Houstonia*, and Smoky Mountain ragwort. The wide bed of the trail had become a footpath, narrow and inviting. Strange fragrances drifted across. Rhododendron was in bloom. Vast blue depths opened to the east, while far to the west lay the close-cropped ruggedness of the Alum Cave Bluffs.

As we skirted below the narrow divide, I looked up at the riotous tangle through which Wiley Oakley and I had forced our way in 1926. We were young and vigorous then, but it had taken us six hours to go from Myrtle Point to the vicinity of the Jumpoff. Now, 35 years later, we made it in two hours.

We met only three hikers—sturdy young men, strapping and competent. Otherwise we were alone in this vivid southern extension of the north woods. We saw not another soul until we met Anne a half mile from Newfound Gap, coming to meet us.

At the gap crowds of people were milling around, hot and congested. Why did they stay so close to their cars, which they seemed fearful of leaving? Why had they not gone to the quiet simplicity of the north woods?

December 28 I look back on the year just concluding with somber feelings. There have been some gains in conservation. Three national seashores have been authorized, although not acquired. There is considerable talk about wilderness in the magazines and newspapers. Most of this seems to be externally inspired, rather than emanating from inner conviction on the part of the editors. A wilderness bill passed the Senate—not perfect, but perhaps the best that could be obtained.

In addition to the commercial-use upsurge in the Congress, we find also an almost cynical disregard for past commitments. Congress has done nothing to protect Rainbow Bridge, and there are constant reminders that the Echo Park dam may yet be legislated and constructed. We find dam after dam being proposed without regard to the effect on other values.

Despite brave words by the President and the two land-administering Secretaries, there is no real leadership for additional wilderness. The Administration's majority in Congress is slim. President Kennedy talks of wilderness but is not able to push its protection. And one wonders whether he has an inner conviction about it.

Over all is the specter of excess population running wild with respect to resources. Congestion and crowding and abuse of public reservations, which are already the source of concern, will be frightening in another 20 or 30 years.

Man is becoming more and more involved in his institutions and less and less concerned with the earth and the resource base upon which his culture rests. A culture which loses sight of these things is doomed. There are examples in the ruins of former civilizations all over the world. There is no reason to suppose that history has seen the end of this. Motivations are personal and self-centered.

Why do we not awaken each day to the wonder of life, to the miracle of existence, vouchsafed, as it is, by the scantiest of fluctuations in moisture and temperature? The miracle is not that weather is so capricious and occasionally so harsh and destructive, but that it is so benign. The miracle is that life is so good, that most people are so healthy. We have had the great boon of existence. Should not the life that surges within us make us strong and self-sufficient?

$\mathscr{N}$INETEEN SIXTY-THREE

January 29   Time scales are curious things. On Crackshot Lake with Ober in 1956, it seemed that we had gone back, far back, in time. To Jim Banks, our Indian guide, we must have been canoeing in an era of shocking modernity. The Indian ways were old and timeless, running back into the dim beginnings of a long past— a world in which there was no written history, only legends and stories.

It was with a start, then, as I read James Dyson's *The World of Ice*, that I realized even these longstanding "cultures" have an unbeliev- able youth compared with the ice ages. It was but 10,000 or 12,000 years ago that the Minnesota canoe country lay deep under the northern ice sheet and the Tennessee highlands were covered with a northern forest much like that through which we camped and canoed on the Crackshot Lake trip. Measured against the glaciers, the sta- bility and vaunted age of each human culture melt into nothingness.

Wilderness people want to preserve the environment of the past. What past? Is it the past of our immediate forebears? Of the Indians whom Ober knew? Is it the past of the last ice age, the age of Leif Ericson, or of John Smith, or of Sir Francis Drake, or of De Soto, or Attakullakulla? Is it the age of George Washington, Jefferson, Lewis and Clark; or of Bernard De Voto, Bob Marshall, Aldo Leopold; or of Murie, Oberholtzer, Zahniser?

From what past do we start? Or could it be that we always start from the present, whatever the age—whether of Thoreau, Muir, Teddy Roosevelt, Zahniser—and work back? Is it really any particular past environment we should seek to preserve, but rather the freeing again of the forces which produced it?

March 17 Yesterday Lloyd and Billy Lundin and I hiked from Indian Gap to Fighting Creek Gap.

The previous day was clear but a great barometric low was pushing "weather" toward east Tennessee. The prediction was for predawn rain, a letup by midmorning, and more rain by late afternoon. This exact prediction involved a precision seldom attained. It called for considerable faith on our part, for Lloyd and I were just getting over colds and neither of us relished walking all day in the rain.

The rain started about 4:30 a.m. but had slackened somewhat when I arose at 5:00. By 6:00 there was again a steady downpour. By the time we reached Gatlinburg there was a small break in the clouds. We decided to leave the Lundin car at Fighting Creek Gap for our return and then drive our car to Indian Gap, where Anne would leave us and drive back to Knoxville. We hoped that a trend in the weather could be discerned before we finally committed ourselves to the long hike. At Indian Gap we were encouraged to find the rain had become simply heavy mist.

From a study of the maps I thought the trip would be about ten miles; Lloyd thought nine. At Fighting Creek Gap the trail sign to Indian Gap had read thirteen and a half miles.

The winter barrier was still across the road at Indian Gap. This would force us to hike three more miles, mostly on the highway. So we pondered the day's weather on the basis of predictions now twelve hours old and our present observations. In that damp, dark, enveloping mist I was almost ready to call it off. But Lloyd said he was game, and that threw the balance.

We set off in thick mist observing the erosion along the road, the soil structure and washes, and the huge chunks of rock pried loose in the freezes. We were uncertain where the Sugarland trail took off, so after 40 minutes of hard hiking we left the highway for the Appalachian Trail which paralleled it. This trail was badly eroded. There were long slabs of dirty ice in its gulleys despite a week of warm weather and much rain. We encountered a few slushy places where openings in the trees had let in the sun. But the appearance and feel of the woods were predominantly of winter.

After we had been hiking about an hour we came to the intersection of the two trails and turned off on the Sugarland trail. I felt we were only then beginning our hike of thirteen and a half long miles.

We started north on the icy trail through woods chiefly of fir. The ground cover was mossy and there was little undergrowth. The trail to the Park Service shelter was eroded and spongy. A hitching rack explained the raw condition of the trail. After inspecting the shelter, which was set on a large level bench in beautiful, rich woods, we turned north again and found no more evidence of horse travel. Here was a path of promise, much of it still new to me.

The first few miles of the Sugarland trail were almost level and the mountain crest itself was only a couple of hundred yards across. Thousands of young balsams, beginning their cycle of life, occupied the ground under the older trees. The slope rolled off on each side into dense forests and misty unknowns. I knew in general the watersheds which flanked Sugarland Mountain; but in this dreamy fog world it served my sense of isolation to ignore these memories and to wonder, after all, what was down in those gray depths.

I had been over the upper section only twice before— once on a frigid day in November 1928 when there was a skiff of snow on the ground, and once in heavy rain about twenty years later. Both trips had been taken from the other direction. My memories were widely separated in time and were fragmentary in detail. Hence I felt a rich expectancy. I remembered only a few landmarks—Bear Pen Gap, the turn-off to the Chimneys, and somewhere a rocky outlook which looked down into the Sugarland valley. I knew there was a Huskey Gap and a trail up from Rough Creek, but I remembered little about either. So in a sense it was a new venture into a massive unknown.

As steepening slopes on each side pressed the trail to the center of the ridge, we could look down into ranks of colossal spruces. Rhododendron crowded the path, and I thought we must be approaching Bear Pen Gap. But we passed through several minor gaps before we reached that first remembered landmark. I looked down a barely discernible ravine to the east which had been all but closed by laurel and rhododendron. The graded Park trail we were following was grassed over in many places, whether from natural succession or exotic grasses brought in by horse parties was not clear.

Here and there we encountered the flat upended root system of a great spruce. In these windfalls we could see evidence that their side roots had been severed when the trail was constructed.

But despite these ill-starred windfalls the woods were thick. Their density was something to be experienced, not told. Rising out of the deep fog, their bounds were unseen. One had the feeling there was nothing else but greenness and brownness and grayness reaching to the end of the world.

As we passed into the domain of the great yellow birches, the tone of the wind deepened into a throaty growl. The valley on the left had been logged 40 years earlier; but a band of virgin timber had been left uncut along the crest for later exploitation, which the establishment of the Park had happily forestalled. I tried to define the limits of the logging operations. But the fog, heavy timber, and resurgence below kept me baffled.

We were strangely alone. A few flocks of juncos flashed the inverted white V in their tail feathers. We saw occasional scats in the trail (from foxes, we thought) and fresh lime and chalk droppings of ruffed grouse.

We moved faster than I had thought possible and came unexpectedly upon a tiny sign with the one word "Chimneys." This intersection was once choked with briers, rhododendron, and spruce. A huge old birch had been the only landmark. Now there was a visible opening in the rhododendron where the rough trail dropped off very steeply. We followed the Sugarland trail a couple of hundred yards farther and craning our necks looked through the screen of vegetation and the thinning mist for our second landmark. It was an act of faith, but out there in the grayness we spotted the irregular shadow of the Chimney Tops.

Loops of saw briers now crept into the edge of the trail on our left where logging and fire had reached the crest of the mountain. The trail had a certain harshness. The pad of wild grasses was thinner, and we could feel and hear the grating of gravel and mineral in the soil under our feet.

The wind was increasing in power, and maintained a continuous mighty roaring in the young trees. Turbulent winter winds delight me. They come out of a vast unknown. They stir our lives and then they are off beyond the ridges.

I began to look for landmark number three, an open ledge where we could look down into the Sugarland valley. But it was not until the trail passed around and to the left of a huge knob on the main ridge—a deviation which carried us through patches of laurel and galax, of trailing arbutus and wintergreen, of pine needles and peaty soil under the young forest—that we came to the ledge.

There we stopped. We had been pressing our luck. So far, we

had hiked in a clinging mist. We wanted to get as far as possible before the afternoon rain came, which I felt was inevitable. It had been six hours since breakfast and we had been moving fast.

Tired, we dropped to the trail to eat lunch, and then inched over behind a ledge out of the wind. Overhead the fog began to get lighter, collecting itself into masses of scudding white clouds. We saw a patch of blue, and on the far slope sunshine lit up a bit of Le Conte. The clouds seemed to be breaking instead of deepening. We relaxed.

After lunch we moved on, proceeding through a band of hemlocks. I thought we would not see any more spruce. But the trail made another right-angle turn to the north, and in small pockets we found more spruce. Mostly, however, the vegetation was xerophytic —ground pine, wintergreen berry, galax, pine, laurel. On the left, where a forest fire had swept up the ridge years before, greenbrier vines coiled along and in the trail. However, the trees were recovering and both the ground and trail were well covered.

We passed several clefts in the main ridge and looked east down steep slopes into the great moist mixed forest. The trail then circled the high eminence of Sugarland above Huskey Gap and we caught glimpses down the west slope through open woods to Little River.

The woods had healed amazingly from the fire and logging of 40 years ago. In southern mountains fire prevention insures quick recovery. Even high on Sugarland we crossed several small streamlets. We passed two superb camping spots. Once we flushed a grouse and watched its plump body hurtle like a brown bomb through the trees.

There were silverbells and a black cherry. We saw a few young cherry trees eight to twelve inches in diameter. Whence had these trees spread? Then we saw a great gnarled, hollow cherry tree which probably was not worth the cutting in the 1920's. It was the seed tree for this remarkable regrowth.

In stands of pine the needles occasionally lay two inches thick on the trail. I had expected the lower part of the trail to be dry and uninteresting, but none of it was uninteresting. The new growth was an exhilaration and the vegetational changes were diagrammatic. Huskey Gap, which seemed to lurk around every bend but which we were a long time reaching, was green and healed. Inviting paths led down on each flank.

The Sugarland trail extended three and a half miles farther and surprisingly had several steep, upward pitches. This climbing at the downhill end I could not understand until I looked at a map. The ridge splayed at the lower end, and our route had either to follow around all these foothill ridges on grade or to climb across some of them to reach the central divide.

Our trip provided a notable experience through a succession of ecological provinces, along a trail which was barely disturbed except at the upper and lower ends.

April 21 Whittling—the piecemeal alteration of our natural environment—goes on everywhere. I note changes along the Road Prong, which has been healing for nearly 50 years, and the slicing into the humus on the lead south of the Chimneys which gave the appearance of having been undisturbed for eternities. Now the new one-way road from Cherokee Orchard to the Roaring Fork cuts through virgin hemlocks in Spruce Flats. And there is a clamor for manhandling certain balds. Some of these changes are being effected with emergency relief money. Such forced work makes me shudder should the Youth Corps be established. Man's capacity for destruction often far exceeds his desire to preserve. It is more than "desire" —comprehension, understanding, and knowledge are involved also.

And now two great new tools—I was tempted to say "toys"—have been discovered. One is the mass use of pesticides, and the other is the "controlled" use of fire.

A curious aspect of all this, and one that conservationists have been winking at for years, is that long-term resources and processes are being viewed and handled with short-term perspectives. Trees 75 and 100 years old are slashed for a view. A road is bulldozed through a forest. Ground cover is disturbed and huge drainage ditches channel water which used to be dispersed over an entire ridge.

We do the same thing with our rooftops, collecting and carrying off all the water which falls on hard and impervious roofs, and then complain of the dryness of the earth in the summer doldrums. We do the same thing with parking areas, interrupting the slow processes of absorption and assimilation for the immediate goals of dry parking lots. Shortcuts produce problems.

Years ago Aldo Leopold, speaking from a lifetime of rare and questioning observation of his environment, said that we should try everywhere to preserve natural conditions. In another place he wrote that conservation is a state of harmony between man and his environment.

Implicit is the thought of adjustment, of accommodation, of a living in harmony with the land. It would require exhaustive study to live in complete harmony, but given a modicum of understanding and good will (not toward men but toward the earth) every individual could do much toward attaining this harmony.

Leopold has said that the greatest discovery of the twentieth century is not television or the radio but the complexity of biological processes. All around us this complexity is evident. In our small lawn unexplained bare spots make a calico and not a carpet of our grass. A tree which is healthy looking one day is kissed with the brown of death the next. Some ricks of firewood lie for years hard and firm in the weather, and others disintegrate almost in a season.

A paper-plant executive says we have not been able to keep pollution from our streams because we have not learned to live without producing waste. Could man in some unseen era learn to live without waste? Could his activities become so efficient that he could live simply as a natural part of his environment, like the various constituents of a terrarium?

October 8 Anne and I slept on the hills above Emerts Cove. The scene was dream-like. Mists had gathered in the valley and, under the moon, seemed like a mystic lake with arms reaching back into the ridges. Beyond the lake, in a pale wash of gray, stood the great walls of the Greenbrier Pinnacle and of the Stateline. All the night through we would raise our heads and look down at the "lake," and all the night through we were bombarded by acorns breaking loose from their caps.

But for the acorns it was one of the quietest of nights. No clouds, no wind. In the moonlight, we could look up into a myriad of leaves. There was never a movement, never a flutter. But on occasion there would float against my face the sheerest of sensations, a slight coolness which touched my face but hardly brushed it—a movement so imperceptible, that though it could be felt, it left the leaves and branches undisturbed. It was a gentle and elusive night, with just the suggestion of fall in the air. If we think of the fall as involving the dropping of the acorns around our faces, there was more than a suggestion—it was compelling. If we think of it as the change of the seasons, we were not yet there; but we were on balance. These serene days and nights are a buffer between the extremes of summer and the carnival of autumn color and the downpouring of leaves and fruits.

Day follows day in an endless procession of perfection. Dreamy blue skies, cloudless and soft, interlard a succession of crisp, crystalline nights, when the thermometer drifts a little lower. We are sinking into winter-time temperature, but slowly. There is no more discomfort at midday. There is a slight tang in the evenings. One is carried along with it, until the feeling arises that it can never change, that it will go on forever. Ruby leaves glow in the sunlight and the curtains of green are interspersed with gold as the trees, too, inch along with the weather. Two golden hickories have already turned from cap to root, standing like orange-yellow silos. Pink globes of fruit dangle from the persimmons.

I live each day in wordless foreboding. We are now in the twenty-second consecutive rainless day. Leaves are explosively dry. Even though there are shows of color from every window—the lambent green and red of the sourwoods and the scarlet of the dogwoods as well as the golden column of the hickory—there are innumerable trees upon which the leaves are already twisted and brown. There has been no rain to beat them to the ground and there is an ominousness in the windless air.

When we staked out our small lawn, I blithely said we wanted a little belt of insulation around us in case the woods should catch fire. Now that a woods fire is an imminent possibility our lawn seems frighteningly small. True, there is yet much green in the woods, but the crackling carpet of the fallen leaves has spread uniformly over our two acres. The very calm in the air has an appalling quality, as though an unannounced storm were about to break.

The desiccated pastures and the prospect of fires in the mountains produce unspoken dread. I recall the great bands of green and of blackened forests along the Alaska highway. I got accustomed to it and accepted the spectacle as a characteristic of a far-reaching wilderness. But here I cannot be so philosophical. As a part of humanity I am much too involved. It is difficult to face with equanimity the prospect of charred hillsides. We live in uneasy quiet.

November 3 On my trip to Silers Bald with Guy and West the mountains were suffused with a soft haze which erased the boundary between earth and sky. The vaults of space and the rolling blue ridges met in misty fantasy.

We drifted down the trail at the focus of perfection. Air and sun and shade touched us but to caress. Scents of balsam and drying grasses drew out old nostalgias. The lonesome queries of the nuthatches, the tiny enthusiasms of the chickadees, and the quivering scoldings of the squirrels spun the feel of the wilds. Leaves rattled around our feet and were pulverized as we walked, raising memories of a thousand fragrant autumn days.

We rested on the south-facing grass of the Narrows bald. Small pits and basins and rollings in the underlying earth received our bodies and the sun dropped a blanket of warmth over us. Rest came easily, naturally, and completely. All of nature was in a languorous pause between the surges of summer and the bitter stringencies of winter. We were wrapped in contentment. A little sapling raised a pleasing oriental pattern against the pale wash of the hills. A sourwood, sheltered from the frost, splashed a bit of color from the edge of the grass.

We moved on through the place of the beeches. Slopes as steep as roofs supported stunted forests. Aisles of gray opened on every side. Gnarled trunks were rough with lichens. Horizontal limbs were brown with leaves of soft leather which quivered in the breeze. One felt a tenseness in their strumming. The Narrows was the corridor of the winds which in spring and early winter boom across in hoarse-voiced roars.

Why had these trees found this exposed place? Do they too delight in the gales? Do these pygmy trees belie their toughness? At many places in the Smokies the gentle beeches have found these boisterous wind paths. We came to these groves with affection; we left them with veneration and respect.

A new shelter has been constructed at the Double Springs. The trees on the south side have been felled leaving a yawning view where once a shaded spring gathered in the rocks. On the north, the green pools collecting under tree roots have been faced with raw concrete in which heedless campers have left skims of soap.

Progress had come to the Double Springs by a flat trough of a trail baked as hard as concrete! This triumph of the planner's art had come by a swift decision at a desk hundreds of miles away. The machines rolled and dug and hardened the cushioned trail which the feet of generations of men and animals had shaped.

Only the spruces now lining the pathways of the skidders of 50 years ago seem to be following the earthly rhythms. Money must be spent, and violence again descends upon the ancient slopes of Clingmans and the Stateline, even though the basic National Park act says that the parks shall be kept unimpaired for future generations.

We were witness to other battlefields. The natural opening, where the tiger lilies used to form their summer ranks with their gay orange caps, has been engulfed in briers. We saw the pods of only one lily at that skirmish area. I cannot believe they have surrendered; they are only grouping for another stand in another opening in another summer.

December 29 On Friday I went to Rainbow Falls. I don't know any place where the trail leads so quickly from a roadhead into another world. This is particularly the case when the ground is heavily covered with snow. One cannot see the wear on the trail under the snow.

The break is sharp. One steps as through a door from the open vistas of the orchard to the close gloom of deep woods and stream. The cold is biting. The tree trunks are dark. Boulders along the trail are gray and green with lichens. The crystal stream reflects dark browns and greens and one sees through it to the grays and browns of its bed. Light is subdued. Even the snow is restful and muted.

I like this woodsy prelude to the world farther along. The trail here swings halfway down the bank from the first bench. There is a similar bench on the far side. One has the feeling of moving upward through a wide shallow trough with the soft rush of the creek at the bottom.

There are big trees, both standing and prone. The latter comprise the hulks of the chestnuts which were felled 30 years ago by the Civilian Conservation Corps. In this damp world they have a surprising resistance to decay and retain their outer shapes even as they molder within. Mosses and lichens attach to their surfaces and an occasional seedling finds lodgment. And so by degrees the trunks subside onto the ground and then into it, taking on the color and character of the earth itself. Here and there a round hummock, with a row of small hemlocks lacing their roots through the fibrous mold, is all that is left of one of these giants.

After awhile the trail found the bench. The sounds of the stream dwindled and an awesome silence was in the air. The mist hung above us in a slowly moving stratum. Galax leaves pushed above the snow and globules of mud rolled down from the trail sides into our path. The thin mat of vegetation at the ground surface overhung the muddy trailsides in a hapless furl. This trail was nearly 30 years old. It was still yielding at the edges and one wondered if it would ever stabilize. Never is a long time. We think in decades. Nature operates in millennia.

We saw the old wall which was built 40 years ago at the lower side of the lily field. On the upper side the soil had flowed level with its top. The wall had served its purpose of holding the soil run-off. The trail now pierced the wall's center, making us aware of its height as we passed through. Young spruces grew in the area of the old field in unwonted numbers. The seeds had found easy location there, as they could not on the more competitive slopes higher up. These seedlings were close to 40 years old. I saw no balsams, but the spruces and hemlocks were abundant.

Boulders, flush with the trail, had caught warm rays and had emerged dark and firm amidst a ring of snow. We took advantage of their firmness and would shove mightily as we felt them under foot, in striking contrast to the shifting and crusted snow.

As the snow deepened and the crust hardened we found ourselves stepping into the tracks of the leader. After we crossed the creek the snow was seven inches deep. I broke trail for a while in a short, choppy stride, leaning over and driving my feet piston-like into the snow. There were tracks of squirrels, wildcats, and foxes. Once, the broad palm-like tracks of a bear crossed our route at right angles. The snow had a certain tenaciousness, and a chunk falling off a tree onto a slope rolled up a spiral before toppling flat.

The mist darkened. The winter scene of great hemlocks and birches and shiny rhododendrons was frigid and forbidding.

We could not see the falls from the footbridge. Even the cone of ice was but a gray shadow in the darker murkiness. The air was bitter. As we ate, stamping out little flat places in the snow, the fog thinned for a moment and the sun streamed through the mist, lighting up the boulder field above us and illuminating momentarily the blue-ice of the cone. The grayness closed in and the boulders resembled again jumbled tombstones under several layers of snow.

On the return we met a handsome bareheaded young man coming up. There was rare color in his face. Frost rimed his hair. He was carrying a heavy pack and was going to camp out on Le Conte. He was one of the most attractive persons I have ever met. And how I envied him the night on top! In years past I had spent several nights on Le Conte at this time of year. I recalled the hushed stillness, with occasional explosions from trees whose moisture pockets had burst in the cold. I remembered the whiteness, the excitement of being in a world that was different but one that was appropriate and utterly beautiful. Young men who look forward to such experiences are good for the nation.

INETEEN SIXTY-FOUR

January 21   One of the meteorological miracles of the Southern Highlands occurred two days before I made my second winter trip to Le Conte in recent years. The swirling, spiral wake of the storm which was to bring new snow took an unpredictable course. Instead of freezing rain and snow, we got clear weather; instead of frigid temperatures, we got unexpectedly warm ones.

At the lower elevations the snow was damp and packed under our feet; yet higher in the valley, where the great wall of Le Conte held off the sun, it became powdery. Although the snow was not completely gone from south-facing slopes, it lay in scattered shallow patches. The general aspect was one of warm browns and greens with islands of white. At Rainbow Falls the ice cone at the foot of the falls had almost vanished.

Much of Le Conte Creek was iced over, but there were occasional clear dark pools which had resisted freezing. Domes of ice covered other pools and fluted walls of frozen crystal lined the cliffs.

On the higher slopes the myriad tiny specks on the snow we discovered were not very active snow fleas. Upon what do these almost microscopic creatures exist? How can they survive and preserve their vitality on wastes of pristine snow? Where do they go in summer? How do they reproduce and survive the heat if this frigid cold is their natural world?

The sky was blue and the sun warm where we climbed through one of its beams. But mostly we were in deep shadow. The great wall of the main range was always on our right and almost always stood between us and the sun. (I looked up the first hollow above the falls and thought of my first clawing climb to Le Conte, now nearing a half century ago. That was a different day, a different world, when in 1920 Father and I, with Wiley Oakley and others, forced our way up that hollow to the West Peak.)

We did most of our climbing in the massive shadow cast by Le Conte. A little to our left was the melt line, but we climbed in deep soft snow. I think I have never before been so aware of the extreme steepness of the north slope of Le Conte. It is a stupendous, forested wall about which almost nothing is known. As Herb Pomerance and I moved along the gentler gradient of the creek, I looked up at it and wondered how a forest could find lodgment there.

In other days I had proposed a climb up the face from Le Conte Creek to the ridge crest between West Peak and Balsam Top. It would be equally taxing to climb the grade between West Peak and Cliff Top. The chances are that I shall never do it. But mysteries of slope and grade lie there to be uncovered by someone else. My sadness that that particular climb is not for me mingles with the joy that here is yet a closed book which possibly no one has ever opened.

There were several areas of windthrow and of forest kill around the top of Le Conte. I cannot even guess whether they have been caused in part by the spread of the lodge area which has been opened around the cabins. Perhaps this opening is the natural result of the spring winds, which on occasion strike the tops with great violence.

Herrick is getting wood from a blowdown which occurred nearly 40 years ago between the camping area and Cliff Top. As I looked out toward High Top from the camp, I saw gray patches, two or three of them of some size, indicating kill. But the trees in these gray areas had not yet blown down.

The lodge is using backlogs which came from trees up to 200 years old. Since the bark was still on them, they must have come from recent windfalls. The cycles of growth and decay on Le Conte I have long thought were measured in short decades. But the size of those large backlogs point to much longer spans. Around the camp the forest seems to be grove-like, lacking the aspect of deep woods. But viewed from the valleys, there is nothing to indicate that there has been change in the forest.

In discussing conditions on Le Conte, somebody remarked that there were a lot of blowdowns on Guyot. This is true. But the conditions there are different, in that Guyot was once logged to the top on the south side. Strictly natural conditions do not presently exist there. Le Conte would be a perfect control but for the activities and cutting around the lodge. I cannot be sure that soil compaction has not had its part because of the presence of many people, and that the removal of the down trees may not have interfered with normal reseeding.

I do know that on Cliff Top and Myrtle Point man-set fires destroyed substantial areas of sand myrtle. Revegetation is taking place around the fringes of the cliffs, but there is too much human use to lead one to expect full return on the central outcrops. It is evident that regrowth under the best of conditions will be very slow and hardly measurable against the human life span.

We have become so accustomed to having the Smokies close at hand, few of us can really sense what a boon they are. Some portions are marked with the spare nobility of the primeval. On this trip I remember quiet avenues of snow among the forest giants, interspersed with new struggling seedlings.

We watched the sunset from Cliff Top. The mountains were gray and aloof—washed in a light, penetrable haze which was drawn over all the distant ranges, obscuring detail and revealing outlines mysterious and remote. Man can skin the land and leave it naked and forlorn, but the vast outlines remain. In the Smokies, in time, the air of softness returns to cut-over lands, and with it this seamless wrapping of slate-gray mist.

On the ledges the wind tore at us, drawing tears to our eyes and moisture to our noses. We huddled together against the wind to watch the climax of the day, when a yellowing sun dropped into a band of slate at the horizon. Then we drew our garments closer about us and passed into the woods. We were turning away from the vastness and beauty and aloofness. For all his perception, man is a hopeless oaf in the presence of the sublime.

George Hines and I broke trail out to Myrtle Point on Sunday morning. Snow was deep. There were several crusts, and sometimes we stepped through clear to the ground in snow nearly hip deep.

George is very perceptive. From miles away he noticed the curious twist in the stream bed of Ramsay Prong. It is my thought that a land slippage or earthquake had changed the course of the stream, since Ramsay appears once to have been a tributary of the Buck Fork. We saw a great level splash of snow marking Newfound Gap. I recalled that I had been to Newfound in 1927 when it was but a minor dip in a beech forest.

April 12 The day was bright, sunny, and lazy—not hot, not cool. The west part of Cades Cove had a green loveliness, dreamy and enticing. Expansive pastures were dotted with fat Angus cattle. Back of them rose the mountains in an opaque blue. The sun bounced off the fields into our faces and the warmth was vital and lifegiving. But it was the silence which registered. Somewhere in the forest back of us a woodpecker chiseled at a tree. Before us a few crows flapped over, calling halfheartedly. So far as I could see there was nothing for them to scold. They simply called because they were crows. Both sounds were almost lost in the vastness and they soothed rather than disturbed the prospect before us. . . .

The season is slow. The sarvis was in abundant bloom, but only here and there did we see a flush of redbud. Of dogwood we were not aware. The woods still had the openness of winter and the sun penetrated them freely.

Later we swapped the quiet of the cove for the stir of the rivers. They were full but not in flood. White bubbles roiled to the surface in the pools, and the water had the color and appearance of frosted, fluid jade. The flow had a lively, open incessance. There was vitality and rare beauty, but none of the violence of the floods.

Of floods there was much evidence—leaves and debris clinging in the undergrowth many feet above the surface of the water; and new, yellow gouges in the banks where the current had torn at its bounds. A few places it had filmed over the road. As economic man, we deplored the raw slopes; as ecologic man, we were excited by the evidence of everlasting change.

July 3 Last Saturday I joined the Hiking Club on its trip to Mt. Le Conte via Trout Branch. In 1952 I had hiked the lower portion of it, one year after the great flood. Vivid in my memory was a great flat drift of stones some two acres in extent. The flood had gutted the upper reaches and had deposited the stones as it spent its force.

But now the undergrowth had made deep inroads into this rocky area. Everywhere the young birches (especially) and other vegetation were coming in. The stones lay in loose sieve-like layers which allowed the stream to percolate out of sight. The water was visible only as it flowed over ledges or where the hidden rocks were close to the surface.

The stream is not yet stabilized. This will come, I would guess, only when the banks are completely laced together with the roots of new vegetation, and the stream bed is cleared by later floods. The original torrent was so violent the bed is now made up of large-sized stones and boulders. It will be many years before these raw conditions will disappear and the stream becomes visible again its full length.

On Trout Branch there was a massive cliff over which the water trickled. A similar cliff is found at like elevations in many parts of the Smokies. Were the cliffs, those at Rainbow and Ramsay Falls and elsewhere, possibly created by a colossal earth shift over much of the Smokies? If the country were more open, as in Yosemite, the answer might be obvious. But under the dense vegetational cover of the Smokies, these cliffs are revealed only in the stream courses or along some of the steeper slopes.

A short distance above the ledge on Trout Branch was the so-called "slide." Its base must have extended several hundred yards along the west side of Trout Branch, whence it stretched upward in a triangle reaching an apex perhaps 600 feet above the stream bed. On the slide and waterfall ledge below, the solid old graywacke had given way to slate. The strata overlapped one another much like a slate roof, with loose slivers accumulated on the exposed strata. The pitch was such that one could barely stand erect, with no assurance that his feet would not scoot out from under him. Higher up, the pitch lessened and I tried some biped climbing; but lower down I used arms as well as feet and clung to shrubbery at the edge. I had seen this slide from the Alum Cave trail to Le Conte, but from there had gained no idea of its extent.

At the apex we bore to the left through heavy rhododendron and soon came out into open but very steep alpine woods. Two hours later we pulled up to the trail after negotiating an irregular series of cliffy outcrops—much like the spines on a dinosaur's back. I had reached the top in about five hours.

There is evidence that the sand myrtle and the laurel are gradually closing in on the raw wastes of Cliff Top and Myrtle Point. The paths are becoming narrower and some of the areas where people once wandered seem to be disappearing.

Far below the cliff, where the foot trail had been hacked out of solid rock, Bob and I found dozens of sand myrtle seedlings, some not more than an inch high, taking root in crevices and troughs in the rock.

On Myrtle Point the fire-fractured rock had slid off the slopes and had come to rest in windrows against the encircling rhododendron. It was clear that vegetation is beginning to override these windrows. The myrtle is beginning to barrel out as it once did in buxom curves along the trail to the point.

Someone asked how the myrtle looked on Myrtle Point in the old days. I recalled that it was so thick in 1922 that Frank Fowler and I could run and jump onto it with flying somersaults. That luxuriance is not duplicated today, but there is gain.

Anne, Margaret, Bob, and I got up at 4 a.m. to make the walk to Myrtle Point for the sunrise. I started out ahead.

There was a quarter moon and only the suggestion of daylight. Alone and in the faint light I absorbed the full witchery of the dawn. Everything had a gloss of mystery. The uneven spread of moonlight along the path created a false perception of a third dimension, to which I had to accommodate myself. I stumbled a time or two along the rugged trail through ledges and woods and myrtle.

On the crest was the closeness of the woods; on my right a wavering blue maw—half mountains, half latency and obscurity. In the soft quarter light of the moon it was little more than a lead-colored void in which drifting lines, more shadow than substance, came and went. These were the Great Smoky Mountains in the mystic shroud of dawn.

Are there several Smokies—those of midday, those of midnight, those of predawn, those of spring, of autumn, of winter? Which *are* the Smokies? Who can say?

I turned to the widening flush in the east which was beginning to outline the cone of Mt. Guyot. As the outlines sharpened, streamers of rose and gold appeared in the sky and blue voids to the south and east took on depth and dimension.

In the semidarkness I had found beauty and mystery and untouchable appeal. The ambuscades and surprises of the earlier days had returned on the blue waves of moonlight and on the barely freshening light in the east.

November 15 Yesterday I returned to Silers Bald almost 50 years after I made my first trip there. The grazing which was extensive on the meadows in 1917 has ceased. Logging on the slopes of the Stateline and Clingmans has ended. All the galled and eroded spots have become covered with grass.

Down the Tennessee side from Double Springs Gap, the rough cabin which I visited in 1917 has disappeared and an open-front shelter has recently been constructed on the bulge between the two springs. The shelter is heavily used and the ground around it is trampled and littered.

On the Tennessee side, water still seeps out of a quagmire of mud. The flow has been caught in a shallow concrete basin and conveyed to another basin by a pipe. On the North Carolina side, the tiny spring which rises within ten feet of the crest of the mountain was flowing, but the woods have been cleared from around it, erasing its charm. One bluet greeted the November sun.

I overheard an explorer scout say that the water was better on the Tennessee side because it came out of a pipe. What sanctity is there to a pipe? Are the woods so forbidding that one is not at home unless there is a pipe? Is a pipe the symbol of the ubiquity of man and of the slow retreat of nature?

Away from the trail and the roads, the woods are slowly healing. There are no bare slopes any more, where the loggers and fire were having their way 40 and 50 years ago. But the evidences of those activities have not been erased even by four decades. It is still easy along the upper slopes of Sugarland Mountain to separate the belt of primeval from the once-cut woods. There is a luxuriant uneven-ness and richness to the band of old growth. The contours are rounder and softer. Where there was fire, there is now greenness, but it clings closely, in sharp profiles, to the underlying rock.

On the side of Clingmans we could see the converging bands worn into the surface by the log skidders, now grown up in briers and un-dergrowth. But the spruce and balsams were absent from those belts of use, and grew only in the less disturbed areas between. The broad outlines of the history of man's doings could be read at a glance.

NINETEEN SIXTY-FIVE

February 24 We were looking for Honey Cove Creek, which flows into the Middle Prong of Little River from the east. The maps show a series of waterfalls or cascades, which we spotted; but between us and them was the 50-foot wide, cold and deep-running Middle Prong. We went farther upstream in search of a bridge which Tom Duncan recalled was there fifteen years ago. It wasn't there now. Wading was the only alternative. So we reluctantly hunted out stout poles to assist us and a handy boulder to sit on while we removed our boots. The boulder I sat on was cold; so I sat on my gloves. I rolled my trousers tightly to my upper thighs, tied my boots across my pack, and waded in.

Immediately my toes went numb. The round stones forming the bed of the Middle Prong were hideously slick. The current was strong and I had to jab with my pole several times before it would hold. My feet were so numb I had to thrust them among the stones until they too lodged. It was tempting to head for a large boulder which was just awash. But I soon learned that the current swirled more swiftly around the sides of such boulders and that I would have to fight to get by.

All four of us were in the water by now. As I neared the bank I moved slightly upstream where I could grasp a long slender limb of a hemlock which overhung the river. For the last five feet I had my pole in one hand and a tenuous grasp on this limb with the other. I emerged upon a dry boulder, limped up the bank on benumbed feet, and sat down on some pine needles in the sun. My legs and feet

I rubbed with leaves and needles until feeling inched down toward my toes. The latter I cuffed with my hands until there was a painful tingle. Then I drew on my socks and boots and soon felt a flow of warmth.

I threw away my stick, stood up, and looked back across the stream. There were my mittens lying on the boulder where I had left them! I had nothing except a parka and sweater in my pack—no gloves and no extra socks. Bob lent me a pair of thin dress gloves as we headed for some of the worst thickets of saw briers I have seen in years.

Moving across the flat we intercepted an old logging grade which ascended to our left and after a quarter of a mile reached the valley of Honey Cove Creek above the series of falls.

We estimated that this railroad grade had been last used by the Little River Lumber Company 25 years ago. And like all such grades in the Smokies it was growing up in young saplings, briers, and grasses. We followed this grade for a couple of hours and only once do I recall the washboard footing sometimes encountered from the removal or rotting of the old crossties.

Farther up, by comparison with tulip poplars of known ages in other parts of the Smokies, we estimated young tulips to be 20 to 25 years old.

Early in the hike a fork in the railroad grade posed a question as to the route. We had an altimeter, a compass, and old Park maps. Never did all three agree with the topography at any of these forkings in the railroad grade. After further review of known data we decided to take the left fork. Three times we did this, each time passing through even-growth woods. We found almost no old growth. The logging that was done had been the equivalent of clear-cutting. Few trees, even those as little as six inches in diameter, had been preserved.

At lunch we were still close to water and still, according to the map, about 600 feet below the crest we sought. Doubts that we were on the right route assailed us. The map showed our pathway high on the north flank of Meigs Mountain. There was a high knob back of us and after lunch we climbed its slopes. The going was rough and steep, and as we pushed eastward we began to encounter dense tangles of saw briers. I was punctured and scratched, and the frail dress gloves were no match for the barbs as I tried to snap my way out.

Eventually we gained enough elevation for a view. We could see

Du Pont, the end of Chilhowee Mountain, and the tower on Cove Mountain. The latter was not on our map, so we could not triangulate to determine where we were.

But the suspicion began to dawn on us that we were not on Meigs Mountain but on Curry She Mountain, more than one trailless mile from where we should be. If we were on Curry She, we were only one-third of the way to Elkmont, where three others of our group had parked a car and were hiking toward us. We shouted many times but got no answer from them.

Tom thought we should backtrack. But before doing so, we climbed the brushy and slightly rounded summit of the mountain we were on for another look. Blanket Mountain was in the "wrong" place. We were lost!

There was a maze of drainages in the area. We thought we were on Curry She Mountain because of the altimeter readings. But it is possible for the barometric pressure to shift drastically in the course of a day and throw the readings off.

Returning, we had no difficulty retracing our route of the morning. Two problems were debated. Should we try to descend the cascades and the righthand bank of the main river to the bridge at the old Girl Scout camp and avoid again wading that icy stream? How long should we wait for the Elkmont group who if they got through were now, like us, dependent upon our one car for transportation?

When we got to the cascades, the banks alongside were brushy and precipitous. We voted to wade the stream at the site of our first crossing.

I took off my boots and double-strapped them to my pack. The rocks in the stream bed were so round and slippery I was afraid I might lurch and sling my boots into the water. I had just stepped into the water when my eye caught a movement on the far bank. It was the three from Elkmont, who had made it through. They were motioning me to go upstream, but I was already in the water. They watched me vigilantly as the water surged high above my knees. Ed came down to the edge and took my hand as I neared the bank. I dried my feet, put on my boots, and picked up the mittens I had left that morning.

Meanwhile, the others in my party had walked upstream to the other crossing. By then I had climbed to the road with Ed and Jessie and was sketching a map of our trip in the sand. We heard a shout and saw Dickerman and Tom running toward us, Tom in his bare feet. At first I was afraid that Bob or Charlie had fallen in the stream. But no; Tom had slipped as he crossed and had lost his boots. We lined the bank with long poles hoping to snare them should they float by. They never did!

Tom started the three-mile walk on the graveled road. After a while I suggested that he use my heavy socks in addition to his since I had my boots. He demurred and I then offered him my mittens. He said with a shout, "Why, I've got my gloves and some adhesive tape. I'll tape the gloves to my socks."

Ed and Charlie ran on ahead with the car keys hoping to get the ranger to open the gate. He was not at home, but Ed found Bob's shoes in the car and returned with them for Tom. And so ended an adventurous day in an unfamiliar area of the Smokies.

November 4 Life has never been sweeter—nor the out-world more enchanting. We were at Emerts Cove last weekend for the "spook night" party of the Hiking Club. The colors were rusty, but the canopy of leaves still held. The contours of the earth quivered with leaves, newly fallen; and one looked, between the layers on the ground and those still clinging to the trees, into vistas of open woods. The moon was waxing. The air breathed redolence, vitality, and peace.

Activity had slowed to a crawl. We walked from one cottage to another. There were wood fires in each. A kettle of stew bubbled over a fire at Bob Maher's. At West Barber's we enjoyed the pleasures of full-throated singing.

At Addison Hook's, while we faced the warmth of the great backlog which had awaited 24 years for the occasion of its lighting, we felt sharp breezes drilling at our back. Turning our backs to the fire, we faced the large windows with a glimpse of trees and the dim outlines of mountains beyond. We used an old-fashioned "john," and pumped water from a cistern with an old-fashioned pump.

At breakfast, at a table laid close to that great fireplace, we lingered long, sharing our latest moments and thoughts with long-time friends. Everything seemed in place—all life desirable! We felt the richness of just being alive—the warmth of pure functioning.

Thrust into the back of our minds for the weekend was the prospect that a parkway might rip through these tranquil woods, erasing this retreat and many others. What had existed so long surely could not come to that end! We forgot the unrest in the tier of states to the south and the bewildering antics on the campuses of our colleges. We forgot momentarily Vietnam; the great unrest over all the world; the cramped congestion and hopelessness in our cities.

Out there was uncertainty—violence, unreason—desperation. Around us, in Emerts Cove where the woods were clean and fresh, were calm, warmth, friendship, harmony.

November 10 The proposed new transmountain road between Bryson City and Townsend via Buckeye Gap would slice through one of the most significant botanical areas in eastern United States. The last period of glaciation brought south the conifers of the north country. Fossilized pollen grains of those trees have been found as far south as South Carolina. When the ice age broke, the line of the spruces and firs began a retreat to the north. Its continuous line now extends across northern Minnesota, Wisconsin, Michigan, New York, and mid-New England.

But tongues and islands of conifers remain in the southern states— usually in the highlands where they are now besieged by hardwoods. These islands occur in the high Smokies, Black Mountains, and Balsam Mountains of North Carolina and Tennessee, on White Top and other high mountains of Virginia, and on the heights of still lower mountains in West Virginia. In recent times the westernmost point for spruce in the Smokies, and probably in the Southeast, had been on Miry Ridge near Buckeye Gap.

The line of the conifers which is doubly affected by rainfall and by temperature is a huge natural thermometer and rain gauge. The gauge was battered by the logging and grazing of the last 50 to 100 years. But it still works! It can be read around Double Springs Gap and Buckeye Gap. Some of the lines have been effaced where the trees were cut or the sprouts trampled. A vast bulb of warmth lies to the south and pushes the hardwoods along the high crest of the Smokies to the west of Buckeye Gap. Opposing it is another dome of influence to the north. The two great ecologic masses confront each other in western Smoky along the ecotone that is plain to see. Outpost groupings from each sphere intrude into the other, like patrols of opposing armies.

Engineers have located the crossing of the proposed transmountain road at Buckeye Gap. There is no evidence that any serious ecological studies preceded the decision. The grading, tunneling, filling, alteration of drainages, and induced desiccation will further smudge the markings of this continental thermometer. Nothing could be more tragic. The Park's custodians deem a few views, a few soothed nerves of jaded automobilists as of more consequence than the preservation of this ecotone.

Man has a curious myopia in that he measures all phenomena against the span of his own life. No one knows with certainty whether there is today a discernible trend in the weather. Eleven thousand years ago when the spruce occupied the terrain far to the south there could be no doubt that the average temperature had dropped. Now the hardwoods have pushed back. But Dr. François Matthes, in his studies of the glaciers, has predicted we are entering a new ice age. The critical vegetational markings around Double Springs and Buckeye Gaps should be preserved, to provide readings of the utmost significance to man.

The Pietà was heavily guarded and surrounded with incredibly novel safeguards during its transport from Italy and its exhibition at the World's Fair in New York. But custodians charged with the protection of the Great Smokies casually propose to slash the canvas of the infinite with meaningless new roads.

$\mathscr{N}$INETEEN SIXTY-SIX

May 1 Yesterday Dickerman and I went to Buckeye Gap by way of Silers Bald. For me it was the first time since 1934, and only the fifth time in my life. Our objective was to ascertain whether my memory was correct that certain northern conifers—probably spruce—are found on Miry Ridge near the gap. We did not find out because of a driving rain and heavy fog. The latter lifted momentarily at the gap exposing the massive slope of Miry Ridge. I could see peaked evergreens along the skyline but at that distance could not determine whether they were hemlock or spruce. But by checking carefully we saw that the western spearhead of spruce had advanced along the Stateline to Silers Bald itself.

It was fun poking along through the fog, pausing now and then to look at the north slope where the woods merged into the mist a hundred yards down. We strained our eyes for darker silhouettes which marked the evergreens. Through the Narrows we saw none at all, and then as we turned onto the side trail below Silers we saw a greenish blur down the east slope. Dickerman went down to investigate and found a small spruce—misshapen as though it had been trampled upon by a bear. But its discovery brought the spruce outpost within three miles of Buckeye Gap. An hour later we saw another on the west slope of Welch Ridge, less than three miles from the proposed new transmountain road.

We had started from Forney Ridge in heavy, clinging mist—mist so dense that it collected on our clothes in tiny gray tendrils. Water gushed into the trail from closely spaced ravines and gathered in a continual flow at our feet. Beyond the blackness of the evergreens there was a dim opaqueness which shut out all the world, leaving us to the flooded trail and dripping shrubs and trees. Once, out of the fogginess, the song of a winter wren came spiraling in—so subdued by the mist, it seemed from a different species. The wind tore at our packs, swinging us around. This wind, this mist and rain, were to be with us for 30 solid hours.

Among the evergreens, the litter of needles and small twigs which had been snapped off by the snow and winds made for good footing. But when we reached the beech belt just above Double Springs Gap, the leaves from the beeches held the moisture in a greasy embrace upon which we slipped with neck-snapping suddenness. This drove us, as it had others, to the edge of the trail, which was becoming wider from such use. In addition, shelter building activities had gouged and muddied the trail. Because of the high rainfall, the Park Service should learn to sometimes leave Smoky trails alone.

Reaching Silers, we decided to camp and cook on the west side of Welch Ridge near water. We paused on a narrow rib between ravines. We reasoned that if it should rain, the water would drain off the rib. It did start to rain just as we were lighting our fire under a slanting rock. The rain became worse. I donned my poncho which pinioned my arms as I tried to chop a bit of beech. The beech though sound was very damp. Dick hunted out a dead center, which was dry but doty. We continued to work an hour at building a fire, even lighting a candle end under twigs and shavings, before the flames finally took hold. By this time it was dark and we had trampled the humus on our little rib into a quagmire.

We cantilevered a flat slab of rock out over the fire to protect the cooking. We broiled steaks, warmed a can of beans and one of corn, and had hot tea. Still it rained.

The ground was soft and sodden. To have slept here would have been like sleeping on a sponge. I decided to go to the little overhanging cliff which in 1917 our party had found, and which Anne and Doris had used in 1953. Dickerman elected to sleep on the knoll above the cliff. I gave him my poncho, and planned to wrap my sleeping bag in a nylon tarp.

By flashlight I started for the cliff overhang and wound up in a tangle of rhododendron and blackberry canes. I strained my eyes, looking into the darkness. No cliff. I floundered up the slope toward the knoll and tried again. Between the soft underfooting, the slope, the rain, and the darkness, I was bewildered and annoyed at myself.

Near the top I found the "cave," black but inviting. I even found some firewood we might have left in 1953. The floor of the cave was damp, but it was flat and not soggy. The space was cramped by a shoulder of rock lying at an angle, which caught rain at its upper edge and drained it under the cliff. The roof was of thin vertical strata, arching over the space it sheltered.

It was better than being out in the rain, however; and as I shucked my boots and trousers and hunched into the warmth of my sleeping bag, I flattened myself comfortably against the ground. The tarp was not quite wide enough for both a ground cloth and cover. Drops of water splashed on my face at intervals all through the night and by morning had found their way underneath. But somehow I rested.

At good light Dickerman appeared at the cave. He had used a lull in the rain to get up. For breakfast we had cold left-overs.

Then we packed and started on. Our objective was Buckeye Gap, three and a half miles farther west. En route Dick unintentionally scared a grouse off her nest. The nest had been built on the ground under the slant of a rotting trunk and despite the rain it was perfectly dry. We counted ten eggs.

The open-front Park shelter was soppy and forlorn. No one had camped there the previous night. Since we would be returning from Buckeye Gap by the same route, we discussed leaving our packs in the shelter. But Dick had once lost a knapsack to marauding bears, which find good picking around the shelters. So we took our packs with us. A few hundred yards farther, however, I wrapped my pack in the tarp and parked it off the trail amid an outcropping of rock. Thus lightened, I proceeded gaily westward in the rain, which drove in almost horizontally from the south. The wind bored into my left ear and I tilted my rain hat for protection.

It was the last day of April. Spring was just beginning to touch this mile-high range. Above, the trees were open and leafless. But the ground was beginning to turn green from early spring flowers. Occasional lilies in a favored spot were yellow with bloom. Pink spring beauties appeared in clusters and a few yellow and purple violets were in bloom.

Rain and fog prevented our seeing very far. But the woods had a certain luminousness, as though in their unleafed condition they had been unroofed; and the rolling contours of the earth, green with low growth, provided an aspect of spaciousness. A score or more of colossal earthworms—their bodies bleached white by the winter—stretched across the path in the warm rain and wriggled toward some obscure destiny.

Always the wind drilled at us from the south. Always our ponchos whipped around our legs. Always I could feel water rising higher in my left boot.

Then came Buckeye Gap. Long whips of young birches were fuzzy green with their first leaves. At the gap the earth dipped quickly from the east and rose as quickly to the west, and dropped off sharply to the north and south—all in beautiful, rounded, merging curves, like those of a saddle. It was a perfect hyperbolic paraboloid. This was Buckeye Gap on that day chilled by the wind and scourged by rain.

The mist lifted briefly and I looked down the steep east slope. I tried to picture this wild scene should the Park Service tunnel under the gap for a road—a scant 200 feet lower down. The Park Service says this is all second-growth forest and much of it burned over—that the scenery can't be hurt by a road. Did the administrators who made that statement think of the resurgent wildness of the new forest; of the infinite garden that clung to the contours of the earth at the first touch of spring; of the everlasting skirmish between the northern evergreens and the warm-blooded beeches and buckeyes? Did they think of the shrinkage of the wilderness? This was a total experience of sight and sound, of fresh smells, of the taste of rain, of the touch of wetness, of cushiony humus under our feet, of steepness followed by the surcease of those welcome level spots.

Dickerman clambered out of sight down in the mist, while I strained my eyes toward the east wall of Miry Ridge which rose incredibly steep across the valley. As the mist thinned momentarily its crest was notched by evergreens. Some seemed stubbier in outline than others. I couldn't honestly say whether they were spruce. They could have been hemlocks.

We beat a retreat without knowing. The rain drove us back to the avenues along the crest whose vistas were blocked by the opaque fog. We were now going east. When we reached Silers Bald both of us tugged off our boots and poured a quarter pint of water from each boot.

The shelter broke the spell. We had been down into the heart of the western wilderness which the Park Service proposed to make the heart of something else. It would become tamed by another motor road—bereft of its wildness and challenge, of its mystery and awe-someness. It would be just one more of thousands of places people could go in motor cars. Destroyed would be one more of the shrinking number of places untrammeled by man and by the works of man.

Surface conditions in western Smoky have changed greatly since the termination of grazing, now about a quarter of a century ago. During the grazing era the ground was tough, firm turf. On this most recent trip, each time we left the trail I was struck by the sponginess of the earth all the way from Double Springs to Buckeye Gap.

It was particularly noticeable on Welch Ridge, which was soft with abundant humus—a condition which has built up in 30 years. No wonder everything seemed like a garden. The humus had become a seed bed which many plants found favorable to growth. And the humus was no doubt alive with living, crawling, tunneling things. Barring underlying roots or stones and barring rain, we could have slept anywhere on any level spot on Welch Ridge. When we left the trail, it was like walking across a deep pile carpet, so different from the worn, compacted, and muddy ground around the shelters.

July 4 I have been to Le Conte on the last three weekends, twice by Alum Cave and once from the Greenbrier via Trillium Gap and down by Alum Cave. It was probably the first time in twenty years that I had been to Trillium Gap. Most of my memories of the gap went back 30 years to the plot studies we had assisted Stanley Cain in making in the Greenbrier. The trail is filling in with humus and pine needles, and is soft to the feet.

The double barn which 30 years ago stood 50 feet off the trail below the Fittyfied Spring had collapsed and was engulfed in vegeta-tion. The cabin at the spring had fallen in. The spring itself was unchanged.

One had to search to find the trail up Long Branch. The great silvery chestnut trees were falling, and when they fall the aspect of the forest is altered. The young tulips superseding them were now dominating the lower woods.

Around the snout of Brushy we pushed, moving in and out of small hollows as though we were walking around the toes of a great bear. Anne and I each remembered a place among the pines where the trail was open. I had almost concluded that this too had changed, when suddenly we came upon the spot. In an area of ledges the trail had been routed over a great flat rock which resisted encroachment.

We sat on the rock and looked out across the valley and over one great ridge to Myrtle Point. But for the trail we were free of the signs of man. Nothing but the muffled sound of the stream, the primeval southern forest, and above it the airy serrations of the northern forest near Myrtle Point.

The overcast may have given this great forest an added mystery. But in its varied tapestry and in the long nap of its growth it had a gorgeous beauty. There were giant tulips, hemlocks, peawoods, horse chestnuts, maples (red and sugar), ash trees, cherries. All the great trees of the Smokies were there. Irregular colonnades enclosed vast vistas between the awning of the leaves above and the thick jungle of the rhododendron and laurel below.

On this moist, north-facing slope is one of the superb forests in the world. On south-facing slopes were the thin-veined pines, laurel, and xerophytic plants—the galax, wintergreens, and ground pines. The two slopes represented two worlds. The one lived richly upon its abundant moisture. The other was marginal, supporting a poverty-line of have-nots. A sharp turn in the trail would end the one and bring on the other. Leaves of a north slope and needles of a south were often separated as sharply in the trail as by the Berlin Wall.

We crossed the stream in a moist ravine. The stones were wet. The water was cold, crystal, and sweet. We drank not because we craved it, but because, with such gorgeous water, it seemed that we should.

Predecessors had stuffed the remains of their lunch under some roots. The bears had carefully dragged out the mess—the only signs of humans on the whole trail. An abandoned canteen had been punctured by a bear.

At Trillium Gap we encountered hosts of another old acquaintance —the pesky no-see-ums. It had been long since Anne and I had had a bout with them. We welcomed them at first, almost as old friends. But when we sat down to eat they swarmed at us from their haven in the grass around the gap, crawled over our faces and arms, and stung our eyelids and cheeks and neck. I could feel the incipient discomfort of slightly swelling flesh. We put on our jackets, swathed our necks and cheeks in bandannas, and swiped at our legs where they crawled up under our jeans. It did not take many minutes for them to wear out their welcome.

That day Anne and I separated at the gap. She went back down to get the car while I slogged up the muddy horse trail to Le Conte. We met about five hours later on the south side of Le Conte at Grassy Patch.

It was a mushy grueling climb from Trillium Gap to the top of the mountain. I met a horseback party of five whose horses wandered all over the freshly worked trail, leaving no firm footing for a hiker. The trail seemed endless. Eventually I emerged on a long level gravelly stretch, which reminded me of the soil around the lodge. But I was not sure even then that I was near until I saw a *Clintonia* plant, which I knew was normally found in the vicinity of the lodge. Then I passed a dripping cliff along whose ledges grew masses of the Grass of Parnassus. The lodge was so well concealed from that direction, I did not detect it until I was less than a hundred yards away.

July 19 Recently I returned to Trillium Gap with Lloyd Lundin. On this second trip Trillium Gap was as notable for the absence of no-see-ums as the week before it had been rendered nightmarish by their presence.

We heard the winter wrens continually. Their song seemed shortened, as though the last high notes from their tiny throats squeezed beyond the range of sound. Those concluding bars were so sweet and tender as to be barely audible. Who knows but that in the last paroxysm they actually passed beyond hearing?

This time we went north from the gap instead of south as I had the preceding week, and threaded a rocky trough between solid walls of laurel and punctatum to the massive flat dome of Brushy Mountain. We sat down in the open sun beside the trail at a spot where the views of Le Conte, Charlies Bunion, Laurel Top, and Guyot were unimpeded.

"This is the life!" sighed Lloyd.

The trail turned east and was quickly wrapped in laurel. In spots it was not visible as we floundered in laurel higher than our heads. Once we crept on hands and knees through a tunnel of vegetation. Scrub pines in fifteen years had become big pines and had crowded into the path, and they lashed back into our faces. We were witnesses to the slow death of the trail. Soon it would be undiscoverable and the thickety path I had known for 25 years would be gone.

We crossed a tiny gap to the north slope. There in the great laurel the shade was deep and life-giving. There were silhouettes of giant hemlocks, and light bounced off the leaves of dog hobble. We had moved in one short scramble from the hot, brilliant, itchy, and thickety south slope into the cooling gloom and open byways of the north.

I could not tell just where we were, but as we scrambled down through the humus and dog hobble and rhododendron I could see light through the screen of undergrowth. We were at the lip of the great cliff. But we were far to the west of where I had hoped we would be. We swung down the wall over a series of great steps, hanging onto a limb of rhododendron and squeezing through chunks of dirty white quartz.

At the base of the cliff we tiptoed along a fabric of humus covering treacherous black holes in the rocks. The going here was over a chaos of huge boulders and sharp-edged cubes which had split off from the cliff above us. Vegetation and vines had crept over them. Leaves had rotted to give a deceptive appearance of safety. I moved slowly, not trusting the footing, for I knew those yawning openings. Twice I broke through "firm" humus to my crotch. Had I been moving fast I would have broken a leg.

We were working down through the rock fall, and the giant talus seemed to have no end. So we moved horizontally to a screen of trees which projected above the hollow. There we found "solid" footing on soil and deep humus. We encountered scattered boulders but the rhododendron was more open and we made progress downward. Great trees interlaced overhead to shade out the undergrowth and we began to see the opposite wall of the valley. Beneath us was the stream, clear, somber, and cold—a tiny feeder of Long Branch from which we drank deeply. We ducked under a prostrate hemlock, avoided a fallen buckeye, and clambered up the opposite slope into open, gently descending woods.

The going, by comparison with the cliff and hanging rock garden, was easy. But in the deep humus jackstraws of fallen trees and sparse clumps of rhododendron crowded us into the stream, and we still had our problems. Eventually the woods flattened out and the sound of a substantial stream struck our ears to the left. We were in the flat of the upper homestead, now reverted after 30 years to forest. In this setting the rotted quadrangle of logs of the old cabin and the unkempt pile of stones from the collapsed chimney seemed forlorn indeed.

Once there had been a good trail through a massive rhododendron thicket to this spot. But now it was overgrown and we followed the flattened stream bed, looking for landmarks. We found none for another scrambling mile, when quite by chance on a bench on the right bank I blundered upon the thin thread of the old trail. It tracked under new blowdowns and vines, but it was firm under foot and I determined to hold to it. We came out on the graded trail near the Fittyfied Spring.

September 25 Yesterday was one of the great days! My memory said there were spruce trees on Miry Ridge near Buckeye Gap. But I could not prove it, and nearly everyone doubted or flatly contradicted me. When Dickerman and I were at Buckeye Gap in April we were in heavy rain and mist and could make no verification.

The Save-Our-Smokies hike, from Clingmans Dome to Elkmont, was scheduled for late October. Dick and I felt we should check the Elkmont end and perhaps take a look at the trail fork at Jakes Gap. We reached the gap about 11 a.m., rested, did a little map reading, and decided to go on up for possible views of Silers Bald.

At 12 o'clock we reached a thin place in the vegetation, possibly near the site of "Pierce's Improvement," where I had slept in 1917. The day was cool and brilliant and the view was immense. We could see every mountain from Clingmans Dome to Thunderhead. Before and below us was a vast shallow saucer-shaped valley—that of the Middle Prong of Little River and its tributaries.

There was color in the trees immediately around us, and an occasional red maple stood out on opposite ridges ahead of the season. But mostly there was a sweep of blue-green as far as we could see, with dark splotches along the Stateline where the evergreens dropped down the north slope.

In front of us Miry Ridge made a huge bend like a giant sickle. The trail moved into a dense wonderful forest of beech, hemlock, cherry, maple, fire cherry, and silverbell. The cluttered, hot, young, and briery vegetation of 25 years ago was gone. In its place was a forest of young and beautiful maturity, interspersed with short stretches of virgin trees which had escaped the lumberman. We were entranced.

The graded trail was soft with a pad of leaves and the glimpses through this vigorous forest were a delight. Along dry stretches of the trail were beds of galax, trailing arbutus, teaberry, and under dense stands of hemlock great patches of partridge berry. Some hemlocks grew so thickly the light was shut out and the ground was a rolling surface of brown needles without vegetation.

We passed the low point of the ridge and progressed onto the curving sickle. All treeless spots were occupied by pure stands of rhododendron more than head high, and offered no views. We moved into a belt of trees. I was unheeding my injunction to Dickerman to "watch for spruce." He was a few paces back of me and suddenly called out:

"Come back here and look. Isn't that a spruce—not this nigh tree, but the one beside it?"

"By golly, it is."

And then as our eyes ranged and penetrated the heavy wall of rhododendron, we saw more spruce—four, five, six, eight trees. Farther along we saw the top of a tall one rising above the vegetation in which it grew. We ducked and wove through the rhododendron and over the crest. Down the west slope we made out its huge trunk. It was over 30 inches in diameter!

I was elated. Here was spruce at least three miles farther west than Silers Bald. My statement to Secretary Udall, that the engineers for the proposed new road had picked the precise point where the northern conifers gave way to the southern hardwoods, was vindicated. The proposed first road tunnel north of Buckeye Gap would go under this outpost stand!

The trail now leveled off on the east slope and we hiked on into a stand of hardwoods. It was getting late. Suddenly we intersected a well-used trail. It was the Appalachian Trail, at a point just above Buckeye Gap.

Dick and I had visited Buckeye Gap from the east in a driving rain in late April. We had now reached it from the west and north in the benign brilliance of an early fall day. From Forney Ridge to Elkmont we had covered the entire route of the Save-Our-Smokies hike. Although on the tough side our proposed route for this hike was feasible. Moreover, it presented great diversity of vegetation and was beautiful its entire length.

As we turned back, I spotted the stand of evergreens I had noted in April. They were the same ones we had passed through an hour earlier on Miry Ridge! Dickerman said: "Let's make a careful count." All told, we counted 25 spruce, from the 30-inch giant down to young saplings.

When we reached our lunch spot we looked back and saw on the west slope of Miry Ridge a wedge of virgin timber which had never been logged. It lay between two ravines. The spruces ranged along the top of this wedge, including a second cluster which had been hidden from us on the trail. This second cluster prompted us to raise our estimate to a minimum of 40. This western island of spruce would be gravely disturbed by the proposed road. The rearguard of the last ice age, along one of the great ecotones of the continent, would be wiped out.

Three subsequent trips, twice with botanists and ecologists from the University of Tennessee, corroborated the find. Borings and measurements have revealed the remarkable size of some of these ridgetop spruce. Living healthy specimens 34 inches and 38 inches in diameter were found. One of the former had 175 rings. A dead snag in the vicinity of these large living trees measured over 40 inches.

By a rough survey we estimated there were over 200 individual spruce trees in the enclave, from seedlings to the giants. The area extends for a quarter of a mile along a north-south stretch of Miry Ridge.

The largest trees are just over the crest on the west slope in an exceedingly rough locale of cliffs, trees, briers, and rhododendrons. The spruce extend down the slope perhaps 400 yards in a triangular pattern intermixed with birch, rhododendron, and briers. The triangle seems to have been too rugged for logging, and this fact probably accounts for the existence of the large specimens which antedate the era of logging by more than a hundred years. The great majority are on the west slope although a dozen or so husky saplings are growing on the cut-over east side.

The existence of these young trees on the east slope raises a speculation as to the limits of the disjunct prior to the logging of 40 years ago. It will require years of undisturbed growth to establish the original boundaries of the enclave.

October 28 On the Save-our-Smokies hike [Sunday, October 23] I was cheered by the outpouring of people. There were fishermen, writers, businessmen, scientists, a forester, housewives, youngsters, and professors. There were many family groups; there was a five-year-old boy. Two businessmen had come down from Ohio. Present was a long-time devotee of the Smokies from New Jersey. These folks had come together from many states on a damp, threatening day to record their desire for the perpetuation, unbroken by a transmountain road, of the grand western wilderness of the Great Smoky Mountains.

After some ceremonies and picture-taking at the Forney Ridge parking area, the hike got under way about 9 o'clock. In the bend of Miry Ridge we were joined by Anne, who had started from the terminus of the hike at Elkmont and who reported she had already met 50 or more hikers.

At the outlook point many stopped for a view into the vast shallow valley of the Middle Prong. Clingmans was hidden in leaden clouds. Thunderhead was a pale contour on the west. It was there I spoke with Reverend Rufus Morgan, age 81, already twelve miles from Clingmans Dome and moving spiritedly along the trail.

More hikers were resting at Jakes Gap. Ed Clebsch and I reached Elkmont at 4:20, but the trail continued to disgorge hikers for four solid hours. We learned with amazement that 576 had signed the roster at Clingmans; nearly 500 had gone the four miles to Silers Bald; and 234 had walked the full seventeen miles from Clingmans to Elkmont.

Many Americans do care for their wild places.

Harvey Broome (1902–1968)

"I have never wanted to leave the top of a mountain."
Original photo by *W. O. Douglas*